To Begin with, God Created . . .

Biblical Theologies of Creation

Karl Löning
Erich Zenger

Translated by Omar Kaste

A Michael Glazier Book
THE LITURGICAL PRESS
Collegeville, Minnesota

A Michael Glazier Book published by The Liturgical Press

Cover design by Ann Blattner. Illustration: "The Flood and Noah's Ark," Beatus Apocalypse, in the John Rylands Library of the University of Manchester.

1 2 3 4 5 6 7 8

Library of Congress Cataloging-in-Publication Data

Löning, Karl, 1938–
[Als Anfang schuf Gott. English]
To begin with, God created— : biblical theologies of creation / Karl Löning, Erich Zenger ; translated by Omar Kaste.
p. cm.
"A Michael Glazier book."
Includes bibliographical references and index.
ISBN 0-8146-5937-3 (alk. paper)
1. Creation—Biblical teachings. I. Zenger, Erich, 1939– II. Title.

BS680.C69 L6613 2000
231.7'65—dc21 99-049576

Contents

II: Personification of the Creative Beginning

III: The World as the Creation of the Merciful God

IV. Creation, Torah, and God's Rule (Psalm 19)

Foreword

This book originated in a lecture series we held together during the summer semester of 1996 at the Catholic Faculty of Theology in Münster. Our intention with the series was not merely to overcome the factual separation in the history of scholarship between the two disciplines "Exegesis of the Old Testament" and "Exegesis of the New Testament." Our purpose was above all to bring the two parts of the Christian Bible into dialogue with one another in such a way that both their many voices and their single basic message would become audible. It is also because of this intention that the book is not arranged in such a way as to place the Old Testament part first, followed by the New Testament part. Rather we attempt to address and develop our theme by approaching it again and again from both parts of the Bible. It would make us happy if we could pass on to our readers the surprise that we ourselves experienced, namely that the witness of the entire Bible is much more strongly shaped by the theology of creation than we had believed.

Even the external aspect of the book permits one to recognize that, on the one hand, it understands itself as the continuation of two books, *Das Erste Testament. Die jüdische Bibel und die Christen [The First Testament: The Jewish Bible and Christians]* and *Am Fuß des Sinai. Gottesbilder des Ersten Testaments [At the Foot of Sinai: Images of God in the First Testament]*. On the other hand, it expands its hermeneutical perspective and seeks to be a partial contribution to a biblical theology that brings into discussion on the horizon of Christian theology the riches of the message of the entire Bible in such a way that the theological dignity of post-biblical Judaism, rediscovered by Vatican II, may not suffer.

The layout of the book does not permit the interpretations presented to be justified in detail or delimited in terms of the history of research. The bibliographical data are limited to what is most necessary. The wider readership for whom we intend the book will understand this. We ask our professional colleagues for their understanding; given the abundance of texts treated, a detailed discussion would have had to go far afield.

Again, the final redaction and printing of this book would not have been possible without the competent collaboration of our "team." Thus we very heartily thank Stefanie Fuest, Resi Koslowski, Sylvia Simon, Kerstin Urbanski, Karin Vieth, Bettina Wagner, and Bettina Wellmann.

Karl Löning
Erich Zenger

Abbreviations

ANRW	*Aufstieg und Niedergang der römischen Welt*
ATD	Das Alte Testament Deutsch
BBB	Bonner biblische Beiträge
BiLi	*Bibel und Liturgie*
BK	Biblischer Kommentar
BN	*Biblische Notizen*
BTB	*Biblical Theology Bulletin*
BThSt	Biblisch-theologische Studien
BZ	*Biblische Zeitschrift*
BZAW	Beihefte zur Zeitschrift für die alttestamentliche Wissenschaft
CThM.BW	Calwer Theologische Monographien. Reihe A: Bibelwissenschaft
FAT	Forschungen zum Alten Testament
FRLANT	Forschungen zur Religion und Literatur des Alten und Neuen Testaments
FThS	Fundamentaltheologische Studien
FzB	Forschung zur Bibel
HBS	Henry Bradshaw Society
HK	Handkommentar zum Alten Testament
HThK, HThKNT	Herders theologischer Kommentar zum Neuen Testament

JBTh	*Jahrbuch für Biblische Theologie*
KuI	*Kirche und Israel*
LD	Lectio divina
NBST	Neukirchener Beiträge zur systematischen Theologie
NEB	Neue Echter Bibel
NStB	Neukirchener Studienbücher
NT.S	*Novum Testamentum.* Leiden. Supplements
NTA	Neutestamentliche Abhandlungen
OBO	Orbis biblicus et orientalis
QD	Quaestiones Disputatae
SBAB	Stuttgarter biblische Aufsatzbände
SBS	Stuttgarter Bibelstudien
StANT	Studien zum Alten und Neuen Testament
ThB	Theologische Bücherei
ThQ	*Theologische Quartalschrift*
ThZB	*Theologische Zeitschrift.* Basel
TThZ	*Trierer Theologische Zeitschrift*
WMANT	Wissenschaftliche Monographien zum Alten und Neuen Testament
WUNT	Wissenschaftliche Untersuchungen zum Neuen Testament
ZNW	*Zeitschrift für die neutestamentliche Wissenschaft*

INTRODUCTION

The Relevance of Biblical Theologies of Creation

That the living God created the heaven and the earth is the first statement of the Bible of Christians and Jews (Gen 1:1), and "the new heaven and the new earth" is the last theme of the two-part but unified Christian Bible (Revelation 21–22). The first article of the Christian creed, too, confesses: "I believe in God the Father Almighty, Creator of heaven and earth." The creed also closes with the theology of creation: "I believe in . . . life everlasting." In looking at the beginning and the end we grasp in a single glance everything that biblical faith has to say about God and God's relation to the world. That the world is God's creation is the first and the last lesson of the Christian Bible and the Christian creed.

Nevertheless, creation theology does not stand at the center either of Christian theology or of theological discourse. It is true that the deepening ecological crisis has led to various new theological initiatives that can be grouped under the label of "ecological theology." In fact, the universal threat has led within "the conciliar process of mutual assumption of responsibility for justice, peace, and the preservation of the creation" to an ecumenical initiative hitherto unparalleled in its scope. Nevertheless, the theological discussion is only marking time or being carried on by a handful of experts.

There are various reasons for this reticence toward creation theology within theology and Church. One of them is certainly the fact that the richness and variety of the biblical theology of creation are too seldom recognized and taken seriously. This is true for both parts of the Bible. One does not often hear that the New Testament texts are relevant to a theology of creation. Whoever seeks biblical material on the theme of creation does not think first of the New Testament. The basic biblical data of a theology of creation are sought in the First Testament, and there on only a few pages, namely in Genesis 1–3. Even when the eye of the investigator penetrates farther, in the background is usually the view that ". . . in the world of Old Testament faith 'creation has no particular weight.'"[1] Therefore it is not surprising that, in contrast to the Bible and the Christian creed, expositions of the "theology of the New Testament" do not begin with the theology of creation.

Walther Zimmerli thus explains the fact that in his *Old Testament Theology in Outline*, which first appeared in German in 1972, the theme of "creation" does not come to be discussed until the fourth part:

> It may seem surprising that the section dealing with Yahweh as creator of the world was not placed at the beginning. In the creed of the Christian faith the first article speaks of the creator and "creation" must in any case be taken as coming at the beginning, standing among the *principia mundi*. But it is hardly possible to overlook the fact that in what the Old Testament has to say the "deliverance of Israel from Egypt," an event in the midst of history, furnishes the primary orientation. With this as the starting point, however, Israel comes to speak ever more clearly of the creator, a confession it was called upon to make in its encounter with the fully developed creation myths of its Canaanite environment. In like manner, the introductory "I believe in God, the Father" in the first article of the Christian creed, which precedes the confession of the "creator of heaven and earth," cannot be understood without the second article.[2]

From the point of view of theology of creation, at least, this concentration on the confession of "Jesus Christ, his only-begotten Son" is not justified, because in both parts of our Bible it is the father metaphor that refers precisely to the Creator-God under the aspect of his "turning to with loving care." This soteriological and christological exclusivity overlooks the fact that the confession of the Creator-God as the God who makes alive by giving a share in the divine life represents the foundation of all further expressions of faith. It is not christology that is the hermeneutic key to understanding the theology of creation, but just the opposite: the New Testament kerygma about God's saving activity in the crucified and risen Jesus is a unique explanation of the living power of the Creator-God. The kerygma of salvation from sin and death that took solid form in Jesus is not to be brought into competition with the biblical theology of creation. The dichotomies "order of creation" vs. "order of salvation" or "nature" vs. "grace" are neither capable of being biblically grounded nor fruitful for systematic theology. They have led to a narrowing and a suppression of biblical creation theology that must be overcome if Christianity (together with Judaism) wants to stand up to the great challenge of making a constructive contribution toward dealing with the great crises of ecology and politics. There are, of course, theological-political reasons for the fact that the Christian theology of the last fifty years has tended rather to marginalize the theme of creation, but those reasons are no longer relevant today.

When, in the fourth decade of this century, great scholars like Gerhard von Rad and Walter Eichrodt subordinated the theology of creation to "salvation faith" and "covenant theology" to such an extent that "the doctrine of creation never attained to the stature of a relevant, independent doctrine" and was "invariably related, and indeed subordinated, to soteriological considerations,"[3] the intention was to draw a clear line of biblical separation against all the attempts being made at that time to legitimize nationalism by calling attention to a (biblical) order of creation. The explosive power of the lecture "The Theological Problem of the Old Testament Belief in Creation," that was given in 1935 at the International Old Testament Congress in Göttingen by the young professor from Jena, Gerhard von Rad, was clearly expressed by Rainer Albertz:

> Against the attempts at that time to use creation to fuse theology and the Church with National Socialist ideology, von Rad denied to "Old Testament creation faith" every bit of independence, consistently subordinating it to "faith in election." In those days there was justification for it; it was a question of safeguarding the core of the faith by insisting that neither for Israel nor for the Church had that ever been "creation."[4]

In order to rescue the theme of "creation" from political misuse (which was at the same time an important theological-political undertaking), Gerhard von Rad had marginalized it in his time:

> *Gen.* I is not an independent theological essay, but one component of a great dogmatic treatise which moves in ever-narrowing concentric circles. The writer naturally takes his own theological stand in the innermost circle, representing the redemptive relationship between Yahweh and Israel. In order to justify this relationship theologically, he starts from the creation of the world and shows how at each stage in the course of history new statutes and ordinances are revealed, which increasingly guarantee the redemption of the people of God. Thus here, too, the creation of the world by God is not being considered for its own sake, nor as of value in itself. On the contrary, P's presentation of it, even in *Gen.* I, is wholly motivated by considerations of the divine purpose of redemption.[5]

Today, after the passing of more than fifty years, we see clearly that this decisive relativization of biblical creation theology signified at the same time its weakening—and the loss of the universal dimension of the biblical message. That God's history with God's people Israel and with the Church stands in the service of the fulfillment of creation, and that there is no salvation that does not affect the creation, has been relegated to the background in the face of the narrowing of the biblical witness. In contrast to this we can and must today emphasize that the world is desired and loved by God for its own sake and precisely as God's creation. And the world of peoples and religions outside Israel and outside the Church is not simply a salvationless void. To formulate this in the view of the Bible itself: The theology of creation[6] outlined in Genesis 1–9 is not simply a prelude to salvation history, but sustains, pervades, and embraces the entire biblical witness to God. The melody of the theology of creation sounds out in continually new variations in the symphony of the Bible from the first sentence to the last. The creation-theological statements of both Testaments name the depth dimension of all of God's activity in the world, and they form the foundation on the basis of which precisely the face of the self-concealing God is sought and recovered.

Biblical creation faith and biblical salvation faith belong together like the two sides of a medallion. Both have statements of their own that must be brought to discussion and heard in all their tension-filled dialectic. According to the Bible and in it there exists something like the self-testimony of creation in whose light the mystery of Israel, Jesus, and the Church are seen in still another manner than in the self-witness of Israel and the ancient Church. Conversely, illuminating light from Israel and from the Church can fall onto the mystery of the cosmos and its relation to God when each of the biblical witnesses is allowed its own words. That is true both in regard to the dialectical relation to one another of the two parts of the Christian Bible and also in regard to individual statements within the same part of the Bible.[7] These individual statements must be heard as "canonical" voices, as a drawing nearer to the great mystery of creation theology, namely that the God of the Bible is profoundly a God of life who as such seeks a living relationship with "heaven and earth."

Notes: Introduction

[1] Horst Dietrich Preuß, *Old Testament Theology.* 2 vols. (Louisville: Westminster/John Knox, 1995–1996) 1:236.

[2] Walther Zimmerli, *Old Testament Theology in Outline.* Translated by David E. Green (Atlanta: John Knox, 1978) 32.

[3] Gerhard von Rad, "The Theological Problem of the Old Testament Doctrine of Creation," in idem, *The Problem of the Hexateuch and Other Essays.* Translated by E. W. Trueman Dicken (New York: McGraw-Hill, 1966) 142.

[4] Rainer Albertz, *Weltschöpfung und Menschenschöpfung. Untersucht bei Deuterojesaja, Hiob und in den Psalmen.* CThM.BW 3 (Stuttgart: Calwer Verlag, 1974) 174.

[5] *Problem of the Hexateuch,* 139. That Gerhard von Rad in the course of his later theological reflections modified the position he so sharply formulated in 1935, almost reversing it in *Wisdom in Israel* (Nashville: Abingdon, 1972), the work of his old age, is shown by Rolf Rendtdorff, "'Where Were You When I Laid the Foundation of the Earth?'

Creation and Salvation History," in idem, *Canon and Theology: Overtures to an Old Testament Theology*. Translated and edited by Margaret Kohl; with a foreword by Walter Brueggemann (Minneapolis: Fortress, 1993) 92–113. Considered in its entirety, this contribution offers a fruitful new orientation in relation to the relevance of biblical creation theology. Good summaries are also given by Christoph Dohmen, "Schöpfer Himmels und der Erde. Christliche Orientierung am Alten Testament?" in A. Hölscher and Matthias Lutz-Bachmann, eds., *Gottes Namen. Gott im Bekenntnis der Christen* (Berlin: Morus; Hildesheim: Bernward, 1992) 32–54; Frank-Lothar Hossfeld, "Schwerpunkte der Theologie," in Erich Zenger, ed., *Lebendige Welt der Bibel. Entdeckungsreise in das Alte Testament* (Freiburg: Herder, 1997) 163–71; Jörg Jeremias, "Schöpfung in Poesie und Prosa. Gen. 1–3 im Vergleich mit anderen Schöpfungstexten des Alten Testaments," *JBTh* 5 (1990) 11–36; Wolfgang Nethöfel, "Biblische Schöpfungstheologie? Ein hermeneutischer Werkstattbericht," *JBTh* 5 (1990) 245–64; Werner H. Schmidt, *Alttestamentlicher Glaube* (Neukirchen-Vluyn: Neukirchener Verlag, 1996) 233–43; Josef Schreiner, *Theologie des Alten Testaments*. Ergänzungsband 1 zum AT (Würzburg: Echter, 1995) 132–63; Odil Hannes Steck, *World and Environment* (Nashville: Abingdon, 1980).

[6] On this delimitation of pre-history, cf. below pp. 99–101.

[7] Only one who thoughtlessly defames, as does R. Mosis in *TrThZ* 106 (1997) 39–59, will oppose such a reading of the two-part but unified Bible as no longer orthodox according to his (mis-)understanding. The interpretations presented in our study are also part of the christology that Mosis condemns in advance, without having read a single page. It is astounding that that kind of action, which is strongly reminiscent of the practices of the Inquisition, is still possible, or again possible in our day.

Part I

Ideas About the Beginning of Creation

CHAPTER ONE

The Interplay of Chaos and Cosmos

Creation theology recalls the creation of the world and of human beings "as a beginning" and indeed "from the beginning" as a good, beneficial, and indestructible life-context with God as the creator and king of "his" world. From the perspective of the Jewish-Christian Bible this is not primarily related to beginning in the chronological or causal sense even though in the conventional understanding of creation these aspects are so dominant that they are considered to be the primary message. In his efforts on behalf of a new biblically-inspired theology of creation Michael Welker has critically described the commonly accepted notions about "creation" in the following manner:

> Secular common sense as well as religious consciousness in the Jewish-Christian tradition understand and refer to "creation" as the totality of the world and nature insofar as they are considered to be *brought forth* and *dependent*. The character of that which is brought forth is persistent, independently of whether creation *(creatura)* is attributed to one god or gods or to other more original, absolutely superior worldly or supernatural powers and authorities. Creation—that is the totality that is essentially thought of as nature, or in fact even as only the nature that was brought forth by an authority superior to it and that, because of being brought forth, is dependent. But the act or activity of bringing forth this "totality" of the world or of nature is also called "creation" *(creatura).* The summary concepts and ideas about this act of bringing forth and that which is brought forth in this way are generally very vague and even unclear. In our Western cultures they have already for a long time been pulled together into a very abstract and spare idea of a final causation and being-caused that can be neither investigated nor questioned.[1]

At the point where "creation" is narrowed down to these two aspects of being-brought-forth by God and being-dependent-on God, the theology of creation comes, on the one hand, into close proximity with questions posed by natural science, but without being able to answer them.[2] On the other hand, at the same time it distances itself from the way in which the Bible speaks of the creator. Though the Bible certainly speaks about the creator God as giving "his" world its beginning, this "beginning" is not simply the beginning of the world; it is the beginning of a relationship between God and the world.

Creation as Origin and Goal

The creation is a beginning that alters and determines God's own life history. And it is a beginning that aims to reign over and transform everything that exists. It is a beginning whose dynamism grows out of the fact that it is constituted by the goal toward which the relationship that links the creator and "his" creation is aimed.

As an origin *(Ur-Sprung)* that is *real* only as a goal, this beginning is not chronologically or causally determinable. It is certainly the beginning of time, but as such it is outside of time. As the primal time it is at the same time the final time, which is as such recalled, invoked, wished for, and dreamed of in order to allow the time of the world and of human beings so to be brought into the "time" of God that a final meaning may shine forth—in the midst of danger and sorrow, but also in the longing for care and security.[3] Therefore this remembered "beginning" is not merely a good beginning that happened once at some time in the past, but was lost through "the Fall," "original sin," or "the jealousy of the Devil." Rather it is God's loving turning toward the world that has been present "from the beginning" always related to the world as "his" world and that continues to give it life that is "new" and "good" (Gen 8:22) "as long as the world endures."

What fascinates the biblical narrators about creation is not that there is something there that was not there earlier, but that something new is underway that was not there—nor could have been—before the creation.

That God created the world "out of nothing" is not an ancient Oriental and First Testament understanding. Even the Bible texts 2 Macc 7:28 and Wis 11:17 that are often cited in support of *creatio ex nihilo* cannot be used for this purpose.[4] The people of First Testament times, whether in Israel or in its environment, occupied themselves in the context of creation not so much with the opposites Nothing vs. Something as with the opposites chaos vs. cosmos and death vs. life. While the concept of absolute nothingness is not conceivable for the Old Testament, the references to a dreadful barrenness give the first impression of what creation means, namely good form, good order, rhythm, and life. The contrast is not between nothing and something, but between the hideous and the wonderful.[5] What moved the people of the Bible was not that something was created, but what and why. In order to imagine that and be conscious of it they projected images and stories from the "pre-creation world" so as to be able in contrast to think about and describe the world—and especially its beginning—as creation.

Ancient Oriental Conceptions of the "World Before Creation"

One way of talking about the "beginning" of creation consisted in speaking of an original, chaotic Something out of which and in the transformation of which the cosmos was created. The conception—which sounds absolutely modern—that creation happened or happens as transformation of chaos is, on the one hand, connected with the fact that Semitic culture was able to conceive of neither an absolute Nothing nor of a previous or a subsequent non-existence of something that exists. On the other hand, the process of creation itself could thus be vividly described even in its initial powerfulness and lasting dynamism.

The "pre-creation" original material out of which or through whose transformation the cosmos is created is, in the tradition of Mesopotamia and Egypt, above all an imagined "primal ocean," divergent in its details and conceived of as personified. Thus we find in the *Enuma Elish* myth, the classic creation myth of the Babylonian tradition, the following description of the "pre-creation world": "As Apsu himself, the one of the first beginning, the begetter of the gods, and Mummu Tiamat, who bore all of them, mixed their waters into one . . . ." The "world before creation" is here described as "original ocean" in which the two kinds of water, the sweet water (Apsu) and the salt water (Tiamat) were still chaotically mixed and confused with one another. And the creation then began with this, that two gods came into being with whom or through whom, in the midst of this watery chaos, the cosmogony is set in motion. Correspondingly, in the Egyptian tradition the "world before creation" is conceived of almost exclusively as a borderless expanse of water from which and out of which the appearance of the world takes its beginning in that the original mountain that had been hidden in the original ocean comes to the surface or that the primal lotus that was rooted in it grows up high. Similarly, the creation of the world begins with the creator god rising up out of the primeval ocean and then beginning his creative activity.[6]

That the pre-cosmogonic chaos was conceived as the antithesis of the world recognized as cosmos can be impressively seen from the gods who represent the "world before creation." They are four pairs of primeval deities that according to the Hermopolitan tradition correspond to the dimensions Water (Nun and Naunet), Darkness (Kek and Keket), Endlessness (Heh and Hehet), and Hiddenness (Aman and Amaunet). The chaotic character of these four pairs is iconographically marked by the symbols of water and wilderness (cf. figure 1).

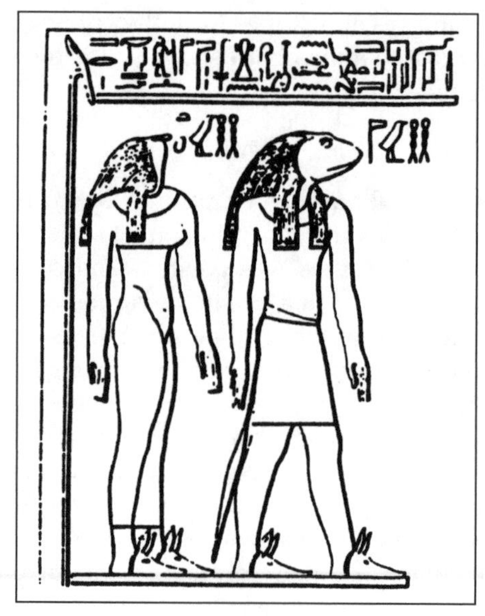

Figure 1

The female deities have heads shaped like those of cobras (desert), while the male gods have the heads of frogs (water). In addition, all the gods have jackal feet (desert/death). Another iconographic tradition (see figure 2) presents the chaotic aspect of the pre-cosmogonic primeval water by showing within it four powerless moving figures symbolizing the four directions in their pre-cosmogonic ineffectiveness, thus marking the primeval water as a not-yet-structured expanse.[7]

Figure 2

That in this picture Atun, the sun god, confronts these four chaotic figures as primeval god and creator already gives an indication of the correct understanding of these images of chaos. According to them chaos is not an imagined preliminary world that corresponds to no reality, but a counterworld that as such possesses continuing chaotic power and threatens the cosmos.

> The unordered expanses of chaos . . . are not abolished by creation, but continually surround the ordered world. Therein lies also a continuing threat, which is reflected for us principally in the myth of the continually recurring struggle of the sun god against the snake Apophis who is "repulsed" but, as an immortal primeval power, never killed. It is therefore understandable that in Egypt the discussion is not about a single creation "in the beginning," but that the creation happened "the first time." Thus we here find the creation of the world referred to as both an action of the first time and as a beginning whose nature demands, if not fulfillment, then repetition! The repetition takes place in the daily carrying out of the creation in the course of nature, especially when "the sun god comes out of the primeval water Nun every morning and with his daily course pulls the cosmic order along with him." But the creation is repeated also in the sphere of the historical, especially with every coronation and temple dedication and in every place where, in response to a hostile incursion, the original order is reestablished.[8]

Accordingly, chaos and cosmos are two tension-filled moments of the simultaneously-experienced world-reality in which the cosmos "since the beginning" and "as the beginning" is nevertheless the more powerful reality inasmuch as creation is a transformation accomplished by God or the gods. There prevails therefore between chaos and ("the world

Figure 3

before or on the other side of the creation" and "the world as creation") an asymmetry of power that, through the intervention of the creator god, is transformed and preserved as a complex and dynamic life process with entirely independent forms of life.

Four images elucidate this dialectic based on ancient Oriental thought about chaos and cosmos.

The first image (figure 3)[9] reproduces an Egyptian papyrus drawing from the 21st dynasty (ca. 1000 B.C.E.). It shows the dramatic struggle in which the sun god must daily fend off and defeat the snake-bodied primeval ocean. In the picture the falcon-headed sun god sits majestically in his boat and is just about to leave his course in the heaven in order to travel through the realm of night to the place where he comes up each morning. It is this intention, which requires the realization of the order of creation, and thus the repetition of the creation of the world, that is opposed by the chaos-serpent, whose body is stylistically represented by high, wild waves. Only with the help of the god Seth, who stands in the bow of the sun ship and jabs at the snake with a lance, and pulled by helpful jackal and cobra demons, does the creator god accomplish the mythical journey of creation through the primeval ocean.

Figure 4

The second image (figure 4)[10] is from the cylinder seal of the Akkadian scribe Adda (*AKK* II, ca. 2200 B.C.E.) The middle of the picture shows the sun god Shamesh as he is about to "cross the mountain of the eastern horizon," just as he "rises from the earth at the dawn of each day and at the beginning of each new year."[11] In his raised left hand he holds the saw that symbolizes the first ray of the sun with which every morning the sun god breaks open the portal of heaven, which is closed every night. To the left of Shamesh, Inanna/Ishtar, the winged goddess of war and love, stands on the mountain peaks. Weapons grow out of her shoulders and she holds a cluster of dates in her hand. In spite of the weapons, it is not her warlike aspect but her heavenly one that predominates, so that she here probably represents the star Venus, whose brilliance precedes the rising of the sun. At Ishtar's side are represented a warlike god with bow and quiver, a tree (symbol of awakening vegetation), and a lion (Ishtar's animal emblem). To the right of the rising sun god comes Enki/Ea, the god of wisdom and ruler of the fresh water ocean *(abzu/apsu)* along with his double-faced visier Isimu/Usumu. Ea, out of whose shoulders proceed floods of water rich in fish, holds an eagle/falcon in his hand and climbs like a conqueror over a reclining steer. The peaceful appearance of the trio of gods, Ea, Ishtar, and Shamesh, according to Pierre Amiet, should be related to a specific point in time: the spring equinox, which coincides with the beginning of the new year: "A sublime general epiphany has taken form in the scene. We may with some justice understand it as a graphic version of the same thought that more recent texts repeatedly express, namely that of the new year."[12] It is the rebirth of the sun god as the giver of life and guarantor of justice who comes out of the winter darkness and the violence of the storms of winter and renews the life-force of the earth.

Figure 5

The third image (figure 5)[13] reproduces a Syrian cylinder seal (18th–17th c. B.C.E.). Its center shows the tree of life, which at the same time bears the heavenly bodies. This signifies the productive polarity of earth and heaven that makes life possible: in other words, the cosmos. It is threatened by the serpent of chaos, which clearly had been about to attack the tree and is prevented from doing so by Hadad-Baal, the god of storm and rain, who strides above the mountains swinging his cudgel. At the left a feminine deity who is identified with Ishtar by the eight-rayed star holds her protecting hand over the tree of life. "Whether the griffin (above, at left) is thought of as guardian of the tree of life, and whether the three men (below left) turn to the goddess in petition in view of the threatening danger cannot be said with certainty."[14]

Figure 6

The fourth image (figure 6)[15] is the reproduction of a cylinder seal from Mari (ca. 2200 B.C.E.). It shows at the center the king of the gods, who is enthroned on the mountain of the gods and the world. He wears a horned crown and carries the scepter as the insignia of divine kingship. At the foot of the mountain of the gods flow two springs of water out of whose streams "grow" two goddesses. They can be identified through their form as tree goddesses (the goddess at the left holds a tree in her hand, the goddess on the right a bowl) and through their attributes as personifications of the fertility made possible by the springs of water. This picture emphasizes repeatedly that the outflowing of the water that makes life possible is a highly dramatic event that can be understood as the metamorphosis—brought about by divine creative power—of the dangerous water of chaos into the waters of life. The springs come out of the mouths of serpents, which are widely-documented symbolic animals of the water of chaos (in the Old Testament as well: cf., for example, Leviathan, Rahab, etc.). They are of course unable to develop their destructive power, for the creator god sits on them. Nevertheless, there is at the left in the picture still another divine masculine figure who sets his foot on the water and holds it down with his lance. That the creation remains a life process because the creator god subdues the waters of chaos and transforms them into good water is a conception that is also developed repeatedly in the Bible.

Notes: Chapter 1

[1] Michael Welker, *Schöpfung und Wirklichkeit.* NBST 13 (Neukirchen: Neukirchener Verlag, 1995) 16.

[2] This is in no sense intended to cast doubt on the necessity of the conversations between theology and natural science about the theme of "creation." Today, after the end of the unhappy misunderstandings, this conversation is meaningful and necessary for both parties. Good examples are the study by Michael Welker mentioned in n. 1, the section "Schöpfungslehre," in Theodor Schneider, ed., *Handbuch der Dogmatik* (Düsseldorf: Patmos, 1992) 1:206–35, as well as Rainer Koltermann, ed., *Universum—Mensch—Gott: Der Mensch vor den Fragen der Zeit* (Graz et al., 1997). That Genesis 1 was read as cosmology already in antiquity, and why this is so, is explained by Clemens Scholten, "Weshalb wird die Schöpfungsgeschichte zum naturwissenschatlichen Bericht? Hexaemeronauslegung von Basilius von Cäsarea zu Johannes Philoponos," *ThQ* 177 (1997) 1–15.

[3] Cf. for this perspective especially Jürgen Ebach, *Ursprung und Ziel. Erinnerte Zukunft und erhoffte Vergangenheit* (Neukirchen-Vluyn: Neukirchener Verlag, 1986) 16–22.

[4] Cf. on this the succinct but informative book by Walter Groß and Karl-Josef Kuschel, *"Ich schaffe Finsternis und Unheil!" Ist Gott verantwortlich für das Übel?* (Mainz: Matthias Grünewald, 1991) 222–23, n. 23.

[5] Horst Seebaß, *Genesis* (Neukirchen-Vluyn: Neukirchener Verlag, 1996) 1:66.

[6] Cf. now the comprehensive documentation of the Egyptian and Mesopotamian ideas on the "pre-creation world," in Michaela Bauks, *Die Welt am Anfang. Zum Verständnis von Vorwelt und Weltentstehung in Gen 1 und in der altorientalischen Literatur.* WMANT 74 (Neukirchen-Vluyn: Neukirchener Verlag, 1997) 155–310.

[7] The illustrations are taken from Othmar Keel, *Die Welt der altorientalischen Bildsymbolik und das Alte Testament. Am Beispiel der Psalmen* (2nd ed. Zürich: Benziger, and Neukirchen-Vluyn: Neukirchener Verlag, 1977) 334 (plates 480a and 481).

[8] Ernst Würthwein, "Chaos und Schöpfung im mythischen Denken und in der biblischen Urgeschichte," in Erich Dinkler, ed., with Hartwig Thyen, *Zeit und Geschichte; Dankesgabe an Rudolf Bultmann zum 80. Geburtstag* (Tübingen: Mohr, 1964) 20–21.

[9] Illustration from Othmar Keel, *Bildsymbolik* (see n. 7) 47.

[10] Illustration from Bernd Janowski, *Rettungsgewißheit und Epiphanie des Heils.* WMANT 59 (Neukirchen-Vluyn: Neukirchener Verlag, 1989) 48.

[11] Pierre Amiet, *The Art of the Ancient Near East.* Translated by John Shepley and Claude Choquet (New York : H. N. Abrams, 1980) 105.

[12] Bernd Janowski, *Rettungsgewißheit* (see n. 10) 49–50.

[13] Image from Keel, *Bildsymbolik,* 42.

[14] Ibid. 43.

[15] Ibid. 39.

CHAPTER TWO

The Beginning of Creation in the View of Genesis 1

Biblical thinking, especially the creation story in Gen 1:1–2:3, also participates in the ancient Oriental conceptual world that regards creation as the beginning of a dialectical tension between Chaos and Cosmos.

The Meaning of the Images of Chaos in Genesis 1:2

That the creation of the world happened "at the beginning" out of chaos is asserted in the following three-part sentence (Gen 1:2) that follows the title (Gen 1:1):

> To begin with God created the heaven and the earth.
> But the earth was still *tohuwabohu,*
> and darkness was over the primeval ocean,
> and God's breath/wind moved over the waters.
> Then God spoke: Let there be light!
> And there was light.[1]

There are therefore four "elements"[2] that were on hand and available to the creator God, who does not create them, but works creatively with them: (1) the *tohuwabohu* earth, that is, the earth inimical to life, (2) the darkness as a menacing evil force, (3) the primeval ocean, and (4) "the waters" as the chaotic figures of the two original waters (see the Enuma-Elish myth mentioned above). In the first three days of creation the creator God then separates "the world" out of the chaos. The pervasive darkness is ended when light is created and divided from the chaotic darkness. The waters of chaos are confined in certain spaces and partially transformed into "good water" (ocean with fish; rivers; rain clouds). At the end the *tohuwabohu* earth is reshaped into a dwelling for life and filled with living creatures.

Probably even the discourse about God's breath/wind in motion over the waters, so mysterious to our understanding, has a quasi-chaotic meaning. As a statement about God's creative life power "before the creation" it means the divine energy and creativity that then become reality in creation. Based on the meaning of the Hebrew word *rūaḥ* (usually translated "spirit" or "breath") is the motherly, creative life power the creator God breathes into his creation "to begin with."[3]

When the biblical tradition describes Gen 1:2 as "pre-creation world" this is not to be reduced to a mere literary necessity permitting the description of the creation as a beginning, as does, for example the great Genesis commentary of Claus Westermann: ". . . its intent is not to describe a state that preceded creation, but to mark off God's act of creation from a 'before' which is beyond words and can only be described in negative terms. The primary purpose of all these sentences is to delimit and not to describe . . . ."[4] That Westermann's interpretation is unlikely is suggested by three observations:

1. The ancient Near Eastern and biblical traditions certainly possess forms of speech for expressing the previous state of an event or a situation in negative terms. It is the well-documented "not-yet style" by means of which, in cosmogonic stories, the deficit that is ended by the creation is described. Sentences in the form "when there was not yet . . ." evoke a proto-world in which are generally concentrated those elements that were experienced as especially important in the created world. Thus it is said in an Egyptian pyramid text: "When the heaven had not yet appeared, when human beings had not yet come into existence, when the gods had not yet been born, when dying had not yet come about . . ." The Babylonian creation myth, Enuma-Elish (= "When above . . .") opens with this figure of speech: "When above the heavens were not yet named, when below the earth still had no name . . . when the dead reeds had not yet accumulated and cane thickets were not yet to be seen, when no god had yet appeared or been named with any name, and no skill apportioned to him . . ." And the second creation story (the so-called Yahwist narrative) in Gen 2:4-25 (or Gen 2:4–3:24) also begins in narrative style: ". . . when no plant of the field was yet in the earth and no herb of the field had yet sprung up—for he, YHWH, had not caused it to rain upon the earth, and when there were yet no human beings to till the ground . . ." (Gen 2:5). These few examples prove that there certainly were linguistic resources available to describe the beginning of creation in as a beginning *in time.* When, on the other hand, the "pre-creation world" is described with "is-statements," a chaotic "reality" is named out of which the world is created. This chaotic counter-world does not then imply any limitation of the creator God. On the contrary, God's creative power is manifest precisely in the divine sovereignty over chaos.[5]

2. It is true that the narrators of Genesis 1 do not say, as does, for instance, the Babylonian Enumu-Elish myth, that the cosmos is made

out of chaos as the material of creation. But the creation of light, of the heaven-firmament, of the ocean and the earth are nevertheless unmistakably told in Genesis 1 as exclusion and as a naming and reorganization of chaos. In a certain sense the cosmos is created within and into the chaos that surrounds and threatens it but is unable to destroy it. It seems that the narrators of Genesis 1 even expressly—although very subtly—imply that the chaotic reality continues to exist "after" or "beyond" creation.[6] God's creative activity begins in Gen 1:3 with the creation of "light," that is, the fundamental and comprehensive requirement of life, by a mere word:

> Then God said:
> "Let there be light!"
> And there was light.
> And God saw that the light was good.
> And God separated the light from the darkness.
> God called the light Day,
> and the darkness he called Night.
> And (then) there was evening
> and there was morning:
> one day (Gen 1:3-5).

If one compares the description of the first day of creation with the days that follow, it is especially striking that the so-called approbation formula does not appear at the end of the first day of creation and that it applies expressly only to "the light." The purpose of this is theological: The darkness here is *not* considered a work of creation, but is, according to Gen 1:2, the chaotic power that had been a given since before creation. It is true that according to Gen 1:3-5, "Night" was taken from it, and is in turn integrated into the Night-Day sequence as part of the life process of creation. But the narrators nevertheless let it be understood between the lines that the chaotic power of darkness continues to exist even after creation, and that the creator God's might is revealed in that power's continuing delimitation.

3. The Flood story in Genesis 6–9, as a narrative of the breaking-in of the pre-cosmogonic chaos into the cosmos, takes for granted that, even after the creation, chaos represents an earth-threatening potential. According to the biblical tradition chaos will not disappear as a threatening counter-world until the history of the cosmos attains the fulfillment set for it "in the beginning," as the Revelation of John describes it in its apocalyptic language of images. When "the new heaven and the new earth" have come, there will be no "sea," that is, no chaos as a threat to the cosmos. As long as *this* earth of ours continues, according to the creation-theological concepts of the Bible (or at least most of them), it will live in an interplay of chaos and cosmos, of death

and life, of self-destruction and self-organization—in the force field of that life that the creator God shares with it "as a beginning."

One can also discover this understanding of creation as a beginning, not one that *was*, but *is*, in the peculiar formulation of Gen 1:1. The exceptional nature of the first sentence in the Bible consists in this: that the Hebrew time statement *bᵉrē᾽šît* followed by the verb-form *bārā᾽* is really not possible according to the rules of grammar.[7] The problem is often resolved by translating Gen 1:1 as a temporal clause: "When God began to create heaven and earth . . . ." However, the unusual form can also be interpreted in the sense that the beginning indicated by *bārā᾽* (create) is characterized as a beginning *sui generis*, so that we can translate: *"As a beginning"* or *"To begin with,"* God created heaven and earth. Precisely by viewing the verb *bārā᾽* (create) together with the unusual statement *bᵉrē᾽šît* are we enabled to paraphrase the intent of Gen 1:1 as follows:

(1) The action of *bārā᾽*, which we know can be said only of God, refers to *creating living things*, and, in fact, living things in the midst of other living beings. It means enabling life by giving a participation of God's own life. In this sense creation means the building up and maintenance of relations of interdependence . . . that are both accessible and inaccessible to human shaping."[8] In particular, the creator God is personally involved, as its ongoing beginning, in the life process of whatever is so created.

(2) Constitutive for God's creative activity *"in* the beginning" is the commitment into which God thereby enters, to remain faithful to "his" creation and to let this "beginning" become reality in its appropriate fulfillment.

A Comparative Look into Egyptian Iconography

We wish to illustrate the concept of the life-giving "beginning" formulated in Genesis 1 by means of a brief look at an Egyptian relief. At the same time, this can reveal something of the capabilities of creation theology. In technical terms it has to do with the important question of the original "Sitz im Leben" (life situation) of creation theology as a whole. The image reproduced[9] in figure 7 shows the relief from a sarcophagus cover from the City of the Dead of Sakkara in the valley of the Nile south of Cairo. The cover dates from the fourth century B.C.E.

Let us first attempt to grasp the overall scheme. In the center of the image is, in outline, the circular disk of the earth, which is divided into numerous concentric fields. It is surrounded by a circular ribbon, the ocean, the "Big Green," as the Egyptian tradition likes to call it. The disk is uplifted and kept in plumb by two angled arms, whose hieroglyphic meaning is "Ka," that is, lifting power, fertility, life power. The

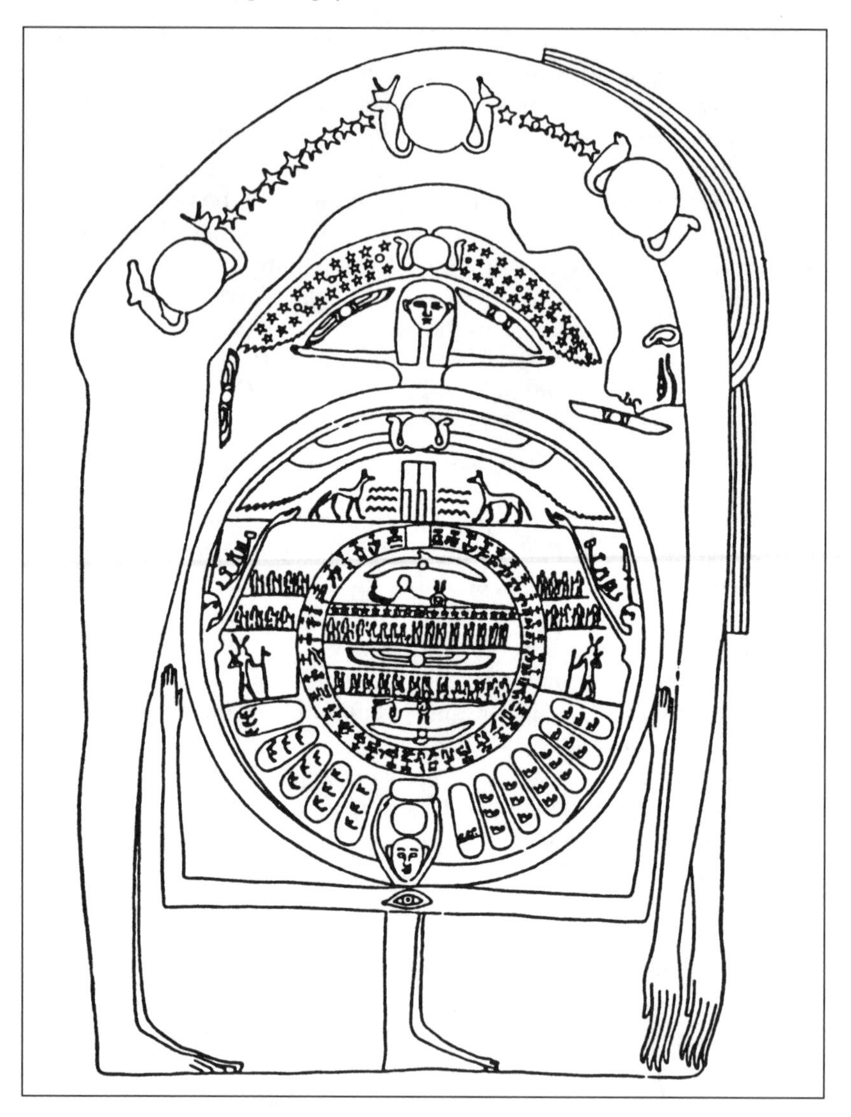

Figure 7

life power, which is characterized as personal power by the eye between the arms and by the two feet, is meant to suggest the experience that had inspired the astonishment of the ancients that the inhabited earth can hold itself above the water of chaos and not be swallowed up by it. The symbol of divine life power is therefore meant to be a theological symbol for the assertion that the world, as an entity maintained by the divine power of life, does not contain its cause within itself. Our image underlines how intensely it is concerned with this perspective when it repeats this interpretation of the world. Directly above the eye in the pair of bent arms a figure consisting only of head and arms rises out of the outermost circle of the disk, that is, out of the ocean. With its head it supports a disk, probably the underworld, and with its arms an oval, probably the disk of the earth. Because this form rises out of the ocean it could well represent the primeval ocean as a divine figure and allude to its function of sustaining the globe.

Above the disk of the earth held up in this way arches the heaven, presented here as a woman who fully embraces it and gives it all her attention. The body of the woman, which at the same time illustrates the beauty of the heavens, is adorned with stars and three suns, symbols of the light that the heavens give the earth both day and night. The picture then again presents the course of the sun in the heavens by placing a little winged sun in front of the pudenda of the heavenly woman as a symbol for the sun's birth in the morning, and a second winged sun before the woman's mouth, signifying the setting of the sun. Between the earth-disk and the woman of heaven bowed above it are once again to be found two symbols for the heavens: above, in the middle, a woman, the ocean of heaven, shown only in half-length, grows directly out of the ocean, and above are stretched a pair of star-studded wings in whose center there is again a disk of the sun. Thus the total composition vigorously attempts to stress and maintain earth's dependence on a divine reality in respect to light, life, security, warmth, beauty, and joy.

We turn in conclusion to the portrayal of the earth-disk and the circle of ocean that surrounds it. The representation is somewhat confusing because of a repeated merging into one another of ground plan and outline. Out of the center of the outermost ring, which denotes the ocean in the grand plan, appear, on both left and right, female figures, each respectively turned inward, and with a long outstretched arm Each of the two figures bears on its hand a hieroglyph which defines her more exactly. The woman on the left has a lance on her head, which identifies her as the East, while the woman at the right bears a feather on her head, a symbol for the West. Thus the two figures again symbolize the rising and setting of the sun, represented this time by the ship of the sun which the woman at the left (East) lifts up out of the subterranean ocean through which she has traveled during the night, and that is again steered downward at the right. At the zenith, in the inside of the middle of the circle of the ocean, the sun is depicted as a sun with wings.

The earth-disk itself is made up of three concentric circles, in the outermost of which a horizontal line once more separates off a segment of the circle. This outer, relatively broad circular band depicts the lands and regions surrounding Egypt, the whole non-Egyptian world, which for the Egyptians was largely identified with desert and chaos. This is suggested in our image by hieroglyphs corresponding to squatting nomads (in the cartouches!) and wild warriors as well as by the two desert gods at the right and left.

At the top of this circular band there is a separate segment that refers to the desert as the place of death and the portal to the realm of the dead, as identified by the symbols shown (animals belonging to the jackal-headed Anabus, god of funerals), two sets of three wavy lines, symbols of the waters of chaos, and the twice-repeated symbol for a tomb. Departing from this tomb, a path leads directly into the innermost circle, which is characterized as the world of the dead (Duat) by the figures within it and by the stars, through which the sun, depicted three times here, passes after it sets.

The last element of the image is still the location from which this interpretation of the world was projected. It is the narrow circular band in the center between the band of the desert people and the realm of the dead—Egypt itself—containing the forty-one symbols of the Egyptian districts.

When one grasps the entire composition it is obvious that this image begins almost analytically, on the one hand, with the multiformity of the sensible world of Egypt, and attempts, on the other hand, a sort of synthetic overview integrating this world into the divine reality of faith in order to give meaning and security to this world, a realm of threatened life. In symbols and ciphers the image attempts to give an answer to the question about the original basis and meaning of the world. It is aware of the threatening reality of chaos and for that very reason invokes the life force of the structured cosmos in order to clear a path past chaos for the dead person.

According to the picture, therefore, the theology of creation springs from the effort to call up and make present the living power of the cosmos in the midst of and against chaos. Precisely this function can be read in the literary form of the biblical and extra-biblical creation stories. They are archaic forms of the myth, or participate in their late form in the linguistic forms and functions of the myth.

Invocation of the Good Beginning: Creation Theology as Theodicy

When creation narratives are called myths, this must be understood correctly.[10] The creation myth is not a pre-scientific and therefore outdated explanation of the reality of the world, or a so-called primitive natural science that uses the figures of gods instead of formulas to describe natural processes. Nor is it, as Rudolf Bultmann said, an illegitimate mixing of what is beyond the world with what is of the world, the divine and the human. The creation myth is not concerned with a rational explanation of world phenomena and their causes, but tells about the good beginnings of the world in the sense of its founding, being given a basis and a foundation to cling to. Thus the creation myth "is . . . no fable about beginnings that no one was there to see. Here, rather, people are looking back from their own time and are perceiving the foundations of their world—what belongs fundamentally to it as it is and what is valid for all time—as being events with which the world was endowed from the beginning, events which laid down what was to be valid for all periods to come."[11] It is a question of the fundamental laws of the world as a whole, which must always apply for the world to exist. While we in our philosophical-theological tradition and expression formulate such normative basic structures and conditions of possibility for the world and humankind in abstract definitions, myth chooses the form of the history of the gods, which it playfully tells as happening "in the beginning." This beginning is not one taking place in time, but a beginning in the sense of an exemplary and normative original event.

The time of the myth is, strictly speaking, a time beyond history. It is original time, the time that actually makes time possible and governs it, original history, which is the source and model of history. The myth tells about an original event that happened *"in illo tempore"* (at that time) and on which all subsequent events are based, against which they are judged, and in terms of which their meaning and goodness can be measured. For the myth, the present life is the necessary repetition of the origin, the anamnesis of life's original image. The ancient Near Eastern creation myths (and analogously the OT primeval histories) do not really tell how the world *came to be,* but rather how the world "really" *is,* how human beings are to see it and themselves in it, and above all what attitude the gods, or in the case of the OT stories the God of Israel, have toward their world, how they are supposed to maintain and protect it. The myth is virtually the plea for a world order directed to the gods honored as creators. It is the narrative discovery of and invocative desire to hold fast to the good beginning with the goal of preserving and forming the world—in accordance with this hidden but self-revelatory and salvific primeval order—as a place of life (and not of death). In the myth, humankind returns to the "beginning," to a paradisiacal world counter to the "real" one, which is experienced as troubled and threatened in many ways. The biblical theology of creation is therefore an answer to anxiety and resignation in the face of catastrophic experiences of the world and of life.

In ancient times the myth developed its fundamental power when it was recited in the language of worship and repeated in ritual. The primary "Sitz im Leben" for the creation myth was the beginning of a new agricultural year or the birth of a child. Both situations are critical moments in the collective and individual life history. When the myth of the creation of the world (New Year) and of the creation of humankind (birth) are recited in those situations it is with the goal of soundly integrating the new person and the new year into the world and life orders established by the gods or God in the good beginning, that is, to give them foundation and meaning as well as to impart to them what always and everywhere is and should be valid, as long as the world and human beings exist.

Sickness and suffering are especially "chaotic" experiences in which creation theology with its invocation of the good beginning seeks to overcome and fend off existential anxiety and threats to life. This is shown paradigmatically by a Babylonian incantation against the tooth worm (see the text given below).

"As we can gather from the structure of the text, the meditation about the original beginning of the earth-event is integrated into an incantation that a dentist shouts out during the treatment (cf. line 20). If the tooth has to be pulled anyway, then at least that will also be the end of the 'worm' (representing the piercingly painful nerve)! By no means does it belong there, after all. Although as a part of Nature the worm, too, emerged during the world-genesis, but it is working in the wrong place. A misuse of power causes misery and disaster. For this reason it is necessary to trace its course back to the fateful crossroads where its actions began to be self-willed. Up to this point the world had still been intact. From that point the thing that has gone astray must be brought back, in this case by magic power."[12]

1 After Anu (= Sumerian god of the heavens) had created (the heavens),
2 the heaven had "created" the (earth),
3 the earth had "created" the rivers,
4 the rivers had "created" the (small) canals,
5 the (small) canals had "created" the mud,
6 the mud had "created" the worm,
7 the worm went weeping to *Šamaš* (= the sun, god of justice)
8 before Ea (the high god of Eridu) his tears flow without ceasing:
9 "What have you then given me to eat?!
10 What have you then given me to suck out?!"
11 "But I have given you the ripe fig,
12 the apricot, the apple!"

13 "What am I to do with these—a ripe fig,
14 an apricot, an apple?!"
15 "Lift me up and let me
16 take my place between the tooth and the gum,
17 so that I suck the blood of the tooth
18 and so that on its gum
19 I can gnaw at its pieces!"

20 Set the forceps firmly and grasp the (tooth's) root! —

21 "Because you have said this, worm,
22 Ea will strike you with his mighty
23 hand!"

24 —Incantation against toothache—

The gods are reminded of the order of creation they have established; the tooth worm is therefore to be defeated as a "chaotic element." "Creation theology" is here in a certain sense invoked as medicine and at the same time the physician's acts are given a creative-constitutive function.

Biblical people appeal to the good order of creation at the moment of extreme existential trouble, or recapitulate, in terms of the theology of creation, the good beginning of their own experience in contrast to their experience of reality as painful and contradictory. This is impressively documented by the vital function of the theology of creation in the tension between death and life, in confrontation with chaos, and in an intellectual invocation of the cosmos. To use theological terminology, creation theology's particular "Sitz im Leben" is theodicy. It attained its first "great" epoch in Israel during the crisis of the exile, when both Deutero-Isaiah and the Priestly document composed their versions of creation theology.

Four examples from the Bible will make concrete the "Sitz im Leben" of creation theology's discourse about the beginning:

1. In the face of unspeakable suffering the petitioner praying Psalm 22 appeals in the following manner to his or her God:

> On you I was cast from my birth,
> and since my mother bore me you have been my God.
> Do not be far from me,
> for trouble is near
> and there is no one to help (vv. 10-11).

2. Similarly, with the exilic lament in Isa 63:7–64:11 Israel, in the night of greatest collective abandonment by God, invokes the relationship posited as "beginning" between YHWH as Father/Creator and YHWH's people:

> . . . you have hidden your face from us,
> and have delivered us into the hand of our iniquity.
> Yet, O LORD, you are our Father;
> we are the clay, and you are our potter;
> we are all the work of your hand (Isa 64:7-8).

3. Then the promise, deliberately grounded in the theology of creation, goes out to the Israel that laments to its creator God out of the chaotic darkness of the exile:

> I have put my words in your mouth,
> and hidden you in the shadow of my hand,
> stretching out the heavens,
> and laying the foundations of the earth,
> and saying to Zion, "You are my people" (Isa 61:15).

4. The book of Job, especially, is a controversy with the interplay of chaos and cosmos in the creation. On the one hand it is certainly correct that on the level of the narrative it is Job's existential suffering that constitutes the focus of the book's account. The comforting answer of the book to this is that false explanations and attributions of the purposes of suffering are to be rejected (such as suffering as punishment for sin, suffering as a providential act of God by which God means to educate and purify, etc.). It is also positively promised that God will put an end to the suffering of those who suffer innocently and that God's final word to those who suffer is love. It cannot be ignored, however, that the book of Job uses the paradigm of Job, whose life becomes chaotic, as the vehicle for a Wisdom reflection on the problem of creation as a whole becoming chaotic. In Job's discourses chaos is problematized in two ways:

(a) Job denies that the concretely observed world is an ordered world. It is, on the contrary, so shot through with chaotic powers and events that it would be better that it fall back totally into chaos (if it is not on the way there anyway!).

(b) Starting from the theological thesis that all good and evil comes directly from the hand of an almighty God, Job accuses God of being the cause of his experiences of life-destroying chaos (illness and crime). Job's accusation says: *God* is a criminal and anarchist!

Both accusations are rooted in a static image of the world, God, and humankind that wants to assign clear responsibility and is unable to leave room for any process of becoming chaotic and structured or of returning again to chaos that is not precisely determined by God even in its details. In contrast, the book of Job pleads in its fictitious literary divine discourse for a worldview and a way of dealing with the world in which there is still room, alongside God and humankind as active characters, for a certain independence of Nature and its powers. Sounding almost modern, the book protests a concept of order that is too narrow and schematic and, especially, too much an exclusive product of human perspectives and interests. And it pleads for a new view of those aspects of the world disqualified as "chaotic" by calling into question and rejecting the leading perspectives of such disqualification, namely, their usefulness to humankind.

The first of the two divine discourses (Job 38:1–39:30) develops the theme that the world is meant to be a dynamic organism brimming with life and not merely a sterile and static regimentation of elements that have only to serve human beings. In its first part (38:1-38) it sketches the principal features of the ancient image of the world, through a series of questions posed to Job, in such a way that the dialectic of making chaotic and making structured appears. God admits to Job that there are processes and areas in the world that, because of human beings' limited vision, seem to be only useless chaos. But God denies that they discredit either the competence of the creator or the earth as a world designed by God to be a world of life. On the contrary, in its second part (38:39–39:30) the divine discourse, while taking up the ancient Near Eastern motif of the "Lord of the wild beasts," describes God's approval of those regions of wilderness or primeval forest condemned by humans as "non-world" or as useless or aggressive chaos. By means of this constellation of images so unfamiliar to us the book of Job promotes in the fourth century B.C.E. a view of the world in which those regions that are not clearly understood or planned for must have their place if the creation is not to degenerate into a world-machine or a garden-gnome idyll. One of the imaginable consequences of such an initiative would be a creator God who enters so fully into the tension- and conflict-filled process of making chaotic and structuring chaos as even, within that tension and conflict, to enter into and participate in the experience and suffering—if one may be permitted such an anthropomorphic expression.

It would be fascinating to document in detail the ancient Near Eastern and Egyptian background of the constellation of images used in the divine discourse.[13] Ten animals (the number of completeness) are introduced one after the other, sometimes at length, sometimes briefly, and in such a way that an image of wild, disordered, and yet fascinating vitality emerges. Of this the creator God says that they are all controlled and controllable by God—but this is done precisely with the kind of free latitude that these animals need for their respective manners of living.

What these animals, assembled here in pairs (lion and raven, ibex and hind, wild donkey and bullock, ostrich and horse, peregrine falcon and vulture), all have in common is that with the exception of the horse they are animals whose habitat is not the cultivated landscape but the barren waste and the wilderness. Above all, however, they represent a dimension of creation withdrawn from the dominion and utility of human beings and that may, in fact, even seem to them strange and "useless." And yet they belong to the world as constituent parts of the creation of the living God. It is, namely, the thesis of the poet who wrote Job that what escapes human insight, calculation, and control by no means contradicts an interpretation that understands the world as a life-community with God. What appears to be chaotic and is experienced and resisted by humankind as endangering the cosmos can perfectly well belong to the life process whose real "beginning" becomes visible only in its purpose, whose beginning is, in fact, real only as a goal.

Notes: Chapter 2

[1] On the translation problems in Gen 1:1-3 see Erich Zenger, *Gottes Bogen in den Wolken. Untersuchungen zu Komposition und Theologie der priesterlichen Urgeschichte.* SBS 112 (2nd ed. Stuttgart: Katholisches Bibelwerk, 1987) 62–66. I would no longer hold to the literary-critical delimitation of Gen 1:2b suggested in that book (81, n. 97). A detailed discussion of the various translation models is offered by Michaela Bauks, *Die Welt am Anfang. Zum Verständnis von Vorwelt und Weltentstehung in Gen 1 und in der altorientalischen Literatur.* WMANT 74 (Neukirchen-Vluyn: Neukirchener Verlag, 1997) 69–92. She concludes that Gen 1:1 presents a titular motto verse that anticipates Gen 1:2, 3ff. (ibid. 145). From a strictly grammatical perspective v. 1 is an anacolouthon: "In the beginning, when God had created the heaven and the earth. But the earth was . . ." (ibid. 92).

[2] It is difficult appropriately to identify the "chaos elements" named in Gen 1:2. It is evident that they cannot simply be understood as the preexistent or even necessary raw material of creation. On the other hand, one may not reduce them to a "stylistic figure" as Michaela Banks, *Die Welt* suggests on p. 317 (and frequently): "The narrative definition in Gen 1:2 contributes to the description of the scope and quality of God's work of creation in the cosmos and history through the stylistic figure of contrast." On the other hand, the concept of "metaphor(s) for the environment" Bauks introduces into the discussion (ibid. 314) seems to me to be a good beginning for thinking further about the "counter-reality" referred to in Gen 1:2.

[3] Cf. Helen Schüngel-Straumann, *Ruach bewegt die Welt. Gottes Schöpferische Lebenskraft in der Krisenzeit des Exils.* SBS 151 (Stuttgart: Katholisches Bibelwerk, 1992) 79–84. Michaela Bauks, *Die Welt* 132–41, correctly emphasizes the polyvalence of the "wind/breath" of God in Gen 1:2 and attributes to "'wind' in Gen 1:2 both a creation-preparing and a chaotic connotation. The *rūaḥ* implies a moment of transition from the former world to creation without itself causing or forcing the creative act." Thus one could evaluate "the wind in Gen 1:2 in the sense of a not-yet-revelation of God . . . whose not-yet narratively anticipates the revelation that will occur in the (primeval) history" (ibid. 285–86).

[4] Claus Westermann, *Genesis 1–11.* BK 1/1 (Neukirchen-Vluyn: Neukirchener Verlag, 1974) 63 (English: *Genesis 1–11: A Commentary.* Translated by John J. Scullion [Minneapolis: Augsburg, 1984] 46).

[5] Cf. on this also Manfred Görg, "'Chaos' und 'Chaosmächte' im Alten Testament," *BN* 70 (1993) 48–61.

[6] Thus agreeing with Walter Groß, *"Ich schaffe Finstermis"* 37–38.

[7] Cf. n. 1 above.

[8] Michael Welker, *Schöpfung und Wirklichkeit.* NBST 13 (Neukirchen: Neukirchener Verlag, 1995) 29.

[9] Illustration from Othmar Keel, *Die Welt der altorientalischen Bildsymbolik und das Alte Testament. Am Beispiel der Psalmen* (2nd ed. Zürich: Benziger, and Neukirchen-Vluyn: Neukirchener Verlag, 1977) 30; our interpretation follows that of Keel, ibid. 31–34

[10] Of fundamental importance is Hans-Peter Müller, *Mythos—Kerygma—Wahrheit.* BZAW 200 (Berlin and New York: de Gruyter, 1991).

[11] Odil Hannes Steck, *Welt und Umwelt* (Stuttgart: 1978) 71. (English: *World and Environment* [Nashville: Abingdon, 1980] 91).

[12] Text and interpretation according to Manfred Dietrich, "Die Kosmogonie in Nippur und Eridu," *Jahrbuch für Anthropologie und Religionsgeschichte* 5 (1984) 166–68.

[13] On this see Othmar Keel, *Jahwes Entgegnung an Ijob.* FRLANT 121 (Göttingen: Vandenhoeck & Ruprecht, 1978) especially 61–125.

CHAPTER THREE

The Effects of the Beginning Continue: YHWH, the Good Ruler, Cares for the World

With the hope-filled confession that God created the world "as a good beginning," all affirmations about human beings and the world, about Israel and its history with God stand under the sign of the royal rule of God over creation. Despite all the chaotic and chaos-bringing threats and endangerments that exist in the cosmos, within the horizon of biblical creation theologies this fact remains the basic constituent of human experience of reality: "From eternity to eternity," from primeval time to end time, the loving care of God, the good ruler of the world for *God's own* creation is the enduring, sustaining, and life-giving power of the cosmos, which can be recognized and received as such at certain places and in certain life contexts.

The Jerusalem Temple and its worship are recognized as an especially privileged place at which the creative life-giving power of YHWH is at work. The expression of this in Psalm 93 is virtually classic.

The Royal God of Creation as the Tamer of Chaos (Psalm 93)

1a The LORD is king,
1b he is robed in majesty;
1c The LORD is robed,
1d he is girded with strength.
1e He has established the world;
1f it shall never be moved;
2a your throne is established from of old
2b you are from everlasting.

3a The floods have lifted up, O LORD,
3b the floods have lifted up their voice;
3c the floods lift up their roaring.
4a More majestic than the thunders of mighty waters,
4b more majestic than the waves of the sea,

4c majestic on high is the LORD!
5a Your decrees are very sure;
5b holiness befits your house,
5c O LORD, forevermore.

The psalm, which programmatically introduces[1] the composition including Psalms 93–100,[2] a cycle revolving around the theme of YHWH's world reign, sketches a poetic image of the king of the world, who sits on his throne clothed in his royal regalia, and who since the beginning/from eternity and until the end of days (vv. 2ab, 5c) so subdues the chaos that the globe of earth can carry out its function as living space for Israel and the nations. The idea that the Temple is in a certain sense the place where heaven and earth intersect, and that the throne of YHWH the heavenly king rests in the Jerusalem Temple, is presumed. At the same time the Temple mediates the mythic original time with the respective present time, giving the latter, in the midst of its imperilment, enduring strength from eternity (v. 2) to eternity (v. 5c: "forevermore").

One option for reading the psalm is to see the twofold assertion about the eternal nature of YHWH's royal rule (v. 2) and about the eternity of YHWH (v. 2b) as the structural center of the psalm. For the interpretation this means that it is the royal reign of YHWH, which is grounded in YHWH's own person (so must the parallelism of v. 2a/2b be understood) that gives the globe of earth its steadfastness so that it does not fall apart (v. 1ef) and effects the power against which the streams of chaos-water break (vv. 3-4).

One also has the option of dividing the psalm into two sections, vv. 1-2 (four two-part phrases) and vv. 3-5 (three three-part phrases), whereby the statement about YHWH's firmly grounded royal throne (v. 2) and about YHWH's demonstration of power in the Temple, or in YHWH's reliable testimonies, are set in parallel. Each of the two strophes then shows a specific image of YHWH's power as creator. The first "strophe" applies motifs from the king's investiture in order to portray YHWH as a warlike king. YHWH wears neither magnificent regalia nor the sovereign's robe of light, but a garment that expresses readiness for battle and military power—and in fact since the "eternal" assumption of divine royal power. "Here lies the inner reason why YHWH is superior to the powers of chaos, so that they are not able to harm the world."[3] This is then developed in the second strophe, which expressly invokes the primeval and every contemporary subduing of the waters of chaos by YHWH. It is precisely this strophe that distinguishes YHWH's rule from the kingdom of the gods that was usual in the ancient Near Eastern world of ideas. While there the kingship was achieved in the struggle with chaos, so that the victory over chaos is a *prerequisite* of royal rule, YHWH's creative battle against chaos is the *result* of YHWH's royal rule, which is from the very beginning. Because YHWH is the royal God, YHWH tamed the wildly foaming floods of chaos at the very beginning (v. 3ab: past tense verbal forms, "have lifted up") and has tamed them ever since (3c: verb in the present tense, "lift up" [continually]).[4] While the flood waters of chaos constitute a reality that permanently menaces[5] the world as creation, they break against the mightiness of YHWH, the sovereign of the world. YHWH's throne is "in the heavens" and is at the same time powerfully present in the sanctuary and not least in YHWH's people, who permit themselves to be led by the "decrees" that can be experienced and learned in the sanctuary. Thus the destructive power of chaos finds its limits where human beings allow themselves to be led by the "sure decrees" that go out from the sanctuary of YHWH, the sovereign of the world. What the psalm has concretely in mind with the chaos-battling "decrees" is difficult to determine. Probably what is meant is every kind of instruction, proclamation, and liturgy to be found in the Temple or in the Temple cult.

Psalm 93 attributes to the Temple and to its liturgy a constitutive role in creation. This applies primarily to the Temple in Jerusalem. It is also true, however, of Jewish communities that allow themselves to be brought into the liturgical service of the God of Zion. And it is true of Christian communities that as liturgical congregations are aware of their solidarity with Israel. Where Jews and Christians, whether as communities or as individuals, allow themselves to be inspired and motivated by the biblically-attested chaos-taming power of the creator God to involve themselves in the battle with chaos, there the "beginning" of the creation is itself their goal.

The life-giving care of the creator God for the world is not, however, according to the biblical writers, mediated exclusively through the theology or liturgy of the Temple, as Psalm 93 verifies. God's creative care is also effective and can be experienced apart from the Temple or any cultic institutionalization, as is emphasized by Psalm 104, a deliberate counter to Psalm 93.

Longing for the Continuing Care of the God of Creation (Psalm 104)

Psalm 104,[6] which originated after the exile (fifth century B.C.E.), is related to Psalm 93 in three respects: (1) Although in Psalm 104 the royal title for YHWH that thematically opens Psalm 93 is missing, nevertheless the metaphors sketched at the very beginning of the psalm doubtless bear the stamp of royal theology (vv. 1c and 2a: splendid royal clothing and garment of light; investiture of YHWH as king of the world; 2b-4b: construction of the royal palace, ascent of the royal chariot, commissioning of the heavenly court). (2) Although Psalm 104 primarily portrays YHWH's royal rule as the provision of everything necessary for all YHWH's subjects, that is, all living things, the theme of the subduing of the chaotic primeval ocean, the basic theme of Psalm 93, is nevertheless not absent. (3) Both psalms agree that the earth is fundamentally unshakable, which can be seen in the fact that it cannot be made to waver.

> Psalm 104 takes up the world-view of Psalm 93, but modifies it above all in two respects. *In the first place,* in Psalm 104 the powers of chaos are much more strongly "domesticated," and as a result the ambivalences of the experience of the world are attributed to YHWH himself. *In the second place,* Psalm 104 does not (at least not expressly) name the Temple as a place of mediation between myth and experience.[7]

Psalm 104 is much more strongly oriented to awareness of the daily world than is Psalm 93, pointing out its interdependent connections, especially the constitutive interdependence of *all* life in the world *and* the living God. The emphasis on interdependence culminates in vv. 29-30:

> When you hide your face, they are dismayed . . .
> When you send forth your spirit, they are created;
> and you renew the face of the ground.

Psalm 104 is a creation hymn from Old Testament Wisdom literature. This characterization is verified by the following three aspects of the psalm:

1. The psalm is a typical Wisdom psalm in its manner of perceiving the world. Almost systematically it describes the concretely experienced world. The psalm writer makes a list of all he knows about natural history. In loving detail (we modern observers of the world are also continually fascinated by the variety and beauty of every "individual example" of minerals, plants, animals, and human beings) the writer of Psalm 104 describes the world as he sees it. He strides through the environments of his three-part world, the heaven (vv. 2-4: briefly), the earth (vv. 5-23: at greater length), and the ocean (vv. 25-26: briefly). As our interpretation will show, he not only traces the individual environments and periods of life, but sees life virtually in its functional contexts. Thus he also connects statements about the creation of the world (vv. 5-9) with those about its preservation (vv. 10-23).

2. All of this happens, not in the distant description of an empirical scientist or of the interested "lay person," but in hymnic praise. It is not only the self-invitation to songs of praise at the beginning and the end of the psalm, not just the participles typical for the hymn that allow one familiar with the tradition of hymnic forms to sense immediately that the interest from beginning to end is in praise of God, the

good creator. The entire "sketch" of the worldview aims at the central assertion of vv. 27-32: all living things owe their common life to the generous hand, the lovingly inclined face, and the life-giving breath of God—to a "thou" before whom and to whom the one who prays the psalm enthusiastically sings his or her praise of creation.

3. In tension with the affirmation of the world as God's creation that marks this psalm is a mood of doubt and anxiety that also permeates the composition. The psalm is aware of the perils of life in this world. Certainly chaos is not so dramatically named as in Psalm 93. But according to Psalm 104, too, chaos is present in many ways. The threatening primeval waters can be experienced in the present "when, for example, water stands 'above the mountains' in the form of clouds (v. 6b), in storms (v. 7) falling as rain and running through the valleys toward the ocean (v. 8)."[8] Also in the theophany motifs of the shaking and smoking of the mountains the psalm lets one sense the drama with which the creator God realizes, day after day, the order of life established as "beginning." In the hustle and bustle of sinners and the godless, too, whose disappearance the psalm asks for in v. 35ab, chaos is present in creation. Finally, the threatened nature of life becomes totally visible in vv. 27-30, which go to extremes to emphasize that everything *per se and in itself* is or would be doomed to die without the God who gives life. It is precisely this tension between life and death that makes plain that the psalm feigns no naïve optimism; its intention, typical for Wisdom literature, is to lead to the correct way of living.

Orienting oneself by the genre pattern of the hymn, one can characterize v. 1a as self-incitement to praise *(Aufgesang)*, with vv. 33-35 as "closure" *(Abgesang)*: (vv. 33-34: dedication of the psalm; v. 35ab: petition for "delivery" from the evil that willfully threatens creation; v. 35c: self-incitement to praise, like v. 1a), and both sections together making up the frame of the psalm:

1a Bless the LORD, O my soul

33a I will sing to the LORD as long as I live;
33b I will sing praise to my God while I have being.
34a May my meditation be pleasing to him,
34b for I rejoice in the LORD.
35a Let sinners be consumed from the earth,
35b and let the wicked be no more.
35c Bless the LORD, O my soul.
35d Praise the LORD! (Hallelu-Jah!)

The remainder of the text can be classified as *corpus hymni,* that is, the real principal part of the hymn, in which two hymnic message levels overlie one another.

The *first message level* marks the *corpus hymni* at the beginning (vv. 1b-2a), approximately in the middle (v. 24), and at the end (vv. 31-32) with motifs from the ancient Near Eastern theology of divine kingship. Verses 1b-2a celebrate YHWH who presents himself in his royal regalia and majestic garment of light:

1b O LORD, my God, you are very great.
1c You are clothed with honor and majesty,
2a wrapped in light as with a garment.

Verse 24 celebrates the earth as the "realm" of King YHWH, created by the application of YHWH's wisdom, the royal charism *par excellence,* and accepted as YHWH's possession for which YHWH bears responsibility:

24a O LORD, how manifold are your works!
24b In wisdom you have made them all;
24c the earth is full of your creatures.

That is the creation-theological "primeval experience" of Old Testament people, about which they are continually amazed: in other words, that life is simply there, simply inexhaustibly given, and, of course, that they are continually obliged to receive it ever anew because no living thing is able to make it for itself. Thus for the author of the psalm the natural world, as far as and in the measure that it is a living thing, is a highly positive experience of power that makes him aware of the foundational and continuing turning of the creator God toward the world. All is made "in/with" wisdom and is a part of God's own realm of life.

The "wisdom" spoken of here is not only an attribute of God, but also and at the same time an attribute of the world with which God has endowed it. It is the secret by means of which it touches human beings and speaks to them as an "I." It is not the I of YHWH—Israel had always known of the immovable boundary between creation and the Creator—but it is the sentient dimension and the beauty of creation insofar as it is formed and loved through YHWH's Wisdom. Whoever listens to this "Wisdom" of the Creator gains the wisdom with which life comes to itself.

At the end of the *corpus hymni* in vv. 31-32 YHWH's royal care for the world is implored for the whole time of the world's existence. Here the psalm uses motifs with which the appearance of gods is described in the tradition of the ancient Near East. The seemingly conflicting statements of the two verses (v. 31: positive inclination; v. 32: shaking of the earth) underline the continuing difference between Creator and creation. In specialized theological terms: they emphasize God's transcendence precisely in view of God's immanence experienced in the world:

31a May the glory of the LORD endure forever;
31b may the LORD rejoice in his works—
32a who looks on the earth and it trembles,
32b who touches the mountains and they smoke.

The *second message level* of the *corpus hymni* becomes visible in the sections that appear literarily between the texts at the first level, which has just been described. They form the bulk of the *corpus hymni* of the psalm and, in the narrower sense, develop the "worldview" and creation theology of the psalm. The whole reads like a religio-historical *florilegium* of Phoenician-Canaanite, Egyptian, and Assyro-Babylonian traditions, but also of genuine elements from Israel, on the two themes "taming and transformation of the (water)-chaos by a royal divinity" and "the (divine) king as mediator of life and nourisher of his realm." Both themes are blended in the psalm within the tension-filled perspective of life and death. The psalm paces through the triad of Heaven, Earth, and Ocean (the poet calls attention to this structure by placing each of these words in the first line of the corresponding section) and thereby depicts the earth as a firmly-grounded and well-ordered house overflowing with life. Certainly in the poet's view this is a mysterious interaction among the creatures, who, full of longing for life, stretch themselves out toward the creator God, YHWH, who as a good king gives gifts of life to all, turning to them a loving countenance and, especially, giving them a share of the life-giving divine breath. As a totality these creation-theology sections are three-dimensional images of the *exercise of YHWH's royal sovereignty.*

In the first section of the *corpus hymni* (vv. 2b-4b) the psalm describes how YHWH assumes and exercises this life-constituting rule in heaven:

2b You stretch out the heavens like a tent,
3a you set the beams of your chambers on the waters,
3b you make the clouds your chariot,
3c you ride on the wings of the wind,
4a you make the winds your messengers,
4b fire and flame your ministers.

YHWH makes three instruments of royal power: palace, chariot, and royal court. Of course, all of them are determined by YHWH's royal activity of being giver of life through the gift of the water necessary for life. YHWH builds a royal palace in the midst of the waters of chaos, thus taking away their power and at the same time establishing a reservoir of water with which to water the earth (cf. v. 13a). YHWH's throne is a chariot like that possessed also by the Canaanite weather god Baal and like the analogous vehicle for YHWH in Ezekiel 1. YHWH's "royal court," too, the storm winds and the lightning (v. 4a: messengers; v. 4b: ministers) is appropriate for cooperation in the royal activity of giving water, or life.

Verses 5-23 describe YHWH's royal activity in and on the earth. This takes place in several phases. First the section in vv. 5-9 describes the beginning and still-active establishment of the earth, with a retrospective glance at images of the battle against chaos:

5a You set the earth on its foundations,
5b so that it shall never be shaken.
6a You cover it with the deep as with a garment;
6b the waters stood above the mountains.
7a At your rebuke they flee;
7b at the sound of your thunder they take to flight.
8a They rose up to the mountains, ran down to the valleys
8b to the place that you appointed for them.
9a You set a boundary that they may not pass,
9b so that they might not again cover the earth.

That the chaotic primeval ocean has here lost all its destructive potency, as is sometimes said, contradicts not only the worldview proposed in vv. 29-30 but especially the Wisdom perception of the world characteristic of the psalm. A boundary is laid for chaos that it is not able to cross, but only because the creator God daily summons up the divine chaos-taming might. In almost three-dimensional view the poet allows one to participate in the experience of how the dragon of the primeval waters hastens on before the commanding voice of YHWH, over the mountains and valleys, until it reaches the ocean, where it is allowed to "stay," though from there it continually threatens the world and makes the inhabitants anxious.

The creator God's taming of the chaos-waters is not, however, based solely on taking away its "character as flood." In the next section, vv. 10-18, the poet celebrates YHWH as the good king even more for the manner in which YHWH provides from heavenly water reserves both springs and rainwater for the earth's varied landscapes. This section is divided into three subsections: vv. 10-12 direct the eye to the wild places "between the mountains" (uncultivated "Nature"); vv. 13-15 look at the fields and arable land "in the mountains/hill country" and vv. 16-18 contemplate "the high mountains" with their plant and animal life (thus once more "uncultivated Nature").

10a You make springs gush forth in the valleys;
10b they flow between the hills,
11a giving drink to every wild animal;
11b the wild asses quench their thirst.

12a By the streams the birds of the air have their habitation;
12b they sing among the branches.

Not reflected in the "creation image" of vv. 10-12 is the experience of the great riverine cultures of Egypt and Mesopotamia, where the rivers were the vital nerves of settlement and agriculture, but that of the Syro-Palestinian rivers and not least the Jordan, whose banks remained until this century lined with jungle-like and luxuriant thickets that offered an environment for wild and feared animals. The wild donkey (v. 11b) represents the animals of the steppes and deserts, to whom YHWH also gives water essential to life by means of spring-fed rivulets in the wadis. The water in the wilderness rivers and wadis flows so abundantly it gives rise to bird paradises resounding with calls and melodious songs. Thus this section (vv. 10-12) praises YHWH as giver of overflowing life. Although to the people of those days these regions and the animals who lived in them did not seem useful, but rather threatening, our psalm perceives here the same life-giving hand of the creator God at work as in the world of human beings, of which vv. 13-15 says:

13a From your lofty abode you water the mountains;
13b the earth is satisfied with the fruit of your work.
14a You cause the grass to grow for the cattle,
14b and plants for people to use,
14c to bring forth food from the earth,
15a and wine to gladden the human heart,
15b oil to make the face shine,
15c and bread to strengthen the human heart.

The spaces for cattle and humankind are so well provided with rain by YHWH that through the life force thus given (YHWH is the actor in vv. 13-15) the ground brings forth all the good things necessary for life: pasture for the cattle as well as plants and trees from which humans can produce bread (for eating), wine (for drinking), and oil (for anointing) by their work (vv. 13-15)—not just daily bread (mentioned twice because it is so important), but also wine and oil, gifts of abundance and of the culture of celebration. There is nothing perceptible here of the tribulations of Palestinian farmers lamented in Gen 3:17-19; on the contrary, what is expressed here is astonishment at what the earth can produce of the good and beautiful when it has the blessing of a kind creator God. The poet emphasizes thereby that these gifts of the earth that was established and looked after by God make glad people's hearts and faces; that is, they can make them strong, happy, and beautiful.

In the section about the mountain world (vv. 16-18) the psalm begins a third time, by means of the motif of the water of life, to praise YHWH's creative, positive inclinations toward creation:

16a The trees of the LORD are watered abundantly,
16b the cedars of Lebanon that he planted.
17a In them the birds build their nests;
17b the stork has its home in the fir trees.
18a The high mountains are for the wild goats;
18b the rocks are a refuge for the coneys.

The mighty cedars of Lebanon, already ancient at the time, whose trunks can reach a height of forty meters and a diameter of four meters, are in the Old Testament tradition a symbol for power and might (cf. Ezek 17:22-24). Such gigantic trees are trees of the gods. The psalm calls them "trees of YHWH," for YHWH planted them and they are in a special way an expression of YHWH's life force. Even the trees of the mountain region are marvels for the poet, "trees of life" for birds. Yes, there is life even where the forested region ends; there ibexes and rock badgers romp.

After the differing life habitats of the earth's creatures are paced off in vv. 10-18, the section in vv. 19-23 describes their various "seasons of life." It does so artfully by describing the basic unit of time, a full day (see also the time-theology of Genesis 1):

19a You have made the moon to mark the seasons;
19b the sun knows its time for setting.
20a You make darkness, and it is night,
20b when all the animals of the forest come creeping out.
21a The young lions roar for their prey,
21b seeking their food from God.
22a When the sun rises they withdraw
22b and lie down in their dens.
23a People go out to their work
23b and to their labor until the evening.

There is in Psalm 104's perception of the world an important prerequisite for the earth to continue being the "house of life" willed by the creator God, that is, that the various life forms respect the environments and seasons of life assigned to them. It is for this reason that in vv. 19-23 the life-ordering times established by the creator God are brought into the discussion, first by a description of the moon and the sun as the bodies that bring order to time; then the psalm speaks of the life rhythms of the wild animals, then of human beings (and the world of animals who live with them). The moon reveals the underlying order of "year" and "month" (the ancient Near Eastern calendar originally had a year made up of moon cycles) as well as the great agricultural feasts and cultic life (for example, festivals of new moon and day of the full moon, but also Passover, the Feast of Weeks, and the fall festival). The sun, which is named in second place, structures the time into day and night and establishes the seven-day week that came into being in Israel with its fundamental distinction between work and rest. The fact that the setting of the sun is named first has to do with the reckoning of the day that had come to prevail in post-exilic times, which has the day begin at sundown (as in Judaism and in the Christian liturgical calendar down to the present). Only when attention is paid to the times of work and rest, the times of Nature and festivals, but also to the differing rhythms of animals and humans (vv. 20-23) can the life common to all of them develop in its richness—that is the wonderful concept behind this section, which seems to us highly modern in this age of ecological consciousness.

After the description of the heavens and the earth as spaces of the creative royal rule of YHWH the psalm turns again briefly, in vv. 25-26, to the ocean, which, according to the ancient Near Eastern view of the world, surrounds the disk of earth:

25a Yonder is the sea, great and wide,
25b creeping things innumerable are there,
living things both small and great.
26a There go the ships,
26b and Leviathan that you formed to sport in it.

In its form as ocean, the primeval sea has lost its mythic-chaotic threat through God's creative activity. It teems with great and small aquatic animals that live in it. Even ships can "go back and forth" on it. Because ships are not living things they seem out of place here. But they fit very well within the psalm's perspective because the ships on the ocean impressively document that, as a part of the creation cared for by YHWH, the ocean has lost its chaotic (not its dangerous) power. That so little is made of this has to do with the fact that the average Israelite knew the ocean and ocean travel only from hearing the comments of others (but cf. Prov 30:18-19; 31:14; Sir 43:24-25). To the psalm writer what is important is that YHWH holds an ordering hand also over the ocean. Leviathan, the chaotic ocean dragon of Canaanite and ancient Near Eastern mythology (where it appears with various names) had once and for all been stripped of its power by YHWH as creator God (cf. also Job 40:25–41:26). YHWH plays with him like a tamer with a dolphin!

While the psalm describes the prerequisites and conditions for the life of creation on the creation-theological statement level we have gotten to know, in vv. 27-30 it turns to the mystery of life itself, specifically *the shared and separated life of God and God's creation*. In a wonderful image the psalmist takes the earth with all its living things into the completion of YHWH's very life:

27a These all look to you
27b to give them their food in due season;
28a when you give to them, they gather it up;
28b when you open your hand, they are filled with good things.
29a When you hide your face, they are dismayed;
29b when you take away their breath, they die
29c and return to their dust.
30a When you send forth your spirit/breath, they are created;
30b and you renew the face of the ground.

This section fundamentally asserts that all creaturely life is *received life*—and that all breath is a participation in God's breath. The psalm formulates this dialectically: "when you take away their breath, they die—when you send forth your spirit/breath, they are created." The Hebrew word used here, *rūaḥ*, which is usually translated "spirit," is the breath as power of life, both human and divine.[9] The "old" earth owes it to the creative life power of YHWH, who turns a loving face to it, giving it abundantly of everything that it needs to live, and who breathes life-giving breath into it so that it daily becomes "young" and as fresh as on the "morning of creation."

This is the principal creation-theological assertion of the psalm: In their longing and hunger for life and in the joy of life, creatures and creation as a whole seek community with the life-giving creator God. By the fact of their life they say "yes" to their creator God, out of and through whose love they live, as the book of Wisdom emphasized half a millennium after the writing of our psalm:

> . . . you love all things that exist,
> and detest none of the things that you have made,
> for you would not have made anything if you had hated it.
> How would anything have endured if you had not willed it?
> Or how would anything not called forth by you have been preserved?
> You spare all things, for they are yours, O Lord, you who love the living.
> For your immortal spirit is in all things (Wis 11:24–12:1).

Notes: Chapter 3

[1] On Psalm 93 cf. also Thomas Podella, *Das Lichtkleid JHWHs: Untersuchungen zur Gestalthaftigkeit Gottes im Alten Testament und seiner altorientalischen Umwelt.* FAT 15 (Tübingen: Mohr, 1996) 226–32, and also Jörg Jeremias, "Die Erde 'wankt,'" in Festschrift for Erhard S. Gerstenberger (Münster, 1997) 166–70.

[2] On this composition see especially Norbert Lohfink and Erich Zenger, *The God of Israel and the Nations: Studies in Isaiah and the Psalms.* Translated by Everett Kalin (Collegeville: The Liturgical Press, 2000) 168–83.

[3] Podella, *Das Lichtkleid* 231.

[4] In spite of Podella, *Das Lichtkleid* 227, n. 323, this contemporary understanding is to be maintained.

[5] This important dramatic aspect is lost when one joins Bernd Janowski (*ZThK* 86 [1989] 408) in seeing realized here the "stylistic form of rectifying the crisis." So also is justified Jörg Jeremias, "Die Erde 'wankt'" 169, n. 10: "This has to do with a permanent crisis (v. 3b) that each time encounters its limits in Yahweh's superiority (v. 4)."

[6] On Psalm 104 cf. also Erich Zenger, "'Du kannst das Angesicht der Erde erneuern' (Ps 104:6). Das Schöpferlob des 104. Psalms als Ruf zur ökologischen Umkehr," *BiLi* 64 (1991) 75–86. Krüger, "'Kosmo-theologie' zwischen Mythos und Erfahrung. Psalm 104 im Horizon altorientalischer und alttestamentlicher 'Schöpfungs'-Konzepte," *BN* 68 (1993) 49–74; Thomas Podellla, *Das Lichtkleid* 232–40.

[7] Krüger, "Kosmo-theologie," 71.

[8] Ibid., 67.

[9] Cf. Helen Schüngel-Straumann, *Ruach bewegt die Welt. Gottes Schöpferische Lebenskraft in der Krisenzeit des Exils.* SBS 151 (Stuttgart: Katholisches Bibelwerk, 1992) 70–75.

CHAPTER FOUR

The Eschatological Establishment of God's Rule as the Deliverance of Creation53

The Place and Value of the Creation Theme in New Testament Theology

The New Testament tells no stories of creation, offers no ideas about the beginning of creation, about the creation of the world and humankind, about a good and indestructible life connection, reaching back to the beginning of everything, between the creature and God as the sovereign of creation. At the center of New Testament theologies stands rather the concept of the saving activity of God at the end "of the age," whose time is running out. "Heaven and earth will pass away" (Mark 13:31) when, after the last great tribulation, the Son of Man, judge of the world, comes to gather the chosen ones from the four corners of the earth (Mark 16:27). Is the principle of creation to be abandoned, given this conception of the proximate end of the world? What relationship is there between the "new heaven" and "new earth" (cf. Revelation 21–22) and the heaven and the earth that the living God created at the beginning (Gen 1:1)?

There is only apparent tension between the hope that at the end God will establish divine rule by means of a judgment of the world and the creation-theological interpretation of humanity and world. In the ancient Near Eastern and Egyptian creation myths creation is understood as a taming of chaos, whereby chaos is not conceived of only as a "world-before-creation" but as a continuing threat to the created world and its order of life. Creation must continually be protected and preserved before the threatening inroads of chaotic forces and powers. The living space of creation must be wrested from chaos ever anew. This begins with the daily rising of the sun god, whose coming up out of the primeval waters reestablishes the cosmic order for the day just beginning. Politically this happens in the continuing historical struggle of the sovereign for victory against threats from foreign nations with different political systems.[1] The expectation of God's rule in the near future and the proclamation of its dawning in the present are understood against this background. They are an expression of the hope that at the end of a long history full of catastrophes and chaotic endings God will attain and make real the goal that was established at the beginning of the creation. The coming rule of God is the deliverance of creation from the ultimate and all-encompassing threat posed by the powers of chaos and death.

In the apocalyptic transformation of creation theology we find in the New Testament texts the point of departure for estimating the chances for life is not a trust in the stability of the creation as a basis for life, but rather the trust that the present menacing and intensifying crisis will not lead into the seemingly unavoidable and definitive catastrophe, and that, although the powers of chaos were dominant until now, God will put them forever in their place through the final and apocalyptic establishment of divine rule over the entire creation. Such an assessment of reality by no means sees God's creation in prevailing conditions, but rather its perversion. It nevertheless awaits its deliverance with confidence because it is God's creation, established from the very beginning to be a place of life.

This apocalyptic calculation of realities came into being at a time when the cultural identity of early Judaism was in extreme peril, namely at the high point of the conflicts over the fundamental principles of post-exilic Judaism, Torah, and Temple, precipitated after 175 B.C.E. by the reforming efforts of the Hellenists in Jerusalem.[2] After repeated violations of the high-priestly succession of office, after the conquest and plundering of Jerusalem by Antiochus Epiphanes in 169 B.C.E., after the Temple had been consecrated to Zeus Olympios in 167 B.C.E. and the practice of a manner of life consistent with the Torah had been forbidden by royal edicts concerning religion, a situation existed that, in the eyes of the pious who were true to the Torah, could no longer be made good without the intervention of God. The historical picture of Daniel 2,[3] which originated during that time, does not commence either with the absolute beginning of creation or with the Exodus and the revelation at Sinai as the foundations of Jewish existence, but counts off the succession of heathen world powers that had ruled over Jewish people with increasingly destructive power since the destruction of Jerusalem by the Neo-Babylonian Empire (cf. Dan 2:37-43). In this history nothing more can be perceived of God's rule among God's people or of divine care for creation. But although God's rule had disappeared behind the regime of secular empires, one initiated into the mysteries of divine rule knows that it is God who determines the length of the reigns of the heathen world rulers (cf. Dan 2:21) and who reveals the knowledge of this to those who are truly wise (cf. Dan

2:22). A part of this knowledge is also to recognize that at the end, without a touch from human hand, a stone will begin rolling that will strike the colossus of the world powers on its feet of clay and topple it. It will then be replaced by God's own eternal rule, which will never be handed over to any other nation (cf. Dan 2:44).

The working hypothesis of apocalyptic, whose dynamism continues unbroken even in the theology of the New Testament, is not understandable when it is seen as nothing more than an attempt to calculate the date of the end of the world in order to be able to take the appropriate precautions. The point at issue in Daniel 2 and in the traditions linked with it is not primarily the calculation of dates, which belongs, after all, to the unfathomable mysteries of the plans of God, the knowledge of which is given to no one (cf. Mark 13:32; Acts 1:7). It has rather to do with not giving up the thought of the righteousness of God in the midst of an unprecedented and worsening crisis situation. It is rather to make the worst crisis experience the criterion for believing in the judgment with which God will establish his universal rule over against the powers of chaos. The working hypothesis of apocalyptic, that presents the rule of God as the final deliverance of the believers out of the most extreme crisis, can be rightly assessed in its claim and its motivating power only when it is understood as a radically critical expression of trust in God as the Creator and perfecter of the world. This implies, on the other hand, that the theme of creation does not always appear expressly in the context of theologies marked by apocalyptic. The idea of the proximity of the coming rule of God is primarily a soteriological concept. God's redeeming action is expected in the near future.[4] But this soteriological conception has a creation theological dimension. The rule of God is the deliverance of the creation out of the most extreme endangerment from chaos, the definitive completion of the creation according to the measuring standard of God's righteousness. For this reason, the soteriology oriented to the rule of God in the end always also implies a basic creation-theological concept.

Motifs of Creation Theology Within the Framing Conception of the Gospel of Mark

The Gospel of Mark is an especially instructive example of a theological framework whose soteriological principal theme is constructed on a creation-theological foundation. This connection will be established in the exposition of the Gospel of Mark, namely in that portion of the book in which the course is set for the entire reading process.

Title

1:1 The beginning of the good news of Jesus Christ [the Son of God].

Exposition

First Summary

2a As it is written in the prophet Isaiah,
2b "See, I am sending my messenger ahead of you,
2c who will prepare your way."
3a The voice of one crying out in the wilderness:
3b "Prepare the way of the Lord,
3c make his paths straight!"
4a John **appeared** baptizing in the wilderness
4b and proclaiming a baptism of repentance for the forgiveness of sins.
5a And people from the whole Judean countryside and all the people of Jerusalem **were going out** to him,
5b and **were baptized** by him in the river Jordan, confessing their sins.

Second Summary

6a Now John **was clothed** with camel's hair, with a leather belt around his waist,
6b and he **ate** locusts and wild honey.
7a He **proclaimed,**
7b "The one who is more powerful than I is coming after me; I am not worthy to stoop down and untie the thong of his sandals.
8a I have baptized you with water;
8b but he will baptize you in the Holy Spirit."

First Episode

9a And it **came to pass:**
9b In those days Jesus **came** from Nazareth of Galilee
9c and **was baptized** by John in the Jordan.
10a And just as he was coming up out of the water,
10b he **saw** the heavens torn apart and the Spirit descending like a dove on him.
11a And a voice **came** from heaven,
11b "You are my Son, the Beloved;
11c with you I am well pleased."

Third Summary

12 And the Spirit immediately **drives** him **out** into the wilderness.
13a He **was** in the wilderness forty days, **tempted** by Satan;
13b and he **was** with the wild beasts,
13c and the angels **waited on** him.

Mark's gospel begins with a title (Mark 1:1) that presents the whole book as "the good news [gospel] of Jesus Christ." There follows a kind of motto identified as a quotation from the book of the prophet Isaiah. Thus the Gospel of Mark places itself in the context of another, already existing text. In reality what we find here is a combination of textual elements from Mal 3:1 (= Mark 1:2) and Isa 40:3 (= Mark 1:3), treated here as a single text. This is consistent with a certain understanding of Scripture in which the individual books of Sacred Scripture are read as a single document of God's revelation. In addition to the literal meaning of its text, the Scripture also contains untapped mysteries. These have to do, as the knowledgeable readers whom the text presupposes can immediately perceive, with the plans of God for the end time. The quotation from Mal 3:1 is an extract from a dialogue[5] in which two persons who are not more precisely identified discuss the announcement of an event that the readers can only relate to the appearance of God in the end time, the inbreaking of God's time[6] and the coming of God's royal reign. The speaker ("I") takes the role of the one who sends, the royal role, which in this context is appropriate to God. Who is addressed is at first not precisely stated.

Immediately after the motto-like Scripture quotation follows, without a sign[7] of any higher text ranking, the beginning of the events narrated by the evangelist in his book. The action related in the "gospel of Jesus Christ" is positioned within the context of a plan projected long ago that now comes to fulfillment. As has been discussed in heaven from eternity, that is to say, "as it is written in the prophet Isaiah," there appears in v. 4 the one who, in the dialogue of the heavenly beings, cries in the wilderness. The Scripture quotations are not, therefore, merely placed before the action like a motto, but belong to the first narrative sequence[8] that briefly describes the activity of the Baptizer.

With v. 6 the narrative begins anew. The Baptizer is introduced a second time and given special attributes. Once again his activity is made the theme, this time not by unnamed dialogue partners in heaven, but in his own words about himself in the context of earthly events. Thereby it becomes clear to what extent the baptism of all the people in the Jordan is the preparation for another figure. This figure is here for the first time called "the Stronger," and specifically in relation to the strong Baptizer, as the one who comes after him and who will not baptize merely with water, but in holy Spirit.

After this announcement (v. 7) comes the appearance of Jesus. But does this constitute a sequence? Does the one whom the Baptizer announces come to fulfill the announcement? While the narrator expressly puts Jesus' coming to be baptized together in time with the announcement by John of the Stronger one ("In those days Jesus came

. . ."), he just as explicitly has Jesus come from outside into the scene of the action that has already begun (". . . from Nazareth of Galilee"). The reader is invited to interpret this appearance as the coming of the Stronger one, but his role is not yet defined by this. What is announced in v. 8 will never be told in the Gospel of Mark. At this point it is at first only said that Jesus is baptized by John in the Jordan, just like all the others before him (cf. v. 9b "was baptized" with v. 5b "were baptized"). The sequence—Jesus comes and is baptized (v. 9)—is fully equivalent to that in the first summary (v. 5).

The reader learns in the sequence that follows (vv. 10-11) what role Jesus is to assume in the "gospel of Jesus Christ." Jesus' baptism by John, the feature of the action that takes place on the earthly horizon, is carried forward from heaven. At his *coming up* out of the water of the Jordan the baptized Jesus sees the heavens, previously accessible only through canonical knowledge of revelation but in reality closed, torn apart and the Spirit, God's creative power, *coming down* upon him. The voice from heaven speaks about this again in the dialogic you-form of Mark 1:2, now directed to Jesus. It identifies him with the expression "my Son, the Beloved" as the principal figure of the action, the son of the sovereign, God's Son. In the eternal plan of God it was decided long ago what the role of the Stronger amounts to in terms of content. Jesus enters into it as heaven supplies him with the charism of the Messiah, the royal deliverer of the people, the Son of God—the creative Spirit of God.[9]

The exposition of the Gospel of Mark ends with the so-called temptation of Jesus (vv. 12-13). The Spirit that has come down upon the messianic deliverer immediately "drives" Jesus into the wilderness, which now becomes the scene of a summary that presents a utopian model of the vocation for which Jesus has been equipped with the Spirit of God. The summary sets up in two contradictory statements in tension with one another: on the one hand, the forty days in the wilderness are the time of the direct confrontation between the bearer of the Spirit and the antagonist in the drama, Satan. On the other hand, these days are a time of peace: "and he was with the wild beasts; and the angels waited on him." Jesus appears in this summary as the royal master of the animals[10] and the angel as the powerful guarantor of peace in the previously divided creation against the power of Satan.[11] To establish this peace in opposition to the chaotic powers in creation is the task that is drawn up as the messianic mission of the Son of God before Mark narrates the story of Jesus of Nazareth.[12]

This begins as befits the vision of a pacified creation invoked in the exposition of the book. The agenda of Jesus' mission is proclaimed by Jesus as "the good news [gospel] of God" (v. 15): "The time is fulfilled, and the kingdom of God has come near; repent, and believe the good news." What the realization of this mission means becomes visible "immediately" (cf. 1:21, 23, 28, 29, 30) and "everywhere" (cf. 1:28) with the description of an exemplary day of Jesus' activity in Capernaum. The first programmatic act of Jesus in the public view of the Capernaum synagogue is an exorcism (1:23-28). The public reacts to this with a chorus of praise that appropriately captures the significance of the action.[13] "He commands even the unclean spirits, and they obey him" (v. 27c). With this formulation the individual exorcism is not only generalized but the expulsion of the demon by the exorcist is understood in a constructive sense as the subjugation of the demons to the authority of Jesus. Thus the miracle is interpreted by the public in a manner consistent with the agenda of Jesus' proclamation (v. 15), as a sign of the dawning of God's rule. It has really come near, and the public has recognized it. The healing of the Peter's fever-ridden mother-in-law in the second episode shows that the peace of creation is gaining a place in the human world. The woman who has been healed gets up and "serves" them. Her liberation from the sickness is not merely a rehabilitation so that she can attend to the traditional role of a woman. With the word "serve" the narrator establishes a link with the "serving" of the angel in the wilderness (1:13). The subjugation of demons and the restoration of the sick are therefore the aspects under which the liberation of the creation through God's rulership is described. The day in Capernaum ends with a summary that appropriately generalizes both of the individual episodes (1:32-34). What more, after all, can still be told when the hoped-for ending has already appeared as the good beginning?

The Gospel of Mark does not end in an idyll of creation peace. What begins with the victory of the empowered Son of God over the powers of chaos ends with the death of Jesus on the cross, his kingship rejected and ridiculed. The description of the death of Jesus (Mark 15:33-39) is presented as a time of the reign of chaos, during which, as at the beginning of the world, darkness covers the earth (cf. v. 33) and as a time of God's absence (cf. v. 34) during which the Righteous One is handed over to death without God's assistance. At the death of Jesus the curtain of the Temple, which displayed a depiction of creation,[14] tears into two parts "from top to bottom."

Chaos seems to have come away victorious. But precisely in the most extreme hour of the power of death the narrator opens for the reader a perspective capable of wresting some meaning from the event.[15] For this is at the same time the hour of recognition, in which the dying Jesus is identified as the Son of God by the commander of the Roman execution squad. When Jesus breathes his last (v. 37) the curtain of the Temple opens ("splits") (v. 38). When the centurion sees that "*in this way* [Jesus] breathed his last" (v. 39, repeating a phrase from v. 37), and recognizes and names Jesus before the opening Temple as God's Son, a view is simultaneously opened for the reader to see the Temple as a house of prayer for all nations. Just so had Jesus "taught" (cf. Mark 11:17a), as it "is written" canonically in Isa 56:7 (Mark 11:17b).

Mark's gospel was written toward the end of the Jewish War. In its description of the Passion of Jesus it connects the experience of the destruction of the city of Jerusalem and of the Temple with the recollection of Jesus' violent death.[16] What is at stake in the process is not primarily the attribution of guilt to third persons. Mark's gospel sees the death of Jesus and the destruction of Jerusalem from the perspective of personal consternation at the power of death in the most extreme and, according to the understanding of that time, final and apocalyptic distress (θλῖψις), the "temptation" (πειρασμός) that no one can withstand except the Son of God, and out of which God alone rescues (cf. Mark 1:13). Against this background the history of Jesus of Nazareth is newly recalled in Mark's gospel. It ends with his deliverance from death, which, however, is not recounted as such but proclaimed as the words of a white-clad messenger at the place of death (Mark 16:6). The good beginning of the liberation of creation in the book's exposition shows the reader the whole scope of the Easter faith. Against the background of the catastrophe of the Jewish War the raising of Jesus from the dead becomes even more the symbol of the universal liberation of creation. The Gospel of Mark devises no utopian idyll, but points out to its readers the way of following the Crucified as the introduction to a life lived within the environment of the power of death in the still unliberated creation of God.

Thus the framing concept of Mark's gospel proves to be a project shaped by creation theology. In its portrayal of Jesus' death and of the Easter event the Gospel of Matthew in particular has adopted and developed further the creation-theological element of the Gospel of Mark. In Matthew's description, at the moment when the curtain of the Temple tears from top to bottom, the earth shakes and the graves open for the resurrection of the saints (Matt 27:51-52). The rule of the power of death is broken. The underworld has to release its dead. Here the leader of the men on guard under the cross, who must recognize Jesus as the Son of God, is seen as a representative of the authority that, at the human level, exercises the power of death over creation. This aspect is very clearly accented in Matthew's Easter narrative. The angel who precipitates the earthquake through the opening of Jesus' tomb (Matt 28:2) destabilizes the system concerned with the safekeeping of the dead Jesus (cf. 27:65). He casts the fear of death on the watchmen at the grave while he himself, seated on the stone that was rolled away from the entrance of the tomb, represents the inbreaking of the rule of heaven. All power in heaven and on earth is now given to the Risen One. His messianic rule is fulfilled universally in the instruction of the nations in the Torah[17] interpreted by the messianic teacher until the end of the world (cf. 28:18-19).

Notes: Chapter 4

[1] See ch. 1 above.

[2] Cf. Martin Hengel, *Jews, Greeks, and Barbarians: Aspects of the Hellenization of Judaism in the Pre-Christian Period.* Translated by John Bowden (Philadelphia: Fortress, 1980) 49–82; P. Schäfer, *Geschichte der Juden in der Antike. Die Juden Palästinas von Alexander dem Großen bis zur arabischen Eroberung* (Stuttgart: Katholisches Bibelwerk; Neukirchen-Vluyn: Neukirchener Verlag, 1983) 48–62; Johann Maier, *Zwischen den Testamenten. Geschichte und Religion in der Zeit des zweiten Tempels* (Würzburg: Echter, 1990) 148–52; J. Alberto Soggin, *A History of Israel: From the Beginnings to the Bar Kochba Revolt, AD 135.* Translated by John Bowden (London: SCM, 1984; Philadelphia: Westminster, 1985) 283–320.

[3] For religious-historical classification cf. Rainer Albertz, *A History of Israelite Religion in the Old Testament Period.* Translated by John Bowden (Louisville: Westminster/John Knox, 1994–). Vol. 2: *From the Exile to the Maccabees,* 534–97; Karlheinz Müller, "Abschied von der 'Heilsgeschichte.' Die unterschiedbare Besonderheit des Umgangs der frühjüdischen Apokalyptik mit den geschichtlichen Überlieferungen 'Israels,'" in idem, *Studien zur frühjüdischen Apokalyptik.* SBAB 11 (Stuttgart: Katholisches Bibelwerk, 1991) 175–93.

[4] This conception of the divine rule in the synoptic Jesus-tradition goes back to the proclamation of the historical Jesus. Cf. Rudolf Schnackenburg, *God's Rule and Kingdom.* Translated by John Murray (2nd enlarged ed. New York: Herder & Herder, 1968); Helmut Merklein, *Die Gottesherrschaft als Handlungsprinzip. Untersuchung zur Ethik Jesu.* FzB 34 (3rd ed. Würzburg: Echter, 1984).

[5] This applies only for the text of Mal 3:1 altered by Mark. In Mal 3:1 no "you" is addressed, while in Mark 1:2 it appears twice ("ahead of you" [Greek: "before your face"] and, in allusion to Exod 23:20, "your way?"). The one who cries in the wilderness also demands that the "way of the Lord" be prepared. This makes it reasonable for the reader of this text collage to identify the "you" of v. 2 with the "Lord" to prepare whose way the one crying in the wilderness raises his voice.

[6] This is suggested especially by Isa 40:3 and its context. Cf. Bas van Iersel, *Reading Mark.* Translated by W. H. Bisscheroux (Edinburgh: T & T Clark, 1989) 36–37. Van Iersel calls attention especially to the shepherd motif that characterizes God's coming to save the people and is applied to Jesus in Mark's gospel (6:33-44; 14:28; 16:7).

[7] An episode normally begins with the specification of the scene's place and/or time. Here it is conspicuous that a time reference to the Baptizer's appearance is omitted. The place of his appearance (wilderness) is that named in v. 3. The opening scenic signals are therefore implied in the Scripture references both implicitly (time of the coming of the "Lord") and explicitly (wilderness as place of the crying out).

[8] The Baptizer appears with his agenda (baptism, proclamation); the people come and enter into this program (cf. the link between the phrases "forgiveness of sins" and "confessing their sins").

[9] On the Spirit-motif in the messianic context of the story of the Baptizer (cf. Isa 11:2; 61:1) cf. Fritzleo Lentzen-Deis, *Die Taufe Jesu nach den Synoptikern. Literarkritische und gattungskritische Untersuchungen.* FThS 4 (Frankfurt: J. Knecht, 1974) 127–70.

[10] Cf. below 178–80.

[11] Cf. Robert Murray, *The Cosmic Covenant: Biblical Themes of Justice, Peace and the Integrity of Creation.* Heythrop Monographs 7 (Westminster, Md.: Christian Classics, 1992) 127–29.

[12] On the motif-historical background see below, at v. 4; further D. Husser, "Die Versuchung Jesu und ihr jüdischer Hintergrund," *Judaica* 45 (1989) 110–28.

[13] That the response of the public to the exorcism is adequate becomes narratively clear when the choric ending in Mark 1:27 agrees in its essential points with the narrative comment in v. 22b. The narrator explains the effect of Jesus' *teaching* by means of the *authority* that distinguishes this teaching from that of the scribes. The public emphasizes the same connection after Jesus' authority has become visible in an exorcism: ". . . a new *teaching* with *authority*."

[14] Josephus, *Bell.* V.5.4.

[15] Cf. on the entire conceptual context Reinhard Feldmeier, "Der Gekreuzigte im 'Gnadenstuhl.' Exegetische Überlegungen zu Mark 15:37-39 und deren Bedeutung für die Vorstellung der göttlichen Gegenwart und Herrschaft," in Marc Philonenko, ed., *Le Trône de Dieu.* WUNT 69 (Tübingen: Mohr, 1993) 213–32.

[16] This connection is noticed far too little by scholarly research. But cf. Lloyd Gaston, *No Stone on Another: Studies in the Significance of the Fall of Jerusalem in the Synoptic Gospels.* NT.S 23 (Leiden: Brill, 1970).

[17] See Part IV, ch. 12 below.

Part II

Personification of the Creative Beginning

CHAPTER FIVE

Lady Wisdom as God's Creative Life Force (Proverbs 8)

Since the fourth century B.C.E. "the beginning" that YHWH creatively established and that permeates the cosmos has been personified, first as Lady Wisdom *(ḥokmā)* and then as the Torah, which was identified with her and which took form as YHWH's creative power before the creation itself. She inspires YHWH to and in the act of creation and finally descends to earth in order to inspire human beings also with the creative wisdom to fashion lives consistent with creation. As a general creation-theological concept, personified Lady Wisdom is encountered for the first time in the edition of the book of Proverbs that places Proverbs 1–9; 31:10-31 as a theological framework around the book. The statement about Lady Wisdom in Proverbs 1–9 and the poem about the wise woman in Prov 31:10-31 are to be interpreted in mutuality: the wise woman of Proverbs 31 is a paradigmatic concrete form of a life compatible with wisdom, that is, the life in harmony with creation to which Proverbs 1–9 summons.[1]

The Context and Composition of Proverbs 8:1-36

Proverbs 8:1-36 and 1:20-33 are conspicuous within the first part of the book of Proverbs (chs. 1–9)[2] because both texts contain the first-person discourse of personified Lady Wisdom. Both speeches take place amid similar scenery:

> Does not wisdom call,
> and does not understanding raise her voice?
> On the heights, beside the way,
> at the crossroads she takes her stand;
> beside the gates in front of the town,
> at the entrance of the portals she cries out (Prov 8:1-3).

Divine Wisdom speaks in the secular, political public sphere. The city gate and the square before it are the gathering place of the city. Here the court meets. Here important political decisions are announced. Here the prophets also make their spectacular speeches. Here Lady Wisdom stands and announces her teaching, which applies to *all*. In Prov 1:22-23 Wisdom preaches a sermon of judgment and repentance for the simple and the obstinate that culminates in the promise:

> Those who listen to me will be secure
> and will live at ease, without dread of disaster (Prov 1:33).

In Prov 8:4-36 Lady Wisdom presents a broadly-based *four-part instruction*.[3]

The first part, 8:4-11, is an elaborate call beginning the instruction, by means of which Wisdom seeks her target audience, the men of Israel and the whole human race:

> To you, O men, I call,
> and my cry is to (all) that live (Prov 8:4*).

In the *second part*, 8:12-21, whose new beginning is marked by the emphatic pronoun "I, yes I . . . ," Wisdom presents herself as the art and joy of living and as the power that brings righteousness or salvation, which is offered to all:

> I walk in the way of righteousness,
> along the paths of justice,
> endowing with wealth those who love me,
> and filling their treasuries (Prov 8:20-21).

The tetragram pointedly placed at the beginning marks the introduction of the *third part* (8:22-31). This part stands out against the preceding components (8:4-11, 12-21) by the fact that it is not paraenetic or related directly to its addressees. Now Wisdom speaks of herself as a creative power at and within the creation. She presents herself as the embodied "beginning" of the creation, the beginning of YHWH's way to and with the creation. The first and last words of this part refer to the two entities between whom the personified Wisdom mediates: YHWH (8:22) and humankind (8:31).[4] This part can be divided into four sections that make up a chiastic composition:

> A 22 The LORD created me at the beginning of his work,
> the first of his acts of long ago.
> 23 Ages ago I was set up,
> at the first, before the beginning of the earth.
>
> B 24 When there were no depths I was brought forth,
> when there were no springs abounding with water.
> 25 Before the mountains had been shaped,
> before the hills, I was brought forth—

26 when he had not yet made earth and fields,
or the world's first bit of soil.

B' 27 When he established the heavens, I was there,
when he drew a circle on the face of the deep,
28 when he made firm the skies above,
when he established the fountains of the deep,
29 when he assigned to the sea its limit,
so that the waters might not transgress his command,
when he marked out the foundations of the earth,
30 then I was beside him, like a master worker;[5]

A' and I was daily his delight,
rejoicing before him always,
31 rejoicing in his inhabited world
and delighting in the human race.

While the two inner sections clarify the relation of Wisdom to the "world before the creation" (B) or to the process of creation (B'), the two outer sections describe the relationship of Wisdom to YHWH before the creation (A) or to YHWH, to the world, and to human beings (A'). Each of the four sections has its own linguistic and theological profile:

1. In the first section (A: vv. 22-23) Wisdom refers to herself as a primeval expression of YHWH's very life. On the one hand she was created by YHWH, but on the other hand she is not simply like any of the other works of creation. She was formed "before the beginning of the earth" and "ages ago," that is, she has divine attributes like those that Psalm 93 attributes to the kingliness of YHWH. She is "the beginning of YHWH's way" in relation to the creation, and YHWH's existence as creator begins with her creation. She is "the beginning before the beginning" and as such is the extrapolation of the creative potency of YHWH's very nature.

2. The second section (B: vv. 24-26) characterizes the pre-creation nature of Wisdom in her relationship with the "world before the creation," which is portrayed in the already-described style of "not yet." In the background is a three-part world-edifice (v. 24: underworld/primeval ocean; v. 25: mountains as pillars of the heavens and as foundation pillars of the earth; v. 26: the disk of earth with its two regions of cultivated and uncultivated land) in contrast to whose not-yet existence Wisdom proclaims her own birth. In relation to the world-edifice, Wisdom is preexistent. In relation to YHWH, she is YHWH's child, born of YHWH. Although the text makes use of only passive constructions ("I was brought forth"), the context suggests only YHWH as the one who bears. Because this section and the next describe the works of creation itself with verbs of action from the building trades (partially with juristic connotations),

the special position of Wisdom is emphasized through the imagery of her birth: She is the creative side of YHWH's very self.

3. The third section (B': vv. 27-30a) describes the process of the creation of the world. While the second section had a perspective "from below upward and toward the center," the third section begins twice above and each time leads the eye downward before it comes to rest on the disk of the earth. "In the process two 'world levels' are connected to one another: the heavens (27a) are bound up with the lower limit of human living space (27b). The clouds above (28a), i.e., the boundary between the human and the heavenly sphere, are named in the text in connection with the most extreme depth, the sources of the primeval flood (28b). Then floods of water dangerous to the earth are delimited from the human living space (29ab). In conclusion this space is given a foundation and its bases are firmly set."[6] Thus the creation is here described as "the process of fencing off living spaces while simultaneously connecting them to each other."[7] This is not the main message, however. That is to be found in the first and last lines of the section, where Wisdom proclaims that she was present during the process of creation, and in fact alongside the creator. Wherever the creator was at work, whether in heaven or in the underworld, at the limits of the disk of Earth and at its foundation, there she was "with, i.e., alongside the creator."

4. The fourth section (A': vv. 30b-31), which is distinguished as the climax of this part by its artful chiastic structure (delight—rejoicing—rejoicing—delighting) refines the manner of Wisdom's presence in the creation. That the fourth section intends to proclaim the nature of the presence of Wisdom not precisely clarified in the third part is signified by the reprise of the key phrase "I was beside him/before him" (vv. 30a and 30b). The presence of Wisdom is characterized, through the adoption of Egyptian and Syrian imagery,[8] as the laughing, joking, and dancing of a lively young woman who delights the creator God, inspires and eroticizes so that the divine work becomes a true work of art. This vivacious, wonderfully beautiful Lady Wisdom is in a certain sense a personified idea of creation that makes YHWH one who creates out of fascination—with the goal of copying her form in the artistic work of the creation. For this reason it is only consistent when the section ends with the virtually paradoxical statement that Lady Wisdom wants henceforth, now that the world has been created, to continue her enchanting play among and with humankind, so that through her and with her they may learn the secret of the creation and so be able to live in harmony with it. This is, in any case, the conclusion drawn by the fourth part of the teaching discourse.

In the *fourth part* (8:32-36) Wisdom mixes appeals for her addressees to listen with the kind of beatitudes typical of instructions for living:

32 And now, my children, listen to me:
happy are those who keep my ways.
33 Hear instruction and be wise,
and do not neglect it.
34 Happy is the one who listens to me,
watching daily at my gates,
waiting beside my doors.
35 For whoever finds me finds life
and obtains favor from the LORD;
36 but those who miss me injure themselves;
all who hate me love death.

Because Wisdom was present at the creation and inspired the creator, she knows the secrets of creation. Whoever wishes to understand the creation can learn from her. Those who want to learn the art of living consistently with the creation must keep their eyes and hearts open to keep her in view and to be transformed by encountering her—like a lover who waits and watches continually before the house of the beloved in order to see her and not miss her when she emerges.

Because Wisdom is the creative, loving power of God, as explained in the preceding section (8:22-31), an encounter with her is an encounter with life itself. By linking a key phrase from 8:32 ("happy are those who keep *my ways*") back to 8:22 ("The LORD created me at the beginning of *his work*") the text emphasizes that whoever encounters Wisdom encounters YHWH, and whoever follows her ways meets the creator God as a companion on the way.

The Search for Wisdom as an Art of Living in Accord with Creation

Proverbs 8:22-31 can be read as a poetic variation on Genesis 1. Both texts deal with the contrast between "the world before the creation" and "the creation of the world by means of the creator God's separating and ordering activity." Both texts make use of technical imagery. The creator God constructs the cosmos as one builds a house. It is true that Prov 8:27-29 also applies verbs that otherwise appear mainly in the context of YHWH's lawmaking (establish, mark out, place), whereby the creative activity is simultaneously characterized as the establishing of a world and an ordered life. In both texts a creative power of YHWH that possesses a certain independence plays a role. In Gen 1:2 it is God's *rūaḥ*, that is, God's motherly, creative life power. In Prov 8:22-31 it is *ḥokmā* (Wisdom) that, as the Idea of Creation, guides the creator God and is secretly at home in the created world, desiring to be sought. At the same time the beautiful and life-loving Lady Wisdom of Proverbs 8 is a poetic-mythic commentary on Gen 1:31: "And God saw everything that he had made, and behold, it was very good," that is, beautiful and conducive to life. Proverbs 8 clarifies this statement by personifying Wisdom as the dancing and jesting young woman, who transforms the master of the works into an artist who in turn, in a kind of euphoric creative "high," forms the world as a dwelling place for life.

When one observes the context of Proverbs 1–9, which includes Prov 8:22-31, the different profile of this Wisdom theology of creation, its contrast to Genesis 1, becomes obvious. Like Genesis 1, Proverbs 1–9 desires to give an orientation for life and meaning within a profound crisis of identity. While Genesis 1 is part of a systematic theological concept, Prov 8:22-31 develops its

> creation theology in the context of Proverbs 1–9 as the foundation for a religious ethics in which the figure of Wisdom occupies a central place. For this purpose it develops its worldview in terms of polar opposites. Divine Wisdom is contrasted with the foreign or foolish woman of the underworld. Both feminine figures are active in the human world and attempt to move human beings to follow them. The figure of Wisdom relates her claim to authority to her pre-world origin, the theme developed in Prov 8:22-31. Her claim on her disciples is—in contrast to Genesis 1—very directly linked to human reality: she was present at the divine act of creation, which is described with the help of terms drawn from legal language. Therefore she knows what is right in the world and is capable of guiding her male and female adherents on the right way through life. . . . Wisdom is the criterion of authentic life . . . as an aid in orientation and at the same time content, as teaching about life.[9]

Those who seek this wisdom as guidance for living in accord with creation can allow themselves to be led by the book of Proverbs—that is the claim of this concept of creation theology.

The Torah as Creation's Blueprint

About two hundred years after the origin of Proverbs 8 the theology of creation laid out in it was carried forward significantly in the book of the Wisdom of Jesus Son of Sirach. Sirach 24 especially can be read as a more developed version of Proverbs 8. As in Prov 8:1-3, so in Sir 24:1-2 the scenery is first constructed for the public discourse to be held by personified Wisdom in 24:3-22. In this discourse, presented in the first person, Wisdom describes (similarly to Proverbs 8) her origin in God "at the beginning" (24:3-4), her universal presence at and in creation (24:5-6), and finally her coming down to Zion (24:7-12) and her creative, productive activity beginning from Zion (24:13-17). As in Proverbs 8, Wisdom closes her discourse in Sir 24:19-22 with an invitation to recognize and accept the life that is present in her.

19 "Come to me, you who desire me,
and eat your fill of my fruits . . .
22 Whoever obeys me will not be put to shame,
and those who work with me will not sin."

While the first part of Sirach 24 still remains on the message level of Proverbs 8 (although Wisdom's beginning is no longer portrayed with the imagery of birth, and she no longer acts like a playful young woman), the second part of Sirach 24 clearly brings new emphases in contrast to Proverbs 8. Sirach 24:23-24 identifies Wisdom with the book of the Torah and presents the search for wisdom as the study of the Torah. The Torah of Israel, which "came forth from the mouth of the Most High" (24:3) and which God created "before the ages, in the beginning" (24:9) is the blueprint that guided YHWH at the creation. Whoever understands the Torah understands the world. For this reason the correct interpretation of the Torah contributes to the continued existence of the creation. Life in accord with the Torah is, therefore, life in accord with creation.

This concept, laid down in Proverbs 8 and Sirach 24, according to which Wisdom is "the beginning" of the creation (Prov 8:22; Sir 24:9) then led to a re-reading of Gen 1:1. Common to all three of these texts is that they make use of the word "beginning" in their theology of creation. If one does not read the start of Gen 1:1, *bᵉreʾšît*, in a chronological sense, as "in or at the beginning," but understands the preposition *bᵉ* in the sense of "through or with," a subtle allusion can be found to Prov 8:22 and Sir 24:9: "By means of the beginning = by means of Wisdom or the Torah, God created the heavens and the earth." In fact, Targum Neofiti and the so-called fragment Targum paraphrase the first sentence of Genesis 1 in just this way.

That the Torah was the building plan of creation—and continues to be so—then becomes a central view of rabbinic theology. The classic example of this is the Midrash *Genesis Rabbah*, which says:

> Torah says: I was God's tool. Normally when a king of flesh and blood builds a palace he does not build it according to his own insight, but according to the insight of a master builder, nor does the master builder follow his own opinion, but has parchments and tables on which the apportionment of the rooms and chambers is noted down. Just so God looked into the Torah and created the world. And the Torah says: with *reʾšît (bᵉreʾšît)*, by which nothing else is to be understood than the Torah, God created the world (as can be seen in Prov 8:22).

Notes: Chapter 5

[1] On the connections between Proverbs 1–9 and Proverbs 31, cf. Ludger Schwienhorst-Schönberger, "Das Buch der Sprichwörter," in Erich Zenger, *Einleitung in das Alte Testament* (2nd ed. Stuttgart: Kohlhammer, 1996) 257–58. For the interpretation of these connections cf. especially Claudia V. Camp, *Wisdom and the Feminine in the Book of Proverbs* (Decatur, Ga.: Almond, 1985) as well as Silvia Schroer, "Die göttliche Weisheit und der nachexilische Monotheismus," in Marie-Theres Wacker and Erich Zenger, eds., *Der eine Gott und die Göttin.* QD 135 (Freiburg: Herder, 1991) 156–69.

[2] On Proverbs 1–9 cf. Gerlinde Baumann, *Die Weisheitsgestalt in Proverbien 1–9. Traditionsgeschichtliche und theologische Studien.* FAT 16 (Tübingen: Mohr, 1996).

[3] Ibid. 66–172.

[4] Cf. on this structure Michaela Bauks and Gerlinde Baumann, "'Im Anfang war . . .' Gen. 1:1ff. und Prov. 8:22-31 im Vergleich" *BN* 71 (1994) 24–52.

[5] See NRSV note: "Another reading is 'little child.'" On the discussion of the problem of translation in this passage cf. Baumann, *Die Weisheitsgestalt* 131–38. A detailed discussion is offered by Urs Winter, *Frau und Göttin. Exegetische und ikonographische Studien zum weiblichen Gottesbild im Alten Israel und in dessen Umwelt.* OBO 53 (Fribourg: Universitätsverlag; Göttingen: Vandenhoeck & Ruprecht, 1983) 517–22; I consider his decision for "master of works" to be more plausible.

[6] Bauks and Baumann, "'Im Anfang' . . ." 41.

[7] Ibid. 41–42.

[8] Cf. Othmar Keel, *Die Weisheit spielt vor Gott. Ein ikonographischer Beitrag zur Deutung der mᵉaḥḥäqät in Prov. 8:30f.* (Fribourg: Universitätsverlag; Göttingen: Vandenhoeck & Ruprecht, 1974); Winter, *Frau und Göttin* 522–23.

[9] Bauks and Baumann, "'Im Anfang' . . ." 51–52.

CHAPTER SIX

The *Logos* as the Revelation of God's Creative Glory (The Gospel of John)

The beginning of the Gospel of John is probably the most impressive set of opening lines in the New Testament. The author begins with a prologue whose lyric power radiates into every part of the book. The consensus of research is that an existing hymn has been adapted for use here. The consensus is also that the hymn in John 1:1-18 is not in its original form, but has been expanded with non-lyrical elements. Still disputed are the questions of the original wording and of its function as the opening of the book. The second question is the more important of the two. The creation-theological beginning of the hymn is an indicator that will be of fundamental importance for understanding the Gospel of John in its final canonical form. Consequently, the concern in what follows will not be with reconstructing the pre-Johannine hymn[1] but with its structure and significance in the context of the canonical Gospel of John.

"From his glory we have all received": The Prologue of John's Gospel (John 1:1-18)*

1a In the beginning was the *logos*,
1b and the *logos* was with God,
1c and God was the *logos*.
2 **This one was in the beginning with God.**
3a All things came into being through him,
3b and without him came into being
3c not one thing that has come into being.
4a In him was life,
4b and the life was the light of all people.
5a And the light shines in the darkness,
5b and the darkness did not comprehend it.
6a *There came a man*
6b sent from God,

6c *his name: John.*
7a *This one came as a witness,*
7b *to testify to the light,*
7c *so that all might believe through him.*
8a **This one was not the light,**
8b **but he was to testify to the light.**
9a It was the true light
9b that enlightens everyone
9c that was coming into the world.
10a He was in the world,
10b and the world came into being through him,
10c and the world did not know him.
11a He came to what was his own,
11b and his own people did not receive him.
12a But to all who received him
12b he gave power
12c to become children of God,
12d those who believe in his name,
13a who not from blood
13b and not from the will of the flesh
13c and not from the will of man,
13d are begotten, but from God.
14a And the *logos* became flesh
14b and lived among us,
14c and we saw his glory,
14d glory as of the only-begotten of the Father
14e full of grace and truth.

15a *John testified to him*
15b *and cried out, saying:*
15c ***"This was the one of whom I said,***
15d *'The one who comes after me*
15e *was before me*
15f *because he was prior to me.'"*
16a For from his fullness
16b we have all received
16c grace upon grace.

17a For the Law was given through Moses;
17b grace and truth came through Jesus Christ.
18a No one has ever seen God.
18b The only-begotten God,
18c who is close to the Father's heart,
18d **this is the one who has made [God] known.**

The impression that this is a lyrical text is based on the presence of certain stylistic devices. These are, especially, the repetition of words *(reduplicatio/anadiplosis),* which produces a certain rhythm and thus divides the text into lyrical lines.

The text begins with a tri-colon (v. 1). The structure of the strophe is determined by the distribution of the word *logos* according to the scheme a/ab/ba. The word *logos* is repeated several times *(reduplicatio/anadiplosis)* and thus builds to a climax *(gradatio).* It stands in emphatic position at the end, so that the first and third lines comprise an *inclusio.* Other strophes reveal other variations of the *anadiplosis.* Verse 3 reveals a so-called *conversio/epiphora* with its repetition of a verb form of "become" (scheme . . . a/ . . . a/ . . . a). Verses 4-5 constitute a simple progressive climax (scheme . . . a/a . . . b . . . /b . . . c/c . . . d). Verse 10 is a so-called *repetitio/anaphora* scheme (a . . . /a . . . /a . . .). In vv. 11-12a an *anaphora* is combined with an *anadiplosis* (scheme a . . . /a . . . b/b . . .). In v. 13 there is the stylistic figure of the *correctio* (not . . . but) in which the triple negation at the beginning of lines a-c *(anaphora)* and the *anadiplosis* in lines b-c structure the whole strophe as a climax. The *anadiplosis* is inserted very effectively in v. 14cd.

In light of these observations it is natural to suppose that these are elements of a traditional lyrical work in John 1:1-18. A *logos* poem was assimilated here. That it was an already-existing work that was used and revised, perhaps adopted only partially verbatim and worked into the new context, can be perceived especially in the tensions that the text of the Prologue reveals at those points where narrative prose passages are inserted into the lyric. Those passages are signaled by italics in the translation above (vv. 6-7, 15). It is true that the first narrative passage (vv. 6-7) takes up the keyword "light" from the preceding lyric strophe, and does not, therefore, stand isolated in its new context. On the other hand, not until v. 9 is the light motif taken up again and continued at the lyric level ("the true light that enlightens . . ."). Something similar can be said about the narrative v. 15, which ruptures the keyword links between the lyric vv. 14-16 ("full of grace"—"fullness"—"grace upon grace"). In this respect the narrative passages give the impression of being later insertions into the lyric text. They introduce the figure of John the Baptizer, who will play a special role in the text that follows (from 1:19 onward). It is especially the narrative passages that cause the apparent lack of uniformity in the text of the Prologue.

The bold type in some lines of the translation denotes a third component with special linguistic characteristics. Their common feature is that, by means of a demonstrative pronoun, they refer back to a name previously introduced. These are neither lyric nor narrative passages, but discursive passages, more precisely statements of identification. Introduced by anaphoric demonstrative pronouns, they are to be found both in the lyric and in the narrative passages. Thus they are of special significance for the consistency of the extant text.

These identifying sentences constitute in themselves a referential context. In v. 2 the author identifies the *logos* as the key figure of his text, and in the closing verse, 18d, explains why this figure is so important. This is the one who has brought news from God. With this, the meaning of the entire subsequent narrative of the story of Jesus is located under this aspect. These positive identifications form an *inclusio* that holds together the beginning and end of the Prologue. Within it are two further identifications having to do with the role of John the Baptizer. He is identified as one sent from God whose task is to give witness to the *logos* as the light of human beings (see v. 7 in relation to v. 4). It is striking that in v. 8 a distinction in the form of a *correctio* is drawn between his task as a witness and the content of his testimony. This corresponds to v. 15 with its brief narrative presentation of his appearance as a witness. Here the Baptizer, as a figure of the narrated world, formulates one of the positive identifying statements about the *logos*. Thereby he presents himself in agreement with the role assigned to him in the identifying v. 8. Therefore v. 8 is not to be understood as a criticism of the Baptizer, but rather refers from the outset to the Baptizer's specific function in the Fourth Gospel.

The identifying statements are the key to understanding the Prologue as a whole and its relationship to the subsequent context of the gospel as a book. It is these statements above all that reveal the unified perspective that dominates the Prologue as a whole. The identifications were formulated and arranged by an author who here, before he begins to narrate (from 1:19, again with an identifying opening), communicates with his reader about the conditions of the possibility of what he is about to tell. He speaks here, before the narrative, as an exponent of a group identified as "we" that has at its disposal some special knowledge that they owe to the primordial *logos*, who, becoming flesh, has brought a message from God. The Prologue of the Fourth Gospel, John 1:1-18 in its entirety, is therefore to be interpreted as an etiological reflection on the knowledge of this "we-group," as whose spokesman the author presents himself.[2]

The first sense unit (vv. 1-2) presents the divine sphere as the original location of the *logos*, specifically through three statements about the *logos*. It is assigned absolutely to the origin. Its manner of existence is a relationship to God; it is itself divine in essence. The identifying v. 2, which closes the first sense unit, takes up the first two statements, for they contain aspects fundamental to the quality of the knowledge of the "we-group." The knowledge provided by the incarnate *logos* as Revealer (see v. 18) is absolutely primordial knowledge based on the primordial relationship of the *logos* to God. This knowledge is divine in nature.

The second sense unit (vv. 3-8) contains explicit statements on the theme of creation. It deals with creation as the area of human experience. It includes statements that stand in great tension to one another. Positioned at the beginning are those that view reality as the one creation that came into being through the *logos*. All things were created by the *logos*, and a reality in addition to that which came into being through the *logos* does not exist (see v. 3). Life itself is owing to the creative *logos*, and what makes this relationship visible is experienced by human beings as light (v. 4). But the recognition of life as light takes place against the contrasting background of darkness, a personified entity that stands over against light as the principle of (refused) recognition (Reception). Because the darkness does not accept the light, it asserts itself in opposition to the light as a counter-principle and even appears as the space surrounding the light (see v. 5). Hence the darkness is not viewed as the chaos before creation, out of which the creation proceeds, but as one of two principles that stand in contrast to one another. It is as this contrasting relationship that reality presents itself, as light in the darkness.

In terms of the knowledge of the "we-group" the previous statements of the first two verses of this unit emphasize the essential unity of reality as creation and thus also the essential universality of knowledge as knowing this one reality. This realization appears as a knowledge of creation that is accessible to "people" in general and that is given with "life" as "light." Therefore, at the first moment when the Prologue says anything at all about human beings it draws a parallel between "life" and "light," an epitome of creation reality and a corresponding example that locates this reality under the aspect of awareness or knowledge.[3] Cosmology and anthropology, reality and knowledge thus establish a close relationship in the Prologue of the Fourth Gospel that is, in the first place, portrayed as essentially monistic and universal. It is not until the statement of v. 5 that this creation-theological concept is modified by the introduction of "darkness," the entity that stands in contradiction to "light." The light does not eliminate the darkness, but light and darkness coexist in opposition to one another. The universal knowledge, basically accessible to all humans as created beings, of their lives as a reality created by the *logos*, accordingly appears from the perspective of the "we-group" as a certain way of understanding reality in opposition to a fundamentally different one that proceeds from understanding reality as "darkness." "Light" and "darkness" are principles that correspond to competing views of reality. One of these two views is that proposed by the "we-group." It claims to be the original, the one corresponding to the origin of life from the *logos*.

Still to be explained is the aspect of knowledge in terms of which the Prologue of the Fourth Gospel describes the double nature of reality. It has previously been merely alluded to with the metaphors of light and darkness, which name cosmic principles. At this point the author inserts into the Prologue of his book the first incipiently narrative passage (vv. 6-7) in which the theme of knowledge is first explicitly named. The figure of John the Baptizer is introduced. He is the envoy of God sent with the task of breaking the universality of cosmic darkness by means of his witness to the light. It is presupposed that darkness determines the conditions under which reality is understood, and this without exception and for every human being.

The goal of the Baptizer's mission is consequently universal in its orientation to the objective that "all" should "believe" on the basis of his witness. The concern is, as the word "believe" clearly establishes, not merely for the reestablishment of a natural perception of reality as creation, but for a special kind of knowledge, namely one transmitted at God's direction. Nevertheless, this understanding first initiated and made possible by God's sending is presented as fundamentally open to "all" people. Light and darkness will not coexist forever. The knowledgeable "we-group," as whose representative the author speaks in the Prologue, view their own knowledge in principle as the suspension of the cosmic antagonism, after whose breakup reality as a whole will be seen by "all" in the same manner as the "we-group" sees it at the present. The knowledge of the "we-group," although transmitted through God's sending, as the reader here learns, is universal in that it abolishes the universal dualism of light and darkness.

The second sense unit closes with the identifying statement in v. 8. As has already been said, v. 8 is not to be understood as criticism of the Baptizer, but says that his testimony is itself the access to the primordial knowledge about the light, which formerly had been inaccessible. In his witness, however, that knowledge has not yet been experienced ("seen") as such.

The third sense unit (vv. 9-13) deals with human divisions that follow the coming of the *logos* into the world.[4] While the statements of the second unit claim universal validity (as instruction about creation, about the two cosmic principles with corresponding general anthropological statements about the possibility of recognizing reality as creation and about the frustration of that recognition), the third unit deals with oppositions between human beings that appear depending on their attitude toward the *logos*, whether they accept it or not. Thus the coming of the *logos* into the world leads to the opposition between light and darkness becoming manifest among human beings. The contrast that appears in the second unit as the rivalry of cosmic principles is intensified in the third unit by the movement of the *logos* toward an (eschatological) crisis in the human world.

In the sense of this intensification v. 9 again takes up the statement from v. 4. Now the subject has become the "true light who enlightens everyone" when it comes into the world. Here for the first time the author introduces a concept descriptive of the human world: "cosmos," "world." Hence there exists from the outset a contrast between the light, on the one hand, and the cosmos, on the other, first of all through the fact that "light" is assigned a special quality (it is "true"), thus implying a contradiction that, though never spoken, is debited by connotation against the content of "cosmos." In the crisis-like process of the *logos'* appearance in the human world, the latter becomes the realm of opposition to the *logos* and its truth and so the epitome of the world of unenlightened people closing itself against the *logos*. The following v. 10 reflects this relationship between the *logos* and the cosmos. The world of human beings that is called cosmos is really nothing else but the creation brought about by the *logos* (see v. 10b); but insofar as it fails to recognize the *logos* at its coming into the world (see v. 10c) it proves itself to be the sphere of influence of darkness. These statements about the human being and the world are again varied by v. 11, specifically in an allusion to Israel's special relationship to God as "his own" *(hoi idioi).* At this point motifs of the Wisdom tradition are taken up (see especially Sir 24:8, 12); these will require later attention. When it is said in v. 11b that "his own" *(hoi idioi)* do not receive the *logos*, the statement of v. 10, which was at first a reference to the cosmos, is now applied to the Jewish people, apparently as a totality. But vv. 12-13 place a counter-group in contrast to "his own," namely the "children of God" (v. 12c).

The designations "his own" and "children of God" obviously stand in competitive relationship to one another. The refusal to receive the *logos* by "his own" stands in direct contrast to the reception of the *logos* by the "children of God." To the acceptance *(elabon)* of the *logos* by the "children of God," on the other hand, corresponds the gift *(edōken)* of the *logos*, which marks those who receive the *logos* with the power *(exousia)* to "become" children of God (see v. 12a). This becoming takes place in the process of the division of human beings that is precipitated by the coming of the *logos* into the world. This process is the separation between a believing minority and a majority among those who are the property of the *logos* who close themselves to the *logos*, in other words, the people of Israel.[5] It is simultaneously understood as a crisis of the cosmos. In the confrontation with the *logos* who comes into the world, "his own" are the representatives of the world. Their crisis is the crisis of the cosmos, and the crisis of the cosmos is theirs. It is in this sense that the Gospel of John uses the expression "the Jews" (from 1:19 onward).

In relation to the knowledge of the "we-group," this says that from the very beginning the group with knowledge sets itself in opposition to its Jewish environment. For this group the Jewish majority is equivalent to the "property of God" that refuses the *logos* who has come and has therefore become alien for them, the minority who receives him as *logos*. Their knowledge, in terms of which they define themselves, sets them up as a cognitive minority. This knowledge is, however, their "power." The knowing minority is what it is, or can become, not on the basis of its natural origin but on the basis of its knowledge.

The fourth sense unit (vv. 14-18) deals with the gift of the knowledge of the "we-group." It begins with a lyrical strophe (v. 14) after which follows the second narrative passage (v. 15), and it ends with a reflection on the nature of this knowledge in relation to the knowledge that had been given by Moses as Torah (vv. 16-18).[6]

The culminating statement of the Prologue in v. 14 is structured as a sequence: the incarnation of the *logos* and its "dwelling" among "us" is the foundation for the "seeing" of the "we-group." That the creative, primordial *logos* itself "becomes flesh"[7] is, in the understanding of the Gospel of John, above all the event of the *appearing* of the *logos* among human beings, and is therefore conceived primarily as a revelatory event. God's glory is now seen in the residence of the *logos* in creation. By the fact that the *logos* itself becomes a creature, God's glory becomes visible among human beings.

The last strophe, especially its last line ("full of grace and truth") contains allusions to Exodus 33 and 34 (especially to Exod 33:19; 34:6), to which the statements in the reflective closing verses John 1:16-18 refer. In Exod 33:12-23 Moses pleads to be able to see the glory of God. This request is not granted by YHWH in the sense that Moses made it: ". . . you cannot see my face; for no one shall see me and live" (Exod 33:20b). God's promise to Moses is: "I will make all my goodness pass before you, and will proclaim before you the name, 'The LORD'; and I will be gracious to whom I will be gracious, and will show mercy on whom I will show mercy" (v. 19). This request, the third and last that Moses makes in the context of a dialogue in which he fights for God's presence for his people, explores the question of the closest conceivable approach of the human being to God. The glory of God is understood in the first petitions of Moses' dialogue as the glitter of power that God supplies to God's people to protect them. It is that which the people will experience of God along their historical way. But as the revelation of God's very self it is inaccessible to human beings. Verses 21-23 concede to Moses the most extreme possibility of experiencing the passing by of God's glory, standing in a cleft in the rock and protected by God's hand from the vision of glory, and with the permission to see God from behind.

Exodus 34:1-10 has to do with the renewal of the covenant (after the falling away from YHWH; see Exodus 32) in a renewed encounter with God on Mount Sinai. Here, too, the passage centers on the motif of glory experienced as YHWH's passing by Moses. Now the accent lies on the power of YHWH to save and to destroy, to forgive and to punish (vv. 6-8). These statements, which are of central importance for the post-exilic image of God, open with the statement to which John 1:14c alludes: "The LORD, the LORD; a God merciful and gracious, slow to anger, and abounding in steadfast love and faithfulness." These allusions are, in the first place, a component of the statements of John 1:14. The issue here is not yet in any sense a delimitation of or polemic about the experiences of the glory of God associated with the figure of Moses, but rather the grounding of the knowledgeable groups' own understanding in biblical-canonical knowledge. The "we-group," reflecting on its knowledge, had "seen" in the incarnate *logos* the gleam of that which was inaccessible to humans, the glory of God. The "steadfast love" and "faithfulness"[8] of God were thus experienced in overflowing measure.[9]

In the second narrative insertion (v. 15) the testimony of John is for the first time formulated in a verbal discourse. The Baptizer, identified by the author in v. 8, now personally speaks one of the identifying statements about the *logos* ("This was he . . ."). What is unusual is the time gradient or gradation of various levels of the text. The sentence is the introduction to another that is cited by the Baptizer as something he himself had already said: "This was he of whom I said, 'He who comes after me ranks ahead of me.'" With this the Prologue reminds the group that sustains this literature of the testimony of the Baptizer about Jesus, which is summarized in a saying of the Baptizer, quoted word for word, in which the latter refers to an earlier statement of his about Jesus. This multi-layered *recollection* of the identification of Jesus by the Baptizer is the point of contact for the beginning of the action narrated by the author of the Fourth Gospel in 1:19.

With this obvious violation of the rules of narrative sequence the author summarizes the whole of the Baptizer's activity for the readers. They, as Christians, already have an impression of it, but this summary functions to emphasize the exclusivity of the knowledge that is the a theme of the Prologue. The comment about the *logos* in which the Baptizer quotes himself is an enigma that the reader can easily understand against the background of the Prologue's context. This enigma is not formally resolved until 1:29.

The Prologue closes with reflections on the quality of the knowledge bestowed by the *logos*. The first statement (v. 16), with its use of the Wisdom motif of fullness, links back to v. 14e. The verb "receive" corresponds to the "seeing" in v. 14c. "We . . . all" refers to the "we-group."

The word "all" emphasizes the fundamental significance of knowledge for the community that is reflecting on its knowledge in this text. The initially enigmatic statement that with their knowledge they had received "grace upon grace" is developed in v. 17. Contrasted here are the Law that was "given" through Moses, and the grace and truth that "came [to be]" through the knowledge given by the *logos*. On both sides it is a question of knowledge that is "given," i.e., with revelation. Consequently there can be no intention to play off the *logos* revelation against the Sinai revelation. Obviously, however, the author does not view what Moses sought in his dialogue with God in Exod 33:12-33 as fulfilled until the revelation of the *logos:* to see the glory of God. What even Moses could not experience without dying (see Exod 33:20b) has been made visible through the incarnate *logos* and accessible to the knowledgeable "we-group." The *logos*, having its beginning as the only-begotten in immediate proximity to God, has in an unparalleled way made God's glory visible in the world of human beings. The Gospel of John will tell anew for its readers this authentic "news" that the *logos* has brought.

Early Jewish Wisdom as Tradition-Historical Background

In the Prologue of the Fourth Gospel (1:1-18) the *logos* is a person within the divine sphere, as becomes clear especially through v. 1 and the identifying statements in vv. 2 and 18d. Beyond this, the *logos* is considered as the principle of creation (see v. 3). In the early Jewish Wisdom tradition these two concepts appear principally in statements about personified Wisdom. Personified Wisdom and the personified Word of God can be understood as parallel entities. In Sir 24:3a Wisdom says of herself that she "came forth" (as creative word) from the mouth of the Most High. In the Targum Neofiti 1 the personified Word and (here not personified) Wisdom are seen at the creation in a close relationship: "From the beginning with Wisdom the Memra [Word] of the Lord created and perfected the heaven and the earth."[10]

The knowledge-etiological interpretation of the Johannine Prologue presented above presupposes the early Jewish Wisdom traditions as background. The tradition-historical development[11] that is essential to the Fourth Gospel can be sketched at least briefly here.[12]

Proverbs 8 and Sirach 24 can be a point of departure.[13] In Proverbs 8 personified Wisdom speaks in the first person as a teacher. She seeks to enlist young people whom she can guide into a wise life, that is, one consistent with creation. Her competence resides in the fact that she herself is involved in the "beginning" of creation (v. 22).

Lady Wisdom[14] here has at least the beginnings of a life story. She employs her joy in creation (v. 30) for pedagogical purposes (vv. 32-36), because it is her joy to "play" among human beings also (v. 31b), just as she did before God at the beginning of creation (vv. 30b-31a). Proverbs 8:22-31 is therefore also an etiological text. The perspective that gives it meaning is the invitation to Wisdom and to a life guided by Wisdom. The idea that the search for Wisdom is not in vain because Wisdom, for her part, seeks to be close to human beings and allows herself to be found emphasizes the possibility of fulfilling the philosophical ideal.

Sirach 24 displays the same first-person-singular structure as Proverbs 8, but now "Wisdom" already has a *dramatic* personal history. After she proceeded from the mouth of the Most High as word of creation, after her residence in the heights of the divine sphere and her cosmic rule over all peoples (vv. 3-6) Wisdom seeks and is granted—at the command of her Creator—her own place in the world of human beings: "Make your dwelling in Jacob, and in Israel receive your inheritance" (v. 8cd). In Sir 24:23 (see Bar 4:1) Wisdom, who resides on Zion, is identified with the Torah: "All this is the book of the covenant of the Most High God, the law that Moses commanded us as an inheritance for the congregations of Jacob." With the Torah, therefore, the Wisdom of God appeared upon earth and abides among humans (see Bar 3:38). The knowledge-etiology is in Sirach 24 more fundamentally the structural principle of the whole text than in Proverbs 8. Sirach 24:25-34 reflects on the value of Torah knowledge and Torah scholarship as knowledge of creation. The Torah scholar participates (vv. 30-34) with his or her knowledge in the fullness of meaning of God's Wisdom in the Torah (cf. vv. 25-29), which is as inexhaustible as the ocean (compare v. 29a with v. 31). The interpretive perspective of this classical Torah-Wisdom conception is what, in view of the challenge to early Judaism posed by the Hellenistic concept of education and culture, strengthened confidence in the superiority of Judaism's own religion and invited a self-conscious contesting of Hellenism as a cultural power.

Wisdom's search for her place in the world of human beings is told in Sirach 24 as a success story. According to Bar 3:9-14 Israel abandoned its closeness to Wisdom and suffers as a result the fate of banishment into exile. This theme is consistently formulated as *tragedy* in apocalyptic Wisdom literature, for example in Ethiopian Enoch (1 Enoch 42:1-3), which has an altered slant in contrast with Sirach 24:

1 Wisdom found no place where she could live. She had a dwelling in the heavens.

2 Wisdom went out to live among the children of humanity. And she found no dwelling.
Wisdom returned to her dwelling and took her place among the angels.

> 3 And injustice came forth from her chambers. Those who did not seek her found her. And she dwelt among them like the rain in the desert and like the dew on the thirsty land.[15]

The history of Wisdom and her rival is here reduced to four short sequences. "Wisdom" appears grammatically in the third person. Now she has a *tragic* personal fate. From the beginning she searches in vain and finds nowhere to live. Her dwelling in the heavens is only an intermediate station on a continuing quest for the place she really desires among human beings. At this point the search fails, and Wisdom returns in frustration to her heavenly place. Her rival, Foolishness, personified here as Injustice, triumphs, and in fact in a manner that is nonsensical according to Wisdom's standards: "Those who did not seek her found her (nevertheless)." She had no need to exert herself pedagogically. Injustice thrives by itself. The knowledge-etiological interpretation corresponds to the tragic tendency in history. A cognitive minority reflects on its knowledge and the relationship to its cultural surroundings that this knowledge implies. The tragically disastrous search of Wisdom for her place in the world of human beings is emblematic of the situation of the besieged minority. She fails to find her place in the human world. The context (the metaphorical discourse in 1 Enoch 37–71) engages the basic question of what place there can be for the righteous when the land is occupied by sinners. The answer is: The base of support for the oppressed righteous is the transcendent place occupied by rejected Wisdom when she returned from the world of human beings (see 39:3-14) until the land is free of sinners (see 48:1-6). The interpretive perspective of such a reflection on one's own knowledge and corresponding spiritual home is the self-affirmation of a sub-cultural grouping in its alternative (apocalyptic) orientation and is the invitation to a life marked by decisive (mental) resistance. The present is a situation that has come about through the disappearance of Wisdom. "Then shall reason hide itself, and wisdom shall withdraw into its chamber, and it shall be sought by many but shall not be found, and unrighteousness and unrestraint shall increase on earth" (4 Ezra 5:9b-10). "For I know that sinners lead human beings astray in order to make Wisdom angry, so that no place is found for her and no temptations will diminish" (1 Enoch 94:5b).

In John 1:1-18 "Wisdom" is represented by her sibling, "the Word."[16] In spite of the lyric style, "the *logos*" as well as "Lady Wisdom" in 1 Enoch 42:1-3 are grammatical third persons and thus qualified to assume a role in a narrative. Here, too, the personified *logos* has a *tragic* fate. But in contrast to 1 Enoch 42, the status of the cognitive minority and the quality of its knowledge are *euphorically* formulated. The real difference from all parallels consists, of course, in the fact that the *logos* does not appear here only as a personified aspect of God's reality, but as a real human person within human history: Jesus of Nazareth. The story of Jesus of Nazareth is recalled as the definitive coming of God's Wisdom to her people, a coming that did not merely leave traces in the knowledge of a cognitive minority but really constitutes the beginning of the uncovering of the truth of the creation.

However, the Prologue of the Fourth Gospel has not yet introduced the main character of the book, Jesus of Nazareth. The relationship between the knowledge-etiological reflection and his story is the theme of the gospel's *expositio* (John 1:19–2:11).

Elements of Creation Theology in the Exposition (John 1:19–2:11) and in the First Ending (20:30-31) of the Gospel of John

The narrative conception of the exposition can be demonstrated in the arrangement of the episodes and scenes. The events are divided according to days.

	John the Baptizer episodes	Jesus episodes
1st day (1:19-28)	The Baptizer is questioned by a delegation from Jerusalem.	
2nd day (1:29-34)	The Baptizer (without antagonists) identifies Jesus as the bearer of the Spirit and "Son of God."	
3rd day (1:35-39)	The Baptizer again identifies Jesus, this time before two of his disciples, who then follow Jesus and "remain" with him.	
(1:40-42)		One of the disciples brings his brother to Jesus; the latter is then identified by Jesus as Cephas/ Peter.
4th day (1:43-51)		Jesus "finds" another disciple who, in turn, finds his brother and brings him to Jesus. A mutual identification occurs. Jesus identifies the disciple as "a true Israelite"; the disciple identifies Jesus as

Continued from page 77		
		"Son of God" and "King of Israel."
After 3 days (2:1-11)		The wedding at Cana of Galilee becomes the event of the revelation of Jesus "glory" for his believing disciples.

The transition from the Prologue to the narrative world of John's gospel is in 1:19. With the first subsequent episode, the identifying testimony of the Baptizer of 1:15 is for the first time *dramatized,* and it becomes a component of a dialogue sequence whose structure (threefold refusal to answer questions, two alternative statements) corresponds to the logic of 1:8. The Baptizer is not the light, but testifies to the light. With this begins the major narrative sequence that ends with 2:1-11. It is the narrative version of the reflection in the Prologue. Already in 1:7 the Prologue, by means of two final clauses, delineates the framework that is completed by the narration in 1:19–2:11. The Baptizer gives his testimony about the Light (first final clause) so that all may come to believe (second final clause). The beginning of the exposition (1:19) corresponds to the first final clause. The ending (2:11) corresponds to the second.

The creation-theological implications of the exposition lie along the semantic line laid out by the metaphors "light," "glory," and "seeing" that runs through the exposition. Thereby, and from the very beginning, it is established—through the determination of the role of the Baptizer as witness to the "light" in 1:7-8—that the "seeing" is always related, in the sense of the Prologue and the episodes of the exposition that follow, to the recognition of the original created reality. The exposition develops this aspect as a whole in relation to the works of Jesus and his being recognized by those who witness his deeds.

The motif of seeing is not present in the dialogue with the emissaries from Jerusalem (1:19-28). The Baptizer describes his own role, in accordance with the synoptic tradition (see Mark 1:3), with an appeal to the canonical knowledge of the Jewish religion, as "the voice of one crying out in the wilderness, 'Make straight the way of the Lord'" (Isa 40:3, cited in John 1:23). Concerning the one who is announced, who will come after the Baptizer, he says: "Among you stands one whom you do not know" (v. 26c). With this, the one who is announced is not only *not* identified for the representatives of the Jewish majority, but expressly described as the unknown in their midst. The way to recognition and seeing is not through the majority.

In the scene that follows (1:29-34) the incognito of the *logos* who comes into the world is revealed when the Baptizer—and he alone—*sees* Jesus coming to him and identifies him as the one to whom the riddle in 1:15-16 applies. The saying is now repeated almost word for word, introduced again by an identifying clause: "This is he of whom I said, 'After me comes a man . . .'" (v. 30). Not until later does the narrator describe how this recognition became possible. Jesus' baptism is the event that identifies Jesus for the Baptizer. He *sees* the Spirit, the charisma of the royal Savior, descending and remaining on Jesus (v. 32). The reason why this is the sign of recognition by which the unrecognized one who comes is recognized is expressed later—at least for the readers—by the Baptizer: This knowledge was communicated to the Baptizer by God when he was called to prophesy: "He on whom you *see* the Spirit descend and *remain* is the one who baptizes with the Holy Spirit" (v. 33cd). This identification given directly by God, therefore, establishes the substantive connection between the incarnate *logos* of the Prologue and the principal figure of the book, Jesus of Nazareth. The scene ends with the identifying statement spoken by the Baptizer: "And I myself have seen and have testified that this is the Son of God" (v. 34).

In the first scene on the following day (1:35-39), the Baptizer *sees (emblepsas)* Jesus and identifies him for two of his disciples: "Look, here is the Lamb of God!" (v. 36b), repeating the words of v. 29c. At that point the disciples follow Jesus. With this begins a process that continues in the following episodes of the exposition: the formation of a knowledgeable group around Jesus (vv. 38-39). Jesus sees the disciples of the Baptizer who are following him and asks them the question, "What are you *looking for*?" They answer with the counter-question "Where are you *staying*?" Then Jesus invites them: "Come and *see.*" And so the disciples come and *see* where he *is staying* and they in turn *remain* with him. (The verb variously translated "stay" and "remain" according to the demands of English syntax is the same in Greek: *menein.*) Characteristic of the narrative shaping of this transition from the Baptizer's circle to the circle of Jesus' disciples is the close semantic interweaving of the portrayal of Jesus' baptism (vv. 32-34) with the first encounter of the disciples with Jesus (vv. 38-39). Through baptism Jesus becomes the charismatic on whom the Spirit *remains;* he is seen as such by the Baptizer and is identified for the disciples. Through their search for and seeing of the place where Jesus *stays* they enter a relationship of *remaining* with him. Readers who are familiar with the topoi of Wisdom reflection will recognize here the classic question about the place that God alone knows, the place where Wisdom is hidden (see Job 28:12-23; Bar 3:15-32; 1 Enoch 48:1) and understand this movement of the disciples from the Baptizer to Jesus as the finding and seeing of the Wisdom of God, who appears in the world of human beings in the incarnate *logos* (see Bar 3:38). The place long sought, where the Wisdom of God has found a place to stay (see Sir 24:7-8, 11) is Jesus, the incarnate *logos* who dwells among human beings (see John 1:14).

The following scenes and episodes continue the series of "seeing"-connections between Jesus and his disciples established by the seeking and finding. In v. 41 Andrew tells his brother, whom he *finds,* what he *has found.* He thereby designates the Jesus who has been found as "Messiah." The place sought has become this identified person. Simon, for his part, is *seen* and identified by Jesus as the Cephas (rock) to whom, at the end of the book, the leadership of the congregation is transferred (see 21:15-17). In the last episode of this kind (1:43-51) Jesus *finds* Philip and calls him to discipleship. The latter *finds* his brother Nathaniel and reveals to him, here already in the "we" style of the knowledgeable group: "We have *found* him about whom Moses in the law and also the prophets wrote" (v. 45c). Thus he identifies Jesus of Nazareth with the figure who, according to Scripture, has already been awaited. This new combination of canonical and non-canonical knowledge provokes skepticism in Nathaniel, whereupon his brother invites him: "Come and *see*!" The scene of encounter that follows begins with what for the readers is an unexpected reversal of roles: Jesus *sees* Nathaniel coming and identifies him: "Here is truly an Israelite in whom there is no deceit!"[17] The question that is provoked by this, "Where did you get to know me?" is answered by Jesus' statement that he had *seen* Nathaniel "under the fig tree before Philip called you."[18] In response Nathaniel identifies Jesus: "Rabbi, you are the Son of God! You are the King of Israel!"[19] Jesus assesses this word—not without irony—as an expression of "faith": "Do you believe because I told you that *I saw* you under the fig tree? *You* will *see* greater things than these" (v. 50).

The concluding word of the dialogue (v. 51), still directed to Nathaniel, proclaims these "greater things" as a revelation for all the disciples: "Very truly, I tell you [plural] . . ." and represents an allusion to the story of Jacob's dream of the ladder to heaven (see Gen 28:12) as *seeing* heaven opened: "you will see heaven opened and the angels of God ascending and descending upon the Son of Man." The figure of the Son of Man—it is left to the readers to recognize therein a self-identification of Jesus—is the connecting point between heaven and earth, between the divine sphere and the human world. In order to grasp the meaning of this statement, the readers must in the process also be aware of the connotations of the Jacob episode, especially the words with which Jacob expresses the meaning of his visionary dream: "Surely the LORD is in this place—and I did not know it!" (Gen 28:16).

"How awesome is this place! This is none other than the house of God, and this is the gate of heaven" (Gen 28:17).

This proclamation of *seeing* the connection between heaven and earth already refers to the story of Jesus of Nazareth told in the episodes of the book that follow. The first miracle story, about the transformation of water into wine at the wedding in Cana (2:1-11), is still part of the exposition of the Fourth Gospel, for at its end the narrator introduces a key concept that announces the miracle of the wine as the first example of the *seeing* announced in 1:51 and beginning with Jesus' action: "Jesus did this, the first of his *signs,* in Cana of Galilee, and revealed his *glory;* and his disciples believed in him" (v. 11). The whole chain of semantic allusions that lead to this point is introduced by the climactic statement of the Prologue: ". . . and we have seen his *glory* . . ." (v. 14c).[20] The exposition of the book, accordingly, tells how, within the world of the Fourth Gospel, the circle of seeing witnesses is constituted around Jesus. Their own experience of seeing is narrated as the genesis of the knowledge of the "we-group," as whose exponent the author of the book speaks in the Prologue.

This conception, which uniformly shapes the Prologue and the exposition of the book, is also in accordance with the two epilogues of the book (John 20:30-31; 21:24-25). The first of these book closings is especially revelatory of the Johannine perspective and its implications for creation theology. John 20:30-31 closes the first Easter cycle of the book. It is characteristic that this first Easter cycle of the gospel also works with the leitmotif of seeing (see 20:1, 5, 6-7, 8, 12, 14, 18, 20, 25, 27, 29). The motif is inserted deliberately. The action begins in the *darkness* (v. 1). At the tomb Mary Magdalene first *sees* that something is no longer there, namely the stone with which the tomb had been closed (v. 1). She interprets this in v. 2 as a sign that the dead Jesus has disappeared from the grave (been "taken out"). At the end of the cycle the risen Jesus appears to the disciples, and invites the disciple Thomas not only to *look at* him but to touch him (see v. 27). Between these points runs the sense line *seeing.* What is seen in each instance allows the body of Jesus that is absent from the grave to become, through literary means, a visible person before the reader. "The disciple whom Jesus loved" (v. 2) first *sees* in v. 5 the linen wrappings with which the body was bound. Simon, coming to the grave after him, *sees* not only these strips, but also the cloth "that had been on Jesus' *head*" (v. 7). Then follow the Easter appearances in which the Risen One is himself *seen* (cf. vv. 18, 25) and at first not recognized by Mary Magdalene (cf. v. 15).[21] At the appearance of Jesus before his disciples in the evening (20:19-25) the disciple Thomas is not present. The witnesses tell him (in the "we" style of those who know): "We have seen the Lord." Is the word of the eyewitnesses therefore to compensate for his not having seen Jesus?[22] Would this be the attitude of an ideal student if he had to accept that one of his classmates is taking the place of his teacher? The disciple Thomas, at any rate, responds with the demand to himself see and touch the Risen One, and specifically, intensifying the physical concretization, the hands of Jesus with the mark of the nails and his side opened by the lance of the soldier under the cross. Unless this condition is met, he will not believe (see v. 25). This highly ambivalent statement assigns Thomas some functions that are very interesting for the readers. He refuses to believe for reasons that very probably suggest themselves to the readers (not having been present at the Easter appearance), and makes demands that must seem just as attractive as unrealizable to the readers. The terms to which Thomas does not agree are the same under which the readers read (see also 1 John 1:1-4). Can one accept the word of Jesus' witnesses only under the conditions Thomas formulates here? This disciple wants more than what seems to be his lot under the circumstances of the first Easter appearance. Does this make him a blasphemer, or—in the eyes of the readers—a courageous seeker after truth? The narrator decides this question in the final scene where, through the principal figure, Jesus, he demands of Thomas precisely what he had called for as a condition of his faith. The second appearance of Jesus becomes a special lesson for Thomas whereby a decision is also rendered within the narrated world: because of his previous refusal Thomas is permitted to see what he wanted to see, and he believes. The bold[23] demand to experience the truth about the crucified Jesus with his own eyes and hands is not criticized as blasphemy or weak faith, but rather rewarded. At the same time, nevertheless, even in the narrated world another type of disciple is preferred to the brave student Thomas, one who does not have the opportunity of obtaining this kind of assurance, but believes without seeing.

The narrator makes clear, finally, on the meta-communicative level of the book's conclusion, who is meant by this, namely the circle of readers explicitly addressed in v. 31 as "you." The readers for whom the narratives "in this book" are intended thus find themselves at the end of the book they have been reading as expressly involved in the story. They have always been envisioned within the story as those involved in the action. Now they are further expressly shown that they have been sought throughout the book as Jesus' truly knowledgeable students. Thomas is presented to them at the end as the one who shows them what they have involved themselves in through this reading. The Thomas who sets conditions makes an unwavering demand at the end of the story for the reality-principle: The truth that the eternal *logos* brought into the world with his coming at Easter is no unworldly *gnosis* and no prompting to flee the world out of fear of the majority (see 20:19, 26). Instead, it is the truth about the real world that at its beginning was God's creation. The *logos* came as the Light of this world that has become darkness. The confession of faith in Jesus is the human assent to liberation as a creature of God.

It is no accident that the word "sign" appears again in this context. The entire activity of Jesus is now in retrospect characterized as the "doing of signs." This corresponds to the exposition of the book, which ended (2:11) with the statement that this was the "beginning of the signs" of Jesus. The book has made literarily visible for its reader an exemplary selection of "narrated signs,"[24] beginning with the miracle of the wine at the wedding in Cana and extending to the raising of Lazarus by an angry Jesus, who has the stone taken away from the entrance of the grave in order to have his dead friend freed from the stinking garments of death (11:38-44). The last sign in the story, the body of Jesus marked by his death on the cross, represents the meaning of all the signs and is in itself the sign of the liberation of creation from death. Thomas, the reader's "twin," formulated the conditions for assurance in faith so that at the end the readers will see how concrete is this liberation of created life from death, the subject of this book.

Let us now exemplify this concept through one of these narrated signs. The text I have chosen shows in an especially instructive manner the significance of the creation-theological aspects of the Johannine narrative.

The Healing of the Lame Man at the Pool of Beth-zatha (John 5)

The text of the episode consists of a narrative part (vv. 1-18) and the discourse of Jesus (beginning at v. 19). The text is correspondingly divided here. In the narrative part it is separated *vertically* according to scenes and sequences;[25] verbal discourse is indented *horizontally* toward the right. The words of Jesus, as concrete discourse, are first placed in the second text level, but are also divided *vertically* according to sense units. The structure of the argumentation is displayed in the *horizontal* arrangement. Support for an argument previously made is indented beneath it. There can be a theoretically infinite number of hierarchical relationships. A basic principle is that what needs to be justified precedes its specific justification.

Beginning of the episode

1a After this there **was** a festival of the Jews,
1b and Jesus **went up** to Jerusalem.

2a Now in Jerusalem by the Sheep Gate **there is** a pool,
2b called in Hebrew Beth-zatha,

2c which has five porticoes.
3 In these **lay** many invalids—blind, lame, and paralyzed.

First Scene
5a One man **was** there
5b who had been ill for thirty-eight years.

6a When Jesus saw him lying there
6b and knew that he had been there a long time,
6c **he said** to him,
"Do you want to be made well?"
<
7a The sick man **answered** him,
7b "Sir, I have no one
7c to put me into the pool when the water is stirred up;
7d and while I am making my way, someone else steps down ahead of me."

8a Jesus **said** to him,
"Stand up, take your mat and walk."
<
9a At once the man **was made well,**
9b and he **took up** his mat and **began to walk.**

Second Scene
9c Now that day **was** a sabbath.

10a So the Jews **said** to the man who had been cured,
10b "It is the sabbath;
10c it is not lawful for you to carry your mat."
<
11a But he **answered** them,
11b "The man who made me well said to me,
'Take up your mat and walk.'"

12a They **asked** him,
12b "Who is the man who said to you,
12c 'Take it up and walk'?"
<
13a Now the man who had been healed **did not know** who it was,

13b for Jesus had left because of the crowd that was there.

Third Scene
14a Later Jesus **found** him in the temple
14b and **said** to him,
14c "See, you have been made well!
14d Do not sin any more, so that nothing worse happens to you."
<

Fourth Scene
15a The man **went away**
15b and **told** the Jews
15c that it was Jesus who had made him well.

Fifth Scene
16a Therefore the Jews **started persecuting** Jesus,
16b because he was doing such things on the sabbath.
<
17a But Jesus **answered** them,
17b "My Father is still working,
17c and I also am working."

18a For this reason the Jews **were seeking** all the more to kill him,
18b because he was not only breaking the sabbath,
18c but was also calling God his own Father,
18d thereby making himself equal to God.
<
The discourse of Jesus
Part I: Jesus' symbolic language
1. The acts of Jesus as God's activity in the Son
19a Jesus **said** to them,
19b "Very truly, I tell you,
19c the Son can do nothing on his own,
19d but only what he sees the Father doing;
19e for whatever the Father does,
19f the Son does likewise.
20a The Father loves the Son
20b and shows him what he himself is doing;
20c and he will show him greater works than these,
20d so that you will be astonished.
21a Indeed, just as the Father raises the dead and gives them life,
21b so also the Son gives life to whomever he wishes.
22a The Father judges no one
22b but has given all judgment to the Son,
23a so that all may honor the Son
23b just as they honor the Father.
23c Anyone who does not honor the Son
23d does not honor the Father
23e who sent him."

2. The word of Jesus as *logos* of the new creation
24a "Very truly, I tell you,
24b anyone who hears my word
24c and believes him who sent me
24d has eternal life,
24e and does not come under judgment,

24f but has passed from death to life.
25a Very truly, I tell you,
25b the hour is coming,
25c and is now here,
25d when the dead will hear the voice of the Son of God,
25e and those who hear will live.
26a For just as the Father has life in himself,
26b so he has granted the Son to have life in himself;
27a and he has given him authority to execute judgment,
27b because he is the Son of Man."

3. Appeal

28a "Do not be astonished at this;
28b for the hour is coming
28c when all who are in their graves will hear his voice
29a and will come out—
29b those who have done good, to the resurrection of life,
29c and those who have done evil, to the resurrection of condemnation."

Part II: Approaches to understanding the language of signs

1. The testimonial value of Jesus' signs

30a "I can do nothing on my own.
30b As I hear, I judge;
30c and my judgment is just,
30d because I seek to do not my own will
30e but the will of him who sent me.
31a If I testify about myself,
31b my testimony is not true.
32a There is another
32b who testifies on my behalf,
32c and I know
32d that his testimony to me
32e is true."

2. The witness of John and of Moses

33a "You sent messengers to John,
33b and he testified to the truth.
34a Not that I accept such human testimony,
34b but I say these things so that you may be saved.
35a He was a burning and shining lamp,
35b and you were willing to rejoice for a while in his light.
36a But I have a testimony greater than John's.
36b The works that the Father has given me to complete,
36c the very works that I am doing, testify on my behalf that the Father has sent me.
36d And the Father who sent me
36e has himself testified on my behalf.

36f	You have never heard his voice
36g	or seen his form,
38a	and you do not have his word abiding in you,
38b	because you do not believe in him whom he has sent.
39a	You search the scriptures
39b	because you think that in them you have eternal life,
39c	and it is they that testify on my behalf.
40	Yet you refuse to come to me to have life.
41	I do not accept glory from human beings.
42a	But I know
42b	that you do not have the love of God in you.
43a	I have come in my Father's name,
43b	and you do not accept me;
43c	if another comes in his own name,
43d	you will accept him.
44a	How can you believe
44b	when you accept glory from one another
44c	and do not seek the glory that comes from the one who alone is God?"

3. Appeal

45a	"Do not think that I will accuse you before the Father;
45b	your accuser is Moses,
45c	on whom you have set your hope.
46a	If you believed Moses, you would believe me,
46b	for he wrote about me.
47a	But if you do not believe what he wrote,
47b	how will you believe what I say?"

The episode in John 5 is set off from its context by the locating statements in John 4:54; 5:1 (shift in locale from Galilee to Jerusalem) and 6:1 (change of locale again, this time to the Sea of Tiberias). The episode itself consists of a series of scenes, the last of which includes a lengthy discourse of Jesus.[26] The order of the scenes and the actions that take place in them are shaped from the outset as an occasion for this discourse. The relationship between the healing and the discourse cannot, therefore, be ignored as something secondary. This is clear from two aspects, i.e., the *dramatic* connection among the five scenes and the discourse, and sense line that runs through the entire text and is signaled by the word "do" *(poiein).*

First of all we should sketch the actions in the five scenes in the context of the discourse. In the first and third scenes Jesus and the sick (then healed) man are the dialogue partners; in the second and fourth scenes "the Jews" and the healed man; in the fifth scene Jesus and "the

Jews." The basis of this arrangement is the idea that Jesus, having healed a sick person at the pool of Bethesda, was persecuted and called to task by "the Jews" as culpable because of the healing, which occurred on the Sabbath (v. 16). The first scene (vv. 5-9a) describes the action, the second (vv. 9b-13) the indignation of the opponents at the deed and the beginning of the search for the culprit, which is at first unsuccessful. The third scene (v. 14) gives an ironic twist to the theme of the search in a way characteristic of Johannine narrative style. What is said first is not that someone finds Jesus, but that Jesus finds the man who had been healed and dismisses him with an exhortation to a life in accordance with the healing. In the fourth scene the man who had been healed responds to this by betraying Jesus to "the Jews," guilelessly or unintentionally, by revealing to them the identity of the culprit. Jesus, he says, was the one who had made him well. *Identified* in this way as the culprit, Jesus in the fifth scene (vv. 16-47) is called to account by the opposing party. In a short dialogue sequence (vv. 16-17) the opponents' charge that he has profaned the Sabbath is rejected by Jesus with the comment that his actions on the Sabbath are concurrent with those of his Father. This provocative self-defense brings about in the subsequent second sequence a corresponding escalation of the accusation, to which Jesus' discourse responds. It is therefore an *apologia* integrated into the context of the action. As will be seen, its content also corresponds to this context. Its central statements are related to the action of the Son, to the judgment of God, and to true testimony and accusation before that tribunal.

Of these principal aspects of the content of Jesus' discourse, the one that is here identified by the key verb "do" *(poiein)* is of special interest because it contains creation-theological components. Striking in this context is not only the frequency of occurrence of forms of the verb "do" *(poiein)* but especially its major semantic function both in the portrayal of the narrated action and also in the context of Jesus' discourse.

What is significant in the context of creation theology is first of all the exposition of the episode with its scenic devices. The motive for Jesus' journey to Jerusalem is a "festival of the Jews." In contrast to this time designation, what is first described is the place of the healing. According to vv. 2-3 the pool of Beth-zatha with its two basins and five porticoes[27] is peopled with "many invalids—blind, lame and paralyzed." The lame man whose healing is then described has been relegated to this place ("there") for the entire duration of his thirty-eight-year illness. With this, not only is his healing selected out of many as an exemplary case, but the pool of Beth-zatha with its buildings and its milieu becomes a symbol for a whole world, a sick world. In his novel *The Magic*

Mountain Thomas Mann made a sanitorium a metaphor for the condition of the world. The illness of the lame man in John 5 is not just the manifest appearance of a human being's need to be healed, but also symptomatic of the situation of the human being in the world.

The healing of the lame man as such is stylized in the first scene—in contrast to the formal therapeutic schema—not as a healing touch but as purely a word-event. However, as soon as the healing is called a crime by "the Jews" in the second scene Jesus is called the "offender," and specifically by means of the aorist active participle of *poiein*. The forensic meaning is simply connoted; the principal referent of "doing" is the act of healing ("making well"). This double meaning, including the differing values placed on the action, is maintained in the fourth and fifth scenes. The man who was healed reveals the identity of the one "who had made him well" (aorist active participle of *poiein*), thus delivering him to the charges of the opponents who "persecute" him "because he was doing *(epoiei)* such things on the Sabbath," whereby now for the first time the meaning of "criminal act" dominates. Jesus' answer to this replaces the ambiguous *poiein* with the verb "work" *(ergazomai)* and uses this new word as a semantic indicator for the new aspect of the parallel between Jesus' acts and the acts of God. This the opponents counter with an interpretation that of course corresponds fully to the claim inherent in Jesus' statement, namely that Jesus is "making" himself equal to God by paralleling his action to God's. With this Jesus' real claim is formulated as an accusation of the opponents. Jesus' work in union with God as his Father appears as a point of accusation against him before the human forum.

The discourse, seen as a part of the narrated action, takes issue with this charge when it makes use of the possibility of self-defense before the forum of "the Jews" as an opportunity for the self-revelation of the Son, in whose action God's activity is revealed.

The discourse has two parts. This can be perceived by a twofold beginning, each time with the principal thesis that what Jesus "does" is a true copy of what God "does." Each time it is formulated negatively (". . . the Son can do nothing on his own"), first as a statement about "the Son" (v. 19) and then as an I-statement at the beginning of the second part (v. 30). Both variations of the main thesis employ the basic concept of the imitation of God by Jesus. The first variant develops this concept on the model of artisanal training. The Son "sees" the father and *does* the same thing "in the same way." The explanation (v. 20) shifts this concept to the perspective of the one who trains: The Father "shows" the Son everything that he himself *does*. Thereby the main thesis, which was first negatively expressed, becomes positive.

The Son can "*do* nothing on his own" because the Father shows him "everything" that he himself *does.* This complete equality of action in all things *(panta)* is founded on the comprehensive personal Father-Son relationship. Because the Father "loves" the Son and "shows him everything," the action of the Son is equal to the action of the Father. At the beginning of the second part of the discourse (v. 30) this mimesis relationship is transformed at the level of *communicative* activity. The main thesis ("I can *do* nothing on my own") is here carried forward as a statement about the judgment of the Son *(hē krisis emē).* The judgment corresponds to what the Son "hears," and is therefore "just." In what follows (vv. 31-36) this is made explicit as a statement about the "truth" of the " testimony" that the Father gives the Son by means of the "works" that he has "given" him to *do* (see v. 36).

The sense line signaled by "do"/*poiein* is therefore significant especially for the narrative portion of the five scenes as well as for the first main part of the discourse, and largely determines their semantic interrelation. What Jesus "does" in the narrated action, that is, the healing of the lame man at the pool of Beth-zatha, for which he is incriminated by the Jews, is interpreted in the first part of Jesus' discourse as an imitation by Jesus ("the Son") of the activity of God ("the Father") according to the faithful measure of the love between "the Father" and "the Son." Thus this section of the Fourth Gospel furnishes a good basis for a concrete understanding of what, in this context (cf. most recently 4:54), is meant by "signs." Jesus' action is a "sign" not just in the sense of a *symbolic* action of a prophet with a relation of symbolic similarity to a future action of God announced by the prophetic sign, but rather the action of Jesus is, as the mimesis of God's action, itself the *reproduction* of God's action, which *presents itself and happens* in the action of Jesus. In this respect the action of Jesus indicated by the word "sign" is more than a symbolic act. Jesus' "signs" not only refer to God's activity by means of an interpretable symbolic action, and they are certainly not signs of the fact *that* God is now acting; rather, they *show God's action as such,* they make it visible. This is formulated in Jesus' first answer to the accusation of the opponents: "My Father is still working, and I also am working." The absence of every argumentative element here ensures a typically Johannine shock effect for the reader, who is here clearly and intentionally overtaxed and has to rely on this thesis being made good in the argumentation of the discourse that follows.

That healings not only point to God's action, but to divine privilege, and that therefore they both present and constitute God's own action, is a fundamental premise of the entire biblical tradition, and historically the point of departure for the New Testament christologies that understand Jesus' healings as proofs of God's own power.[28] Apart from this, it is characteristic for the Johannine theory of signs that Jesus' *semeia* identify him not only as a charismatic acting in the power of God, but as the incarnation of the "Word" by which God "at the beginning" in divine wisdom called creation into existence. To a greater extent than in the synoptic narratives of healing, the Johannine "signs" of Jesus call attention to this correlation with creation theology. Where the synoptics emphasize the breaking-in of the eschatological rule of God that becomes visible in the healings and exorcisms of Jesus, the Fourth Gospel accentuates the revelation of the reality of creation through the "signs" of Jesus, the human being in whom the creative *logos* of the beginning now appears in the world in order to lead the world into crisis and to set in motion the rebirth of creation.

The first part of Jesus' discourse in John 5:19-29 gives special emphasis to this connection. Again this can be perceived from the sense line "do"/*poiein.* John 5:20 speaks in the future tense of the "greater works" that the Father will show the Son. The explanatory statement that follows makes this concrete, also in the mimesis scheme ("just as . . . so"), overtrumping "do" or "make" *(poiein)* with "give life" *(zōopoiein). Zōopoiein* is thereby used as a synonym for the raising of the dead. God, who raises the dead, saves the creation from death through the "greater works" of Jesus. In v. 22 this action is called "judgment," which the Father has given over entirely to the Son. Judgment is interpreted in terms of creation theology as the salvation of creation from death through the works, in the world, of the *logos* that has become flesh.

The general resurrection of the dead is initially seen, consistent with the apocalyptic tradition, as a future event, as is also the judgment that the Father has left to the Son as his work. In the second section of the first main part of the discourse (vv. 24-27), however, the judgment and the resurrection of the dead are linked with hearing the word of Jesus, and thus as occurring in present time. The healing of this lame man at the Beth-zatha pool is correspondingly structured. In the first scene (vv. 5-9) the healing as such is, as has already been said, stylized as purely a word-event, thus deviating from the therapeutic scheme, which as a rule includes healing touch. When the lame man hears the voice of Jesus ordering him to "stand up . . . " this is the event that is named and happens in the "sign" of healing that is interpreted in 5:24-25 as the raising of the dead through hearing the voice of the Son.

The healing of the lame man is therefore not only the visible proof of God's present activity in creation, but also the manifestation of the eschatological deliverance of creation from death now occurring in present time through the "greater works" of the Son, who is both the initial *logos* of creation and the Son of Man to whom God has handed over the judgment for the deliverance of the creation. The "Word" and the "Son of Man" are equally figures of creative Wisdom, by means of which God calls creation into existence and with which he also definitively saves it in the end time. This tension-filled union of creation theology and eschatological soteriology is characteristic of Johannine theology and christology, and it cannot be dissolved by separating the elements of this theology into different layers of tradition, thus depriving the entire structure of its dynamism.

The second principal part of Jesus' discourse (5:30-47) brings to an end the theme of the deliverance of creation on the level of communicative action, and so also on the level of knowledge. It should be remembered that the Prologue of the gospel also closes with a reflection on the source of knowledge. Even when the theme of creation and rebirth/resurrection to life moves into the background and we discuss this part of the discourse only briefly, the concluding reflections on the source of knowledge, nevertheless, have to do with the decisive aspect for the readers of the Gospel of John, namely their participation in the narrated action, which is for them above all an action that imparts meaning and in which they participate as those with knowledge.

On the level of reflection on the source of knowledge, three ways of attaining knowledge are brought into relationship with one another, ways that are brought together in a similar manner in the Prologue: the knowledge that is given through the acts of Jesus, the testimony of John, and the word of Scripture (Moses) all testify to one and the same "truth." This thesis is advanced in sharply polemical language that corresponds to the apologetic situation that has been set up in the narrative. Jesus, "persecuted" like a wrongdoer, must justify himself against the accusations of "the Jews." At first glance the discourse impresses the contemporary reader as an anti-Jewish front. It is true that the Fourth Gospel, like Luke's historical work and other New Testament writings, documents the difficult process of separation of the Jesus-congregations from the synagogue at the end of the first century (see especially John 9:35). "The Jews" is used as a term for "others," as if Jesus were no more a Jew than the narrator who speaks in this way. The real situation is most obvious in the polemical sharpness of the contention about the truth attested by Moses (see 5:39). The polemic, which seems at first glance to be directed at Moses (see 5:37b; 1:18a in contrast to 9:29), is not directed within the narrated action directly against Moses, but against a rival interpretation of Moses' authority by "the Jews." It is not Moses who has said not to have heard God's voice or seen God's form, but rather the opposing party in the scene. In the same way the motif of the radiance of Moses' face is not polemicized against Moses as it is, for example, in 2 Cor 3:13, but against "the Jews," who accept "glory" from one another (and are thus called into question as the cognitive majority) instead of seeking the glory that is "from the one who alone is God" (5:44; see 1:14-18). All of this is discussed in connection with the question of the accessibility of the knowledge that is promulgated in the Gospel of John as "truth," that the readers "believe," and by means of which they participate in the "life" (see 20:30) that in the very beginning was in the *logos* and now has again come to light in the signs of Jesus (see 20:30). The Jewish majority, from whom Jesus distances himself in the Gospel of John, is attacked as a group caught up in its own biases to whom the knowledge provided by Jesus is inaccessible (5:44), and who therefore do not understand their own cultural knowledge ("the scriptures," 5:39). "The scriptures" do not testify to the "eternal life" that the majority believes it can find there; the one who "comes to me" (v. 40) will receive it. This correlation is regarded as indissoluble. Without the knowledge of the minority, that of the majority is not "true." For this reason—this is the concluding point in vv. 45-47—"Moses" will stand at the judgment as accuser of the opponents, the majority of "the Jews."

The creation-theological interpretation of Jesus' signs places the controversy about the authority of Jesus on the most general level in order to confront the Johannine readers, who are still grounded and oriented in Jewish Christianity, with the question of their "true" identity. The dispute has to do precisely with the question of the identity of those for whom Moses' testimony speaks. In other words, it is about the question of whether the knowledge on which *Jewish* identity is grounded includes or excludes Jesus. For the Jewish-Christian author and for his readers, who are no longer only Jewish Christians, the faith that the glory of God is revealed in the signs of Jesus for the deliverance of God's creation cannot be separated from the question of Jewish identity.

Notes: Chapter 6

[1] On this cf. Helmut Merklein, "Geschöpf und Kind. Zur Theologie der hymnischen Vorlage des Johannesprologs," in Rainer Kampling and Thomas Söding, eds., *Ekklesiologie des NT (FS-K. Kertelge)* (Freiburg: Herder, 1996) 161–83; Otfried Hofius, "Struktur und Gedanke des Logos-Hymnus in Joh. 1:1-18," *ZNW* 78 (1987) 1–25; Michael Theobald, *Die Fleischwerdung des Logos. Studien zum Verhältnis des Johannesprologs zum Corpus des Evangeliums und zu 1 Joh.* NTA n.s. 20 (Münster: Aschendorff, 1988); idem, *Im Anfang war das Wort. Textlinguistische Studie zum Johannesprolog.* SBS 106 (Stuttgart: Katholisches Bibelwerk, 1983).

[2] In my opinion the order of ideas in the Prologue does not result from a *christology* that describes the way of the *logos* as creator and revealer, thus making christology the

basis of the logical order of all statements in the Prologue. In that case it would be especially troubling that the coming of the *logos* into the world (v. 9c) is spoken of before the statement of the Incarnation (v. 14).

[3] Light is a metaphor that initiates the semantic concept that is established with "seeing" (cf. first v. 14c) that runs through the entire Gospel of John. "Seeing" is the principal metaphor for revelation and understanding in the Fourth Gospel; cf. Otto Schwankl, *Licht und Finsternis. Ein metaphorisches Paradigma in den johanneischen Schriften.* HBS 5 (Freiburg: Herder, 1995) 370–74; on John 1:1-6 cf. there 84–96.

[4] The participle "coming" in v. 9c is not to be applied to "every human being," although this would be syntactically possible, but rather to "the true light," because the motif of coming is related in the entire section 1:9-11 to the *logos* that comes as light. Cf. Michael Theobald, *Im Anfang* 22–23.

[5] Cf. J. Schoneveld, "Die Thora in Person. Eine Lektüre des Johannesevangeliums als Beitrag zu einer Christologie ohne Antisemitismus," *KuI* 6 (1991) 40–52, 147–48.

[6] For this reason the equation of *logos* and *torah* suggested by J. Schoneveld in John 1:1-18 is impossible.

[7] One should note the tension between v. 13b ("not . . . of the will of the flesh") and v. 14b. The incarnation of the *logos* bridges the distance between God and world that is further reflected in the antithetic relationship of the "children of God" to their surroundings.

[8] The translation of *ḥesed* / χάρις and *ʾemet* / ἀλήθεια with "grace and truth" expresses the revelation-theological accent of the Johannine concept; cf. Hartmut Gese, "Der Johannesprolog," in idem, *Zur biblischen Theologie. Alttestamentliche Vorträge* (Tübingen: Mohr, 1983) 152–201; Udo Schnelle, *Antidocetic Christology in the Gospel of John.* Translated by Linda M. Maloney (Minneapolis: Fortress, 1992) 211–27.

[9] Cf. Michael Theobald, *Im Anfang* 58–60.

[10] Martin McNamara, *The Aramaic Bible,* Vol. 1A (Collegeville: The Liturgical Press, 1992) 52; Roger Le Deaut, "Targumic Literature and New Testament Interpretation," *BTB* 4 (1974) 243–89.

[11] On this cf. Rudolf Schnackenburg, *Das Johannesevangelium.* HThK IV/1 (Freiburg: Herder, 1972) 257–69; Michael Theobald, *Im Anfang* 98–109.

[12] I can here only make reference to the apocalyptic-Wisdom instructional text 1QS III, 13–IV, 26 that can contribute most to the understanding of the thematic program of John 1:1-18. After the prescript (III, 13-15a) the text begins with the theme of creation/two-spirit doctrine (III, 15b–IV,1), followed by the doctrine of the Two Ways (IV, 2-18b). These themes correspond to those of the second and third sense units of the Johannine Prologue. The next section (1QS IV, 18c-23c) announces, in an eschatological prospect, the end of cosmic dualism and the struggle between the sons of the Light and the sons of Belial: ". . . truth shall rise up forever in the world which has been defiled in paths of wickedness during the dominion of deceit until the time appointed for judgment." Here the essential difference from the conception of the Prologue of the Fourth Gospel becomes clear; for the latter the appearance of the truth in the world in the form of the *logos* has become an experiential reality. (The translation of the Qumran text is from Florentino García Martínez, *The Dead Sea Scrolls Translated* [2nd ed. Leiden et al.: Brill; Grand Rapids: Eerdmans, 1994]).

[13] Cf. above part 1 of this chapter.

[14] Bernhard Lang, *Frau Weisheit. Deutung einer biblischen Gestalt* (Düsseldorf: Patmos, 1975).

[15] On the distinction between Torah-wisdom and apocalyptic wisdom cf. Max Küchler, *Frühjüdische Weisheitstraditionen. Zum Fortgang weisheitlichen Denkens im Bereich des frühjüdischen Jahweglaubens.* OBO 26 (Fribourg: Unitersitätsverlag; Göttingen: Vandenhoeck & Ruprecht, 1979) 31–113.

[16] Cf. Günter Reim, "Targum und Johannesevangelium," *BZ* 27 (1983) 1–13, at 4–6.

[17] There is a possible allusion here to Zeph 3:13 (cf. also Ps 32:2): "The remnant of Israel; they shall do no wrong and utter no lies; nor shall a deceitful tongue be found in their mouths."

[18] This, too, can be an allusion to 1 Kgs 4:25 [MT 5:5]; cf. Mic 4:4; Zech 3:10. Sitting under the vine and the fig tree is here a symbol of security and peace for Israel.

[19] This can be viewed as an allusion to the LXX of Zeph 3:15: "King of Israel, the LORD is in your midst." As in John 1:49 "King of Israel" stands here without an article.

[20] The assumption that the reader of the book can remember all the way back to the beginning of the text is not improbable. If one estimates the duration of a reading before an attentive public it lasts only about eleven minutes from the first sentence of the book, "In the beginning was the Word" to the concluding sentence about the "beginning of the signs."

[21] The misunderstanding of Mary, who believes that she sees the gardener before her, shows the truth of the Easter experience in an ironic mutation. The notion of the royal Lord of the garden as creator and preserver of the world of living things is part of the grammar of ancient Near Eastern symbolism of royal authority. Cf. K. Stähler, "Christus als Gärtner," in *FS H. Brandenburger* (Münster: Aschendorff, 1994) 231–36. As is still to be shown, the creation-theological aspect in the understanding of the Gospel of John is an implication of the Easter revelation or of the idea of the raising of the dead.

[22] In addition, Thomas is not introduced as a "disciple" but as "one of the Twelve" with his apostolic name "the Twin." Should the Easter appearance be withheld from such a person?

[23] Note here the contrast to the fear motif of v. 19.

[24] The concept of signs is therefore basic for the entire Fourth Gospel, and not just for one part or for the much-discussed Semeia source. Cf. Christian Welck, *Erzählte Zeichen. Die Wundergeschichten des Johannesevangeliums literarisch untersucht. Mit einem Ausblick auf Joh. 21.* WUNT, 2nd ser. 69 (Tübingen: Mohr, 1994); on the pragmatic significance of the end of the book, John 20:30-31, cf. ibid. 279–312.

[25] The smallest element of the dramatic structure, the micro-sequence consists of two parts of the action that are related to one another, the parenthesis calls attention to this relationship.

[26] On the analysis of the miracle stories cf. Welck, *Erzählte Zeichen* 148–57, which emphasizes the unity of John 5:1-16 but neglects the contextual link with the discourse of Jesus. Here we can still recognize the influence of the hypothesis that goes back to Rudolf Bultmann according to which the miracles are to be traced back to a Semeia source and the discourses to a Gnostic source.

[27] On the archeological evidence for this installation, mentioned also in the so-called Copper Scroll from Qumran, cf. Joachim Jeremias, *The Rediscovery of Bethesda, John 5:2.* New Testament Archaeology Monograph No.1 (Louisville: Southern Baptist Theological Seminary, 1966); Gustaf Dalman, *Jerusalem und sein Gelände* (Hildesheim and New York: G. Olms, 1972) 175–77; W. Harold Mare, *The Archaeology of the Jerusalem Area* (Grand Rapids: Baker Book House, 1987) 166–68. The name Beth-zatha/Bethesda corresponds to the name of the part of the city in which the pool lies (close to the Church of St. Anne in the northern part of the old city). Because of the healing powers attributed to its waters the name was interpreted in popular etymology as "house of mercy."

[28] On this see below, ch. 12.

Part III

The World as the Creation of the Merciful God

CHAPTER 7

The Biblical Primeval History in Genesis 1–9 as a Theological Composition

Genesis 9:28-29 as the End of the Primeval History

Where, on the level of the final text, the narrative of primeval history ends and the story of the primeval parents begins is a disputed question in exegesis. This is by no means an irrelevant discussion in our context. At least two questions that are important for the theology of creation are at stake here:

1. Because the conclusion of a narrative is very important for its whole interpretation, this is a question on whose resolution depends the entire concept of creation theology as it is fundamentally developed at the beginning of the Bible.

2. Because the stories of the first parents follow upon the primeval history as Israel's "originary" history, the resolution of the question of where and how these two narrative sequences are related to one another is decisive also for the question of what the Bible sees as the significance of Israel in and for creation.

Normally the end of the primeval history is seen in the transition from Genesis 11 to Genesis 12.[1] Gerhard von Rad finds both the climax and the conclusion as late as Gen 12:9.[2] The primeval history is then read in linear fashion so that the history of Israel grows out of it—as a history of blessing that can and should work against the dimension of curse and disaster in creation that breaks into the primeval history. This perspective, whose exegetical and literary dubiousness cannot be discussed here, has contributed substantially to the fact that primeval history was read mainly from the perspective of "creation and fall" and the "real" creation theology was sought in the two creation stories in Genesis 1–2. For this reason, the story of the Flood in Genesis 6–9 was accorded scarcely any theological relevance. In systematic-theological schemes, at least, this story played practically no role at all.

If, as is here assumed, the end of the primeval history is to be found already in Gen 9:29,[3] this has far-reaching consequences for creation theology. For one thing, Gen 9:28-29 marks a narrative break that gives the primeval history a relative autonomy and demands an interpretation that, in the first place, seeks to understand Genesis 1–9 as a conception that is readable in and out of itself. This is confirmed also by the fact that Genesis 10–11 sets the background or stage for the story of YHWH with Abraham and Sarah as the progenitors of Israel, which begins programmatically with Gen 12:1-9. Genesis 10–11, which narrate the geographic and linguistic distribution of the peoples (to which the story of the Tower of Babel in Gen 11:1-9 belongs thematically) do not constitute, from a *compositional perspective,* the continuation or the conclusion of the primeval history, but mark the beginning of the stories about the patriarchs.

> The YHWH discourse in Gen 12:1-3 and the description of Abraham's move (Gen 12:4-9) to and through Canaan presuppose a narrated world that the genealogy of the peoples and the Tower of Babel story have unfolded. Thus Genesis 10–11 portray the background for a development that moves by way of the patriarchs to Israel's becoming a people (Genesis 12 . . .). The history of the patriarchs is rooted in a scenario in which post-diluvian humanity had already developed into "peoples," "languages" and "tribes," and in which the world disc had been divided among this humanity into fixed places of residence. One line of the development of humanity is initially carefully excluded, precisely that which reaches from Shem to Eber to Abram, who had received no share in the division of the world; it moves purposefully toward the people of the Pentateuch, Israel. The special emergence of the "people" Israel with a great "name" created by God and their own "land" within the region of the "Canaanites" and the significance of Israel for other tribes of people can thus be demonstrated within the scenario at hand.[4]

The significance of the creation theology drawn up in Genesis 1–9 for the role of Israel in the midst of this world of nations must then be deduced from the *correlation* of the Genesis 1–9 unit, which is first of all to be interpreted *in itself,* with the history of Israel narrated beginning with Genesis 10–12.

In the second place, a three-part compositional structure emerges from Gen 9:28-29: Gen 1:1–2:3; 2:4–4:26; 5:1–9:29, whereby, deviating from the usual reading, the third part of this composition, namely the story of the Flood, becomes the *culminating theological statement* about the world as God's creation.

The Three Parts of the Primeval History in Genesis 1–9

As important structural signals in this composition, which are described in detail by Norbert Baumgart in his soon-to-be-published Münster postdoctoral thesis, the following observations should be mentioned:

1. That *Gen 5:1-9,* which forms the third part of the Genesis 1–9 composition, is to be read as a *compositional bridge* is indicated by the genealogical notice in Gen 9:28, which, in terms of the composition, establishes the link with Gen 5:32. If one reads Gen 5:32; 9:28-29 as a connected "genealogical biography" of Noah it is consistent with the structural scheme of the other nine genealogical biographies together with which Gen 5:32; 9:28-29 then produces the succession of ten prehistoric genealogies from Adam to Noah. The genealogy of Noah's sons is no longer narrated in Genesis 10 according to this scheme. It no longer belongs in the time of prehistory, but in historical time. The genealogical biography of Noah in Gen 5:32; 9:29, which on the one hand frames Genesis 6–9 and on the other hand compositionally links the narrative sequence in Genesis 6–9 with the narrative unit that begins with Gen 5:1, says:

> After Noah was five hundred years old, Noah became the father of Shem, Ham, and Japheth. All the days of Noah were nine hundred fifty years; and he died.

When the story of the Flood with Noah as its human protagonist is read in light of its compositional prelude in Gen 5:1-32, it becomes clear at the level of the text that this is a story of creation that seeks to develop a hidden dimension of Gen 1:1–2:3. That a many-layered web of connections exists between Gen 1:1–2:3 and Genesis 6–9 has often been demonstrated. There is an especially large number of semantic interconnections (admittedly with significant variations) between YHWH's blessing of humanity in Gen 1:28-30 and of Noah and his family in Gen 9:1-7. There are also imaginative parallels in the respective descriptions in Genesis 1 of the earth established by God and in Genesis 6 of the ark built by Noah as an organized home for all kinds of living things. From the perspective of creation theology it is especially important that the story of the Flood be read through its connection with Gen 5:1-32 from the perspective with which Gen 5:1-2 begins, in headline style:

> This is the list *(tōlᵉdot)* of the descendants of Adam.
> When God created humankind,
> he made them in the likeness of God.
> Male and female he created them,

and he blessed them and named them "Humankind"
when they were created.

It cannot be overlooked that this is meant to summarize Gen 1:1-12. At the same time, the ten genealogical biographies that follow describe what is in this God-created human being and what it means to be a human being. From this perspective the story of Noah in Genesis 6–9 is a fundamental anthropological narrative: it is a narrative explication of the human beings' God-given destiny to be the image of God in the created world. Noah's life story is, when seen from this perspective, a concretion of the "life story of the human being" (cf. Gen 5:1).

2. Corresponding to Gen 5:1, in the final text we now possess Gen 2:4 marks a new structural beginning. Both verses, which function as titles, are analogously shaped in terms of motif and syntax:

Gen 2:4, 7	Gen 5:1-2
These are the generations *(tōlĕdot)* of the heavens and the earth when they were created. In the day that the LORD God made the earth and the heavens, . . . then the LORD God formed man from the dust of the ground . . .	This is the list of the descendants of Adam. When God created humankind, he made them in the likeness of God . . . when they were created.

The *narrative sequence* Gen 2:4–4:26, which is marked off by Gen 2:4 and 5:1, forms the *second part* of the composition Genesis 1–9. It consists of the two narratives in Gen 2:4–3:24 (Adam and Eve: humans as man and woman) and Gen 4:1-26 (Cain and Abel: humans as brothers/siblings) that, from a structural perspective, are formed according to the same pattern of events (good beginning situation—conflict and offense—worsening of the initial situation/continuing disruption of the conditions of life—concerned intervention of the creator God). The two narratives, their actions linked by the sequence parents–children, the motif of cultivation ("service") of the land, and by the theme of death, develop, as does Genesis 5–9, an anthropologically oriented and interested theology of creation. As a statement about the human condition they portray the human being as a being fundamentally intended for relationships—and at the same time they show the possible or given disruptions of life that result. That the creator God—similarly in both stories—orders a halt to the diminishing of life through these disruptions, or counteracts them (giving protective clothing to the human beings expelled from Paradise and placing the murderer Cain under legal protection by means of the mark on his forehead), makes clear that this God is shown to be creator precisely by remaining allied to the creation. God confronts both Adam and Eve, as well as Cain, with their creation-disturbing behavior, but does not take from them the divine protective closeness. To this ultimately theocentric perspective is added the concluding note of this section: "At that time [in pre-history] people began to invoke the name of the LORD" (Gen 4:26).

3. As the *first part* of the Genesis 1–9 composition, Genesis 1:1–2:3 presents a narrative sequence that is consistently theocentrically structured from beginning to end. It says, as we will later describe in more detail, that creation is to be a home for all—for forms of life created by God and even for God the creator. The three parts of the pre-history in Gen 1:1–9:29 delimited in this way form a complex theological interrelation:

(a) The three parts may be read as three *variations on one and the same theme.* Each shows the God of creation from a different perspective. In all three parts the creation is described from a strongly anthropological perspective. In each part the creation of human beings as man and woman is expressly narrated (Gen 1:26-28; 2:5-24; 5:1-2) and their roles in the world in which they live are reflected. Each of these variations has its own distinctive creation-theological profile. Genesis 1:1–2:3 presents the first nameless pair of humans (i.e., the genus "human") from the perspective of the God who creates, blesses, and assigns tasks. Genesis 2:4–4:26 shows humankind in its basic social condition as family or kinship group. Genesis 5:1–9:29 presents a single family (that of Noah) in its genealogical origins and in its interrelation with the human family.

(b) The three parts can be read as a *concentric* composition. Genesis 1:1–2:3 and Gen 5:1–9:29 correspond to one another in their cosmic scenario, while Gen 2:4–4:26 takes place in and around the Garden of Eden. The two parts Gen 1:1–2:3 and Gen 5:1–9:29 are related to one another by numerous keyword references. The beginning of the third part, with the motif of the creation of human beings as image of the creator God in 5:1-2, mirrors Gen 1:1–2:3. The middle part, Gen 2:4–4:26, distinguishes itself clearly from the other two in that here the human figures act three-dimensionally as troublemakers in creation and do not let themselves be restrained by the creator God. Because of this concentric structure the interpretation of the two external parts must be correlated. At the same time, they form the interpretive framework for the central part.

(c) The three parts are, however, also to be read as a *continuous action narrative* that only attains its intended goal in its third section. It is in this way of reading that Gen 1:1–2:3 in a certain sense narrates the first act of the creation of the world, Gen 2:4–4:26 reflects in two exemplary stories on the disturbance of the creation by humans, and then Gen 5:1–9:29 presents the second act of the creation of the world. The principal creation-theological statement is then that the world was not just created once by the creator God, but that it stands under God's special protection in spite of, or precisely in the face of the disturbances (mysteriously) set off by human beings. It is and remains the realm of divine rule. One sign of this is the bow God has placed within creation, appearing as a rainbow and joining heaven and earth. (See below, Chapter Nine.)

Notes: Chapter 7

[1] In individual cases the positions diverge even more: Gen 11:9 or Gen 11:26 or Gen 11:32 are variously accepted as the end of the primeval history.

[2] Gerhard von Rad, *Das erste Buch Mose: Genesis ch. 1:1–12:9*. ATD 2 (Göttingen: Vandenhoeck & Ruprecht, 1949).

[3] Cf. the detailed proof in Norbert C. Baumgart, "Das Ende der biblischen Urgeschichte in Gen 9:29," *BN* 82 (1996) 27–58.

[4] Ibid. 38.

CHAPTER 8

The World as a House for the Living (Genesis 1:1–2:3)

The story of the creation of the world in seven days depicts, as we have already often emphasized, the utopia of creation theology that has been inherent in creation from its beginning as its goal, as the "idea" that guided the creator of heaven and earth and that will not be abandoned until its end. Because this idea exists, there will be what we call the fulfillment of the world. This means, in theological terms, that Gen 1:1–2:3 has to do with eschatology. What, then, is this eschatological meaning that is established in the world and in everything that has happened in it since its beginning?

The Universe as a Home for All

A first answer to the question of the creation-theological utopia projected in Gen 1:1–2:3 is found when we call to mind the structure of this narrative. The biblical narrator arranges his narrative as a succession of seven days of creation that are not simply set in a row like seven identical pearls on a string. A clear structure can be perceived in the form and content of the seven days.[1]

The sections at the beginning (the first day), in the middle (the fourth day), and at the end (the seventh day) lie like a frame over the narrative. In contrast to the other days, these three days of creation revolve around the theme of time as a basic category of the order in life. The *first* day of creation with its programmatic divine discourse, "Let there be light" (Gen 1:3), states the goal of creation: "Light" is here the power opposed to "darkness," i.e., to begin with creation is endowed with "light" as the dimension within which it will find life and all goodness. Simultaneously with the creation of the light there appears the order of day and night that is the basis of every natural measurement of time and, as such, also makes possible God's creative work as an ordered creative activity. The *fourth* day of creation provides the possibility, through the creation of the sun, moon, and stars, of a numerical and quantitative structure for the time that flows away like a stream; it makes possibility an agrarian, social, and historical calendar. Finally, the *seventh* day of creation brings a further category of time through the resting of the creator God, namely the important distinction between the time of work and the time of rest; it is only rest that completes the creation.

Into this framework are inserted the paired days two and three, five and six. These pairs are artfully related to one another. The first pair, that is, the *second and third days of creation,* tells how the creator God set up the earth, encircled by the ocean, as living space into which then on the *fifth and sixth days of creation* the corresponding living things are placed. How concerned the author is with the view of the earth as a home for all living things becomes clear when one imagines all of this as a continuing process. Out of the primeval waters the creator God separates once and for all a dry earth that immediately brings forth its vesture of plants. "Thus God set the table for all living creatures"—that is the perspective shared by the second and third days of creation. The narrator does not care whether or not there are mountains and valleys on the earth, but only that it is a food-filled table for living things, a table that the earth should always be able to set. The plants and trees are not important here as living things *on* the earth, but are themselves part of the earth, which is essentially a living earth that makes life possible. On the fifth and sixth days of creation this earth is handed over and progressively divided out to the various living things. On the fifth day of creation the creator God gives to the acquatic creatures and winged things the space *around* and *above* the disk of the earth. On the sixth day of creation God delivers the plant-bearing earth to the land animals and human beings. The narrator never tires of emphasizing the themes of "life." Four times he says expressly that the creator God wants "living things" on the earth, beings hungry for life and capable of living, therefore, that stretch themselves out to receive life as a gift that they cannot give themselves but that they find present in the creation. In addition, the creator God calls out a blessing over the living creatures, that is, they are given the capability as living things to pass on their life in the chain of the generations (see also Genesis 5).

The creation appears here in technical artistic imagery. As one plans a house and builds it[2] the creator God plans and then realizes the universe in accordance with a divine plan. First God creates a cosmic cavity in the midst of chaotic masses of water and then, by means of the vault of heaven and earth, gives it the form of a house. This God then divides into individual living spaces and fills them with appropriate objects and living beings.[3] On the ceiling of the house are the bodies of light. On the floor of the house plants grow and different spaces are assigned to animals and humans. God places the fish in the waters that surround the house like a castle moat. And to the bodies of light God at the same time gives the function of serving the house and its inhabitants as a great "world-clock" (Norbert Lohfink).

There is more, of course: The stars of heaven proclaim the glory of the creator God, who is present over this house and in it. *God's* glory shines through and dominates the entire house, as is shown by the "bodies of light," sun, moon, and stars created on the fourth day. It is emphasized three times in Gen 1:16, 18 that this is a house that is "ruled." And Gen 1:18 gives as the goal of this "rule" that, as on the first day of creation, God first of all divided darkness from light, so shall that division be repeated day after day and night after night as constitutive of life. Here is a subtle hint of what is expressly laid out in Psalm 19 (see below). The movement of the heavenly bodies is a palpable expression of the fact that the world stands under the ordering and life-giving rule of the creator God.

Human Beings in the Service of Life (Genesis 1:26-28)

Human beings are admitted into creation's house of life with a special task. In the "house of the world" the human being is the only living creature that can and is obliged to accept responsibility. The narrators of Genesis 1 summarize this with their statement about the human being as an image of God. The effects of this anthropological conception have been multiple, in Judaism and in Christianity, to the present day. The statement about the divine image plays an important role in the discussion about the image and worth of the human being.

In contrast to earlier interpretations that saw here a statement about the essential nature of the human being and especially its *relationship to God,* there is today a near consensus in biblical scholarship that this is a functional statement expressing *the relationship desired by God between human beings and other living things and to the earth as a whole.*[4] This important distinction appears already in the translation, for human beings are not created *according to* God's image but *as* God's image:

> Then Elohim (God) said, "Let us make humankind *as* our image, *as* our likeness, so that they may have dominion. . . ." So Elohim created humankind *as* God's image, *as* the image of God Elohim created them; *as* male and female Elohim created them (Gen 1:26-27*).

The translation itself is sufficient to discredit the opinions that sought to find in Gen 1:26-27 a kind of similarity with God that makes human beings essentially different from the animals. Further attempts to define only "the man" as the image of God because the biblical God is not a woman were positively perverse. This was then said to be confirmed by the fact that Jesus is a man and as such "the image of God" (see 2 Cor 4:3-4; Col 1:1). The consequences of this pseudo-theology are evident in the arguments for the exclusion of women from the priesthood. None of this can be justified on the basis of Gen 1:26-27. Here women and men are, both together and in the same way, "images of God" because they have the same task in the world's house of life. What is meant by the metaphor of the image of God can be summed up in three considerations:

1. According to the meaning of the Hebrew word *ṣelem,* which stands for "image," human beings are to be in the world as a kind of living image or statue of God. According to the conception of the ancient Near East and ancient Egypt an image of God represents the godhead portrayed, and is the agent of its power. It is, as it were, the place out of which the Godhead acts. The image of the god signals the where and how of the living divine presence. Images of God are therefore treated as if they were living beings. They are like a body into which the living Godhead enters in order to be, through it, effectively present in the world. From this point of view human beings, as living images and statues of the creator God, are to be channels of active divine power on the earth.

2. A look into Egyptian and Mesopotamian culture, where the duties of the royal office were often represented by the concept of the king as the image of the creator God, opens up another nuance involved in calling the human being an image of God. Understood in this way, the primary responsibility of the royal office is to defend the order of society against external and internal enemies as well as to help the weak, above all, to attain their rights. While in the Egyptian tradition the *king* is the "image of God" on the basis of his royal office, in the biblical story of creation this dignity and responsibility belong to *all* human beings without distinction. The concept is here practically "democratized": not because of *extraordinary* achievement or responsibilities, but as *human beings* all are royal images of God.

3. An additional key to the image of God proclaimed in Genesis 1 is provided by the more immediate literary context when it is said in Gen 5:1 that Adam fathers his son Seth in his own likeness and image. With this, the father-son relationship is identified as one in which a son by his thoughts and actions comes to be a repetition of his father. The expression "image of God" therefore characterizes the dependence of human beings on God as a kind of relationship to God that obliges them *to act* as good daughters and sons of God, that is, to protect and care for the earth as their Father's house. "The human being is, there-

fore, an image of God to the extent that he acts responsibly in relation to his living space including the living things within it, and not because of the way he behaves toward God."[5]

In order that this functional image of God not become a metaphysical divinity, the narrators add in Gen 1:26: "Let us make humankind . . . *as our likeness.*" Many things indicate that this defining statement is also aware of the resonant words of Psalm 8, which speaks about God having created the human being as "almost God" (Ps 8:5). But Psalm 8 is similarly not pointing to any special status of human beings, but to their instructions at creation (Ps 8:6-8). Also weighing against the "metaphysical" interpretation of the image of God is the biblical prohibition of images, especially in its later understanding, according to which *no* creature can depict the mysteries of God (see Deuteronomy 4).

At the same time, Gen 1:26-28 emphasizes that the relationship, established by the image of God, of the human being to the other living beings, and to the earth as the life-dwelling common to all living beings, continues dependent on the creator God, to whom the dwelling belongs and whose "realm" it is, and that relationship always turns back toward God. This perspective is expressed in the so-called creation commission whose deeper meaning we have not begun to grasp again until recently. This creation commission, so we understand today, is a God-given command to shape the world—but not as unbounded rulership "over all creatures," and certainly not as a destructive war against the earth, as the official translations of the two major German churches seem to suggest: "Be fruitful and multiply, and fill the earth and *subdue it for yourselves,* and have dominion . . ." (Martin Luther). "Be fruitful and multiply, people the earth, *subject it to yourselves* and have dominion . . ." *(Einheitsübersetzung).*

Neither of the translations is entirely wrong, but both are problematic in two respects:

1. They give encouragement to the misunderstanding that the human being is to behave toward the earth like a military general, that is, the human being must actually *fight* against the earth.

2. What is not true to the text in these translations is that human beings are made the sole beneficiaries of contact with the earth: "subdue it *for yourselves* . . ." or "subject it *to yourselves.*" The dative pronoun is not to be found in the Hebrew text. Three brief considerations make it clear that Gen 1:28 implies neither a subjugation of the earth nor a trampling down of the animals (and plants) and that the God of creation does not by any means bless the destruction and plundering of our planet.

(a) The Hebrew word *kābaš,* translated by Martin Luther as "subdue" and by the *Einheitsübersetzung* as "subject," means "to place one's foot on." This gesture, according to the ancient Near Eastern tradition and the use of the word and words related to it in the First Testament, has a many-layered field of meaning. There are pictures (for example, the victory column of Naramsin) in which the victorious Pharaoh or (as in the relief of King Anubanini) Mesopotamian kings stand on their enemies and triumphantly hold them down. Other portrayals show the Pharaoh on his royal throne as he sets his feet on a footstool on which the nations that belong to his area of rule are symbolically depicted. There are pictures and statues, especially from the culture of the Persian empire, in which the universal peaceful rule of the Persian king is programmatically expressed in that he literally stands on human figures symbolizing the peoples he rules (for example, the statue of Darius I discovered in 1972). On seals can be seen a god or a hero who sets his foot on an animal lying peacefully before him, while with his hand or with a cudgel he wards off an attacking lion. Other seals show a royal god who stands on beasts of prey and brings them under control—and nearby grows the tree of life, which means that God controls chaos and thus benefits the cosmos. Beyond this, we know from numerous texts of the First Testament of the gesture of taking possession of a piece of property by walking on it. Even now we appreciate the significance of walking into a new house. All of these aspects are connoted by Gen 1:28: Human beings are empowered by God to walk into "the house," to take possession of it, to protect and defend it as the house of life in contrast to all the powers of chaos—and for the benefit of all the living things for which the earth is destined as living space.

(b) The motif of the defense of the earth as living space fits coherently into the Egyptian and ancient Near Eastern ideals of kingship that shape Gen 1:26-28. To the official duties of the Egyptian king belongs, expressed in greatly simplified language, the defense of the God-given agricultural land against the desert and even its expansion. The Egyptologist Hellmut Brenner describes this official obligation of the king insofar as he represents the creator God or is even "co-creator":

> As the son of God the king is obliged to "expand the frontiers." Only a twentieth-century European would think thereby of words like "imperialism" or "colonialism." But in Egypt, that at the creation was delimited from chaos and, furnished with the fruitful Nile, "created" for the benefit of human beings, every deed that wins a further bit from chaos and adds it to Order is a continuation of the creation. In the same way the struggle against the animals of the wilderness, especially the lion and the wild ox, was reserved for the king, who alone was allowed to hunt them, as he hunted the "savage" peoples around Egypt. Both pictures on the lid of the famous trunk of Tutankhamen show the king en-

gaged in hunting lions and other wilderness animals and also, on its two sides, the battle against Nubians and Asians. The pictures are similar in their structure as well: in the middle is Pharaoh in his war chariot, dominating the scene by his size; behind him in good order and smaller in scale is his retinue, while before him is a wild assortment of animals or enemies. This similarity of composition teaches that these are parallel actions, a "ritual" in the broader sense of the word, even though not with established movements and appropriate speeches. The "expansion of the borders," the widening of the expanses of the created world over against "wilderness" (to simplify the expression) belongs to the rights and duties of the king who bears the name of "Lord of everything under the sun."[6]

It is precisely with this royal task that the imperative deals: "fill the earth and defend it against chaos"—with the single important difference in relation to the Egyptian tradition that, according to the biblical myth, this is not a privilege of the king but a commission given to all humans along with their human existence. The imperative used in Gen 1:28, "place or hold your foot on the earth as living space," in context by no means describes a battle against the earth, but at most a struggle *for* the earth, against everything that threatens and destroys it as a house of life.

(c) In the history of the interpretation and effects of the biblical creation commission, it is above all the imperative ". . . *and have dominion* over the fish of the sea and over the birds of the air and over every living thing that moves upon the earth" (Gen 1:28) that has been interpreted as justification of violent rule by human beings over nature and the world of animals.[7] It is indeed true that the dictionaries give as basic meanings of the verb *rādāh* used in the original text "step on, trample down, rule over." The great monograph by Werner H. Schmidt, Old Testament scholar in Bonn, about the Priestly creation story summarizes what many said until the more recent ecological discussion: the word denotes "an unlimited rule in relation to which there is no resistance (Pss 72:8-9; 110:2), a hard, merciless subjugation (Isa 14:2, 6; Ezek 34:4; Lev 25:53)."[8] Exegetes who wanted to make concrete this "task of ruling" thought about the battle against and hunting of wild, dangerous animals, and of their taming and breeding, about the employment of animals for agricultural work and generally for everything that is useful and helpful to human beings (from experiments with animals to killing them for human food, the latter of course with reference only to Gen 9:3).

Beginning in the 1970s, scripture scholarship has raised a protest against this interpretation. Proceeding from the premise that a metaphor (an image) has here been used to clarify the task of human beings in relation to their living space, a duty that follows from the fact that they bear the image of God, a violent "rule" benefiting only human beings is hardly probable. It would contradict the entire plan of creation that is projected in Genesis 1 of the earth as a house of life *for all*. Destructive, brutal human beings as "images" of the good God of creation—that flies in the face of the entire direction of Genesis 1. Could such a "ruler" be introduced with the phrase: "God (Elohim) blessed them and God said to them . . ."? What is meant (or not meant) with the "task of ruling" can be made explicit through four observations:[9]

First, although the word *rādāh* does have violent connotations at some places in the Hebrew Bible, these instances are then expressly formulated with the more exact modifier "with harshness" (for example, Lev 25:43, 46, 53) or "in wrath" (for example, Isa 14:16). In Gen 1:26, 28 a descriptive phrase of this kind is missing; it is excluded by the context as well.

Second, the Hebrew word *rādāh* ("rule") is historically related to the Akkadian word *redū*, which is to be translated "guide, lead, command," and which characterizes the king's rule in Neo-Assyrian royal inscriptions, especially to the extent that the king, by the authority of the sun god, "guides" the fate of his land and its living things with justice and righteousness. For this function of juristic ordering he of course needs authority and power, but this is anything but destructive, violent rule—at least in the ideal conception (with which Gen 1:26, 28 is concerned).

Third, the peculiar territory of rule in Gen 1:26 has always been conspicuous. It includes the totality of living things, not in their zoological variety but in their assignment to the areas of life in the three-part world: "fish of the *sea*, birds of the *air*, every living thing that moves upon the *earth*." As regards the meaning of the word "rule," this signifies

> that what is expressed is not a real process or special application of power . . . but a concise description of the *universal* ordering function of humankind. "Rule" is necessary *for the sake of creation as a whole and its ongoing future*. It defines the human being as "image of God," as a trustee *of the totality of the natural world of creation*. Part of this is that "they are responsible for the survival and protection of the animals of the created world. The measures taken by Noah at God's direction (!) for the survival of the animal world during the Flood, according to the Priestly document (Gen 6:19-22; 7:13-16), are certainly seen by P as concrete applications of the human beings' duty to govern; the goal of the preservation of life of the threatened animal world that is expressly stated in 6:19, 20 is more than indicative of that!"[10]

Fourth, the task of ruling is a *metaphor* that through the stated relationship of humans, animals, and their living space seeks to make plain the responsibility of human beings for the house of life, to the extent that human beings are themselves care-giving, empowered, protective, and ordering representatives of the creator God. As such they are royal shepherds of living beings, especially since the care of the creative divinities for their creatures is frequently portrayed as the activity of shepherding. The Bible, too, is aware that the human beings are not able *de facto* fully to measure up to this responsibility. But that human beings are nevertheless able *de facto* to fulfill it, and that this contributes to saving life in the house of life is made explicit by the third part of the primeval history with the story of Noah, a "human being."

The Utopia of Cosmic Peace (Genesis 1:29–2:3)

The Jewish tradition emphasizes that Genesis 1 ten times says "And God *said,*" and parallels God's ten words of creation with the ten commandments from Sinai, especially since both are concerned with life and freedom. The significance of the tenth of God's words at creation (Gen 1:29-30) is generally little known to us, and yet it is a kind of synopsis of the idea that God had at the creation. Genesis 1:29-30 formulates the goal of creation that human beings have, in practice, failed to attain (as the story of the Flood explains); nevertheless, it remains valid as the meaning (or vision) of creation:

> God said, "See, I have given you every plant yielding seed that is upon the face of all the earth, and every tree with seed in its fruit; you shall have them for food."

It has often been emphasized that Gen 1:29-30 takes up ancient images and concepts of the Golden Age in order to contrast them with the painful present. But the writer has been unjustly accused of having ruined the tradition of a paradisiacal original peace. "The Priestly document was acquainted with this tradition. As elsewhere, it relinquished the poetry and retained only a 'scholarly theory' about the history of human and animal nutrition. The matter of nutrition interests the author as a priest, for in his religion the commandments and prohibitions having to do with food play an important role."[11] And yet the point at issue here is not, as the gift formula emphasizes, a "food *commandment,*" nor is this divine discourse a further explanation of the character of human beings as the image of God, as if, having received hegemony over the animals, they are now to be given sovereignty over the world of plants as well. Genesis 1:29-30 is not simply the continuation of Gen 1:26-28, but introduces a new theme. This is indicated not only by the introductory formula of the discourse, but also the absence of the motifs from 1:29-30 in God's self-address (Gen 1:26). There are four aspects that the narrator wishes to make clear through the metaphorical divine discourse:

1. The solemn formula of gift ("See, I have given you . . .") stemming from the legal language announces that with this divine speech the earth, furnished with plants, is given over to the human beings, the land animals, and the birds as living space. Just as a royal ruler "gives" his vassals olive groves, vineyards, and fields as a fief (see 1 Sam 8:14; 22:7; 27:6), so the creator God transfers the earth to the living creatures as *their* "home." This aspect, which is stressed by the double statement of purpose, "for food," distinguishes the creation theology of the Priestly document from most ancient Near Eastern cosmogonies, in which human beings are created primarily to till the earth *for the gods*.

2. The gift of the earth is made in such a way that human beings and animals are allocated different living areas. Thus the narrator vividly suggests how the utopia that keeping to the living spaces appropriate to the individual living things could best ensure a fullness of life consistent with the creation event. The fact that the narrator chooses this fundamental differentiation of human and animal living areas for their utopias is related to the experience of the people of that time, for whom the relation of human being to animal was much more replete with tensions than it is for us moderns. Behind Gen 1:29-30 stands the experience that human beings and animals, as inhabitants of one and the same house of life, are in fact simultaneously partners and rivals; the assignment to different living spaces is the utopian alternative to that situation.

3. That the earth was planned as a house of life and intended to continue as such is signaled by the narrator above all by the fact that only the "vegetable" world is given over to human beings and animals. "Whoever understands poetry knows even without the propositions of modern natural science that this story from the golden age is a poem, a beautiful dream of yearning hearts."[12] That human beings live only from the fruits of the trees and plants is also in the story of Paradise (Genesis 2) a metaphor for the God-given fullness of life in prehistory. The narrator expressly extends this conception to include all living things on the earth. And because, according to the conception of the ancient Near East, plants are not living things, but the nutritive and supportive gift of the earth, the imagery intended here is clear: In the creator God's house of life no living thing is to live at the expense of other living things. The earth is not to become a house of death through deeds of violence and blood. The house of peace is not to become a place of struggle and war for the best pieces of meat.

4. In this text there is a resonance of a dimension of criticism of society and rulership. In the tradition of antiquity, "to live vegetarian is to

avoid participation in a hierarchy associated with the consumption of meat. . . . The sharing of meat manifests the position of a human being in the social hierarchy—as the ruler's function is to divide and apportion."[13] The metaphor is accordingly aimed at a shared life without struggle and privileges, a society in which there is no violence and there are no enemies because there is also no rivalry and no enmity. The metaphor aims at cosmic peace on the earth as God's realm.

With Gen 2:1-3, the closing section of their creation story, the narrators show how much they dream of the earth as a house of happiness and peace. This section contains what is perhaps the most surprising of all statements of creation theology: it does not say that God completed the work of creation on the *sixth* day, but only on the *seventh* day:

> And on the seventh day God finished the work that he had done, and he rested on the seventh day from all the work that he had done (Gen 2:2).

That is no mistake of the narrators, but an extremely significant statement that is not obvious at first glance: The world is God's creation only in light of the seventh day, for which all other days are preparation. The six days of God's work (and also of human beings' and animals') exist only and exclusively for the sake of this seventh day, which the Hebrew Bible (beginning no later than the time of the Exile) and Judaism down to the present day call *Shabbat*. Concerning this the principal work of the fourteenth-century Kabbala, the book *Sohar*, says "In truth, all days are ordered to Shabbat, which gives them their existence."

What was it, then, that was still lacking in the house of life created by the creator God even though it was already said in Gen 1:31: "And God saw everything that he had made, and indeed, it was very good"? Midrash Rabbah on Genesis says of this: "It is like a king who made a wedding canopy and decorated it wonderfully with figures and images. What is still missing? Nothing but for the bride to step under the wedding canopy. In the same way, what is still missing in the world? Shabbat." And the very great Bible interpreter of Judaism, Rabbi Schlomo Yizhaqi (called Rashi) writes on this in the eleventh century: "What was lacking in the universe (after the six days of creation)? Silence! Then came Shabbat, and with it came the silence, and the work (of the creation) was complete and concluded." At another place in his commentary (on Exod 31:15), Rashi declares that there are two kinds of silence, namely "the temporary quiet" and "the quiet of completion." The "temporary quiet" is rest from the effort of work as a gathering of strength for continued work. Such pauses of recovery, especially in the evening and in the sleep of the night, are needed so that human beings can do "good" work. According to the narrative of

Genesis 1 there were such pauses of temporary quiet even for the creator God, as intimated by the sixfold repetition of the formula "And there was evening and there was morning . . . ." The quiet of the seventh day is something else. It is a further act of God's creation, as the midrash states: "What was created on the seventh day? Composure, serenity, peace, and quiet." That is the quiet of completion about which is said in the Shabbat prayer of the synagogue:

> For the praise of your greatness and as the crown of salvation you have given your people a day of peace and holiness. Abraham rejoiced (over this day of rest). Isaac shouted with joy. But Jacob and his children find peace through it: a peace in love and magnanimity, a true rest full of trust, a rest produced by peace and composure, imperturbability and confidence. A perfect peace, in which you have pleasure.

For the sake of this "rest of completion" God created the world. One could even exaggerate a bit and say that *God* worked in order to be able to experience and enjoy this rest. In order that the creation experience this rest of completion, God created the seventh day and gives it special honor and rank in comparison with the other days: "So God blessed the seventh day and hallowed it" (Gen 2:3). What the Bible means by this is explained at the high point of its Exodus story. When Israel comes to Mount Sinai the cloud of the glory of God comes down upon the mountain. This continues for six days—and on the seventh day the voice of God sounds out of the cloud and calls Moses into the cloud. As Moses goes into the cloud on this seventh day and climbs the mountain YHWH reveals to him the goal of the Exodus and of creation: All Israel is to construct ("work") a sanctuary—so that it could there celebrate the festival of encounter with its liberator-God and the gift of being a liberated people.[14]

That is the meaning of the seventh day: plunging into the gift of festival, relaxation, and community (with one another and especially with God). That is the meaning and goal of the work and of creation as a whole, namely that there should be "one house" in which nearness to God and to human beings become reality. Shabbat is the day on which this reality of the completion of the creation can be experienced.

Because the world is *God's creation*, living things can and should experience the world as a place of celebration and of rest—according to the example of God the creator.

Notes: Chapter 8

[1] On this construction scheme cf. Erich Zenger, *Gottes Bogen in den Wolken. Untersuchungen zu Komposition und Theologie der priesterschriftlichen Urgeschichte.* SBS 112 (2nd ed. Stuttgart: Katholisches Bibelwerk, 1987) 71–80. A somewhat different scheme is worked out by Odil Hannes Steck, *Der Schöpfungsbericht der Priesterschrift. Studien zur literarkritischen und überlieferungsgeschichtlichen Problematik von Genesis 1:1–2:4a.* FRLANT 115 (Göttingen: Vandenhoeck & Ruprecht, 1981) 199–223. Cf. also idem, "Aufbauprobleme in der Priesterschrift," in Dwight R. Daniels, Uwe Glessmer, and Martin Rösel, eds., *Ernten, was man sät: Festschrift für Klaus Koch zu seinem 65. Geburtstag* (Neukirchen-Vluyn: Neukirchener Verlag, 1991) 288–92.

[2] In agreement with Steck, *Schöpfungsbericht,* the formula "and it was so" would better be translated "and it happened accordingly," which would eliminate the usually posited distinction between "word report" and "action report" in Genesis 1. The so-called "word report" then formulates God's plan/projection, and the so-called "action report" then registers corresponding realization of the plan or projection. On this see also Erich Zenger, *Gottes Bogen* 51–58.

[3] The "construction" of the cosmos corresponds in many ways to the "construction" of Noah's ark.

[4] Cf. the perspective of Walter Groß, "Die Gottebenbildlichkeit des Menschen nach Gen 1:26, 27 in der Diskussion des letzten Jahrzehnts," *BN* 68 (1993) 33–48; idem, "Die Erschaffung des Menschen als Bild Gottes," in Rainer Koltermann, ed., *Universum—Mensch—Gott: Der Mensch vor den Fragen der Zeit* (Graz et al., 1997) 157–64.

[5] Groß, "Die Erschaffung" 161.

[6] Hellmut Brunner, *Grundzüge der Altägyptischen Religion* (Darmstadt: Wissenschaftliche Buchgesellschaft, 1983) 67–68.

[7] Cf. the informative sketch by H. Baranzke and Hedwig Lamberty-Zielinski, "Lynn White and the *dominium terrae* (Gen 1:28b). A contribution to a story of double effect," *BN* 76 (1995) 32–61.

[8] Werner H. Schmidt, *Die Schöpfungsgeschichte der Priesterschrift.* WMANT 17 (3rd ed. Neukirchen: Neukirchener Verlag, 1973) 174.

[9] Cf. recently especially Udo Rüterwörden, *Dominium Terrae. Studien zur Genese einer alttestamentlichen Vorstellung.* BZAW 2150 (Berlin and New York: Walter de Gruyter, 1993); Bernd Janowski, "Herrschaft über die Tiere. Gen 1:26-28 und die Semantik von *rdh*," in Georg Braulik, Walter Groß, and Sean McEvenue, eds., *Biblische Theologie und gesellschaftlicher Wandel: für Norbert Lohfink SJ* (Freiburg: Herder, 1993) 183–98. Hans-Peter Müller, "Schöpfung, Zivilisation und Befreiung," in M. Daniel Carroll, David J. A. Clines, and Philip R. Davies, eds., *The Bible in Human Society: Essays in Honour of John Rogerson* (Sheffield, England: Sheffield Academic Press, 1995) 355–65.

[10] Janowski, "Herrschaft" 191.

[11] Hermann Gunkel, *Genesis* (6th ed. Göttingen: Vandenhoeck & Ruprecht, 1964 [= HK 3rd ed. 1910]) 113.

[12] Ibid. 114

[13] Jürgen Ebach, *Ursprung und Ziel. Erinnerte Zukunft und erhoffte Vergangenheit* (Neukirchen-Vluyn: Neukirchener Verlag, 1986) 33.

[14] Cf. on this especially Bernd Janowski, "Tempel und Schöpfung. Schöpfungstheologische Aspekte der priesterschriftlichen Heiligtumskonzeption," *JBTh* 5 (1990) 37–69.

CHAPTER 9

The World as the House of the Merciful God (Genesis 5:1–9:29)

In the chain of generations described in Gen 5:1-32, beginning with Adam, Noah is number ten. In the biblical tradition that number denotes perfection and completeness; and in fact the work of creation was not completed until Noah. Noah stands literally on the threshold between the (mythical) pre-history and (historical) time. Not until the end of the Noah narrative is the earth the way it is, because not until then does the creator God once and for all clarify and establish the relationship between God, the earth, and its living creatures in the "Noachic covenant" with the earth and all living creatures on it. The creator God—so it is said, in any case—comes to this determination only after the Flood, which was painful for the earth *and* for God.

The Purpose of the Flood Stories

What we have said about the other stories at the beginning of the Bible applies especially to the Flood story, namely that it does not have to do with a one-time occurrence that happened at some time during earth's early history. For this reason, no expedition will ever find Noah's ark either on Ararat or at any other spot on earth. Certainly the stories about floods that exist in many world cultures deal with *historical* experiences of catastrophic inundations and long-lasting, pelting rains that annihilated field plantings, settlements, and thousands of animal and human lives. Even our modern age is, for all its scientific and technical progress, to a large extent powerless and at a loss when such floods break over a given region. Those are the human experiences that constitute the *historical* background for the motifs that make up the *mythical* Flood stories in the Bible and its environment.

Its point is not, however, that there really was a worldwide cosmic flood. On the contrary, the intention of the stories is to overcome the anxiety that there could ever be such a cosmic catastrophe as punishment from the gods or from the creator God. In order to transmit the message of hope that such a flood would *never* happen, the story is told that *once upon a time "in the beginning"* in mythical time (therefore before historical time) there was such a flood and that the gods had thereby learned and sworn that a cosmic flood would *never* happen again. For the "historic" time of creation this means that the gods agree that they will *never* send an annihilating flood, whatever else may happen. In biblical terms, the creator God agrees never to violently destroy creation, not even as a consequence of human wickedness, however great it may be and however justifiably God's anger might flame out because of it.

Thus it is precisely in the story of the Flood that is expressed what creation means as a *theological* category (in contrast to the concept of creation in natural science): that the creator God has a relationship of love and faithfulness toward the earth and says a fundamental and irrevocable "yes" to *this* earth and *these* human beings.

However much the flood stories told throughout the world may differ among themselves, they all have in common that their real theme and message is not just the flood as an annihilating event, but that in and through the flood a human couple together with many/all the animal species were *saved* and that after the flood life on earth continued (or was renewed).

In the story of the Flood the people of the Bible and their environment dealt with the experience that their living space was threatened by inexplicable and incomprehensible catastrophes, but also by human violence and greed. At the same time they thereby faced up to their anxieties that total collapse might come—through caprice, or because of the anger of the gods. Thus in the formulation and recitation of their history they not only gave themselves assurance, but also implored the gods not to allow a cosmic flood. They reminded the gods that the destruction of human beings is of no use to them, but instead hurts them because they need human beings to bring them sacrifices and generally to serve the gods.

Because of this objective, biblical scholarship also calls these stories anti-myths; they are complementary to the myths of creation. "As the creation myths tell why what exists is in accordance with the divine will and thus also has its own right to exist, so the anti-myths of the Flood de-legitimize what may not, or after a prehistoric initial period may now no longer exist, i.e., unrestrained chaos and the annihilation of life may not, or may no longer, exist."[1]

The biblical narrative of the threat to the world by a chaotic flood is also an anti-myth that only when taken *together with* the myth of the creation of the world results in a dialectical statement about the world as God's creation. Precisely as the endangered world threatened by human violence it is loved by God, because it is over this world that God speaks the loving word of creation: "See, everything shall be very good" (Gen 1:31*).

The Biblical Flood Narrative: A Complex Story

It is easy to see that in the final written version of the biblical Flood narrative in Genesis 6–9 at least two narrative currents have converged. It is true that biblical scholarship for the most part sees this story as an example and demonstration of the view that two major narrative works were combined in the Pentateuch, the Priestly document and the so-called Yahwist. This question neither needs to be nor can be further discussed here. In our context it is enough to realize that in Genesis 6–9 at least two textual strata (text levels) can be distinguished, the later of which came into being as a part of the basic Priestly document (about 520 B.C.E.) and understood itself as a kind of commentary on the (older) pre-Priestly Flood narrative. This older Flood narrative, which came into being in pre-exilic times and whose end can be found in Gen 8:21-22, was once the final narrative of a pre-Priestly primeval history in Gen 2:4b–8:22, conceived as an independent composition. Not until the time of the Exile was it set as an overture before the narrative of Israel's beginnings (Genesis through Numbers).[2]

That two overlying narrative strata exist in Genesis 6–9 can be perceived from the unmistakable tensions, contradictions, and repetitions in the details of the narrative, which cannot be attributed to a single narrator. The following four contradictions are the most conspicuous:

1. According to Gen 6:19-20 Noah is to take along in the Ark two of every kind of animal, a male and a female, so that the continued existence of that species will be guaranteed. According to Gen 7:2 Noah is to take seven of each clean animal (i.e., three pairs and an individual animal for the offering after the Flood; the *Einheitsübersetzung* translates "seven pairs," probably incorrectly!) and two of each unclean animal.

2. According to Gen 7:4, 12 the Flood lasts forty days and forty nights; according to Gen 7:6, 11; 8:13 it apparently continues an entire year, since according to Gen 7:24 the waters swelled on the earth for one hundred fifty days, and according to Gen 8:3 another one hundred fifty days passed before they receded.

3. According to Gen 7:12; 8:2-3 the Flood comes about because of a mighty cloudburst. According to Gen 7:11; 8:2 it is precipitated when all the fountains of the great deep on which the disc of the earth floated burst forth, and all the floodgates of the heavens were opened.

4. According to Gen 8:6-12 Noah opens the window of the Ark and sends out first a raven and then three times a dove in order to determine whether the water had gone away and whether the earth was dry so that he could leave the Ark with his family and the animals. In Gen 8:15-17 Noah receives a direct command from God to leave the Ark without even an intimation of the "bird experiment."

In addition to these contradictions there is the fact that all the important phases of the event are told or explained twice in contrasting styles, semantic forms, and images. Twice God sees that the wickedness or violence of human beings is great and therefore makes a decision to annihilate them (6:5-7; 6:11-13). Twice God announces the Flood (6:17; 7:4) and gives Noah the command to go into the Ark and to take the animals along in order to keep them alive (6:17-20; 7:4). Accordingly, it is then also twice said that Noah carries out this command of God and how he does so (7:1-9; 7:13-16). Then there are two descriptions of how the Flood comes (7:10; 7:11), how the water rises and the Ark begins to float (7:17; 7:18), and how the floods of water destroy all life outside the Ark (7:20-21; 7:22-23). Then it is twice stated that the Flood ends and that the waters sink or run away (8:2-5). And twice there is a promise by God, each very differently formulated, never again to send a flood (8:20; 9:8-17).

Both strata of the text can be read as independent narratives. They have, on the one hand, the same event structure. They tell of the rescue of Noah, his family, and all the species of animals from the flood that the creator God sent on the earth out of disappointment/anger at the sins of human beings and animals. Both stories culminate in a solemn "guarantee of continuance" for the earth given by the creator God. On the other hand, each of the two stories has its own narrative profile, which can be established by the following differences: The (pre-Priestly) narrative portrays the Flood as a rain of forty days, has Noah send out the raven (in antiquity the familiar "navigation bird") and the dove (symbolic of the love divinities and in the narrative the symbol of the creator God's care), and closes the event with Noah's burnt offering, whose delightful odor prompts YHWH's creation promise (Gen 8:20-22).

> "As long as the earth endures,
> seedtime and harvest, cold and heat,
> summer and winter, day and night
> shall not cease" (Gen 8:22).

These last details are missing in the Priestly narrative, which depicts the Flood as a gigantic year-long water catastrophe. It is strongly interested in the details of the Ark's construction. The dimensions of the rescuing Ark are here brought into numerological-symbolic relationship with the sanctuary[3] that the Israelites are to construct in the wilderness in order that in it the God of life may be revealed in the midst of the people. Only in the Priestly account is the story of the Flood a covenant narrative. Only there is the motif of the rainbow in the clouds a symbol of the rule of God and God's irrevocable "yes" to creation. Only at the narrative level of the Priestly document is this "yes" of the creator God bound up with commandments for the protection of life (see Gen 9:5-6).

The Creation of the World as the Creator God's Learning Process

Each of the original and independent stories of the Flood that are now woven together into a simple narrative in Genesis 6–9 gives a plausible motive for the flood sent by the creator God. The pre-Priestly[4] version says

> The LORD saw that the wickedness of humankind was great in the earth, and that every inclination of the thoughts of their hearts was only evil continually. And the LORD was sorry that he had made humankind on the earth, and it grieved him to his heart: So the LORD said, "I will blot out from the earth the human beings I have created" (6:5-7).

The Priestly version, in contrast, represents an intensification, especially when one remembers the formulation of Gen 1:31 that comes from this version *("God saw everything that he had made, and indeed, it was very good")*, for it takes up motifs from the Cain narrative in Genesis 4 when it says:

> Now the earth was corrupt in God's sight, and the earth was filled with violence. And God saw that the earth was corrupt; for all flesh had corrupted its ways upon the earth. And God said to Noah, "I have determined to make an end of all flesh, for the earth is filled with violence [cf. Genesis 4] *because of them; now I am going to destroy them along with the earth"* (6:11-13).

Thus YHWH allows a powerful flood to come to destroy everyone and everything. YHWH reacts as the majority of worldly and spiritual rulers did and still do: by punishing and destroying. Against the violence of creatures, *God* now reacts with violence.

Before Israel, the Sumerians and Babylonians had already told how a flood sent by the gods was intended to free them from irksome human beings. The biblical narrators adapted their material. Presumably they even were acquainted with the two ancient Near Eastern versions that we also know today. One was preserved on the eleventh tablet of the Gilgamesh epic, and the other can be found in the so-called Atrahasis epic. In order that we may better grasp the theological message of our narrative it is helpful to know its Mesopotamian predecessor.

In this story, a conflict takes place among *several* gods concerning the flood. It is the god of storms and government, Enlil, who desires once and for all to make use of a flood to wipe out the human troublemakers who spoil his divine repose (his "siesta"). No one dares to protest in the council of the gods against this divine violence. Even the mother goddess (in the Gilgamesh epic she is called Ishtar, in the Atrahasis epic Nintu, "Lady of giving birth") agrees with the decision, though with a heavy heart. But when the flood begins it is said of her:

> Then Ishtar cried out like a woman giving birth.
> The mistress of the gods, she of the beautiful voice, wails:
> Better if that day had become clay (?)
> when I agreed with the assembly of the gods in evil!
> How could I agree to evil in the assembly of the gods,
> to the battle of annihilation against my human beings.
> First I give birth to my dear humans,
> then they fill the ocean like young fish!

In the mother goddess the contradiction within divine violence breaks out: It "is like the experience of a mother who under no circumstances wants to see destroyed what she has borne in travail and pain."[5] Therefore she is overjoyed when, at the end of the flood, she sees that *one* human being with his family has survived the catastrophe. In the Gilgamesh epic he is called Ziusudra or Utnapishtim; in the Atrahasis Epic he is Atrahasis (in the biblical tradition he is called Noah). This one person survived, according to the Mesopotamian tradition, because Enki, the god of wisdom, revealed to him the plan of annihilation and counseled him to build the rescuing boat or the saving Ark.

As thanks for his salvation, the surviving man builds an altar and brings an offering. As the odor of the incense rises up and attracts the gods, the mother goddess, the goddess of kindness, forbids the god Enlil, the god of wrath, to enter the circle of the gods. She proclaims:

> You gods, as surely as I do not forget
> the lapis lazuli amulet on my throat
> I will note for myself the days here
> that I never forget them eternally!

What the Mesopotamian tradition divides among various divinities takes place for the biblical tradition in the head and heart of one and the same God, and in such a way that this God is different at the end of the Flood than at the beginning. To exaggerate slightly, at the beginning he is Enlil, the god of destroying wrath, as well as Enki, the crafty, protective god of wisdom, and at the end he is Ishtar-Nintu, the god of motherly love. What at the beginning of the narrative was the motive for God's violent anger is at the end the basis for merciful divine patience and love. When YHWH smells the reconciling offering of incense that Noah brings after the Flood, he announces:

> "As long as the earth endures . . . I will never again curse the ground because of humankind, for the inclination of the human heart is evil from youth; nor will I ever again destroy every living creature as I have done" (Gen 8:22, 21).

This is a different divine remorse from that shown at the beginning of the Flood.[6] Then YHWH looked at himself; *now* he looks at the humans. After all, they are YHWH's children, whom he wants to love unconditionally and to whom he will hold, not only in good days but also in bad ones. Once he gets involved with human beings he wants to be *fully* involved with them, not with the cold logic of "law and order" but with the generous love of a mother who still holds to her children and helps them when no one else will.

This is the special point of the biblical flood narrative: "The flood did not transform the human being, but God."[7] As the creator, God has a weakness for God's creatures, clings to them passionately and will not abandon them, because God cannot (paradoxically stated) abandon God. This "weakness" of the creator God is the irrevocable connection with creation through which the world becomes the place where divine mercy is experienced daily. That is in fact the climax of the theology of creation developed in Genesis 1–9. That God is the creator of heaven and earth means that God loves them profoundly—against all "reason" and "free of charge" (that is, not in vain, but purely out of grace). The visible symbol of God's mercy is, according to Genesis 9, the "bow in the clouds."

In Genesis 9, the final chapter of the primeval history attributable largely to Priestly narrators, the "yes" of the creator God to creation is made concrete and summarized in the great symbol of the bow in the clouds. First, in Gen 9:1-7,[8] God the creator repeats to Noah and his sons the blessing given to human beings on the day of their creation (vv. 1-2; cf. Gen 1:28-29), and modifies it in view of the violence that had led to the Flood (cf. Gen 6:11-13). In fact, God's worldview is "more realistic" from this point on. God knows about the "war" that prevails between human beings and animals, and the deadly violence with which human beings mutually threaten and annihilate one another. In view of this illusionless worldview God empowers human beings so that they can also fulfill their role as trustees on the earth, when necessary, with "responsible" violence—so that the violence that destroys *everything* can be banned. Unlike in Genesis 1, the killing of living things now comes into view: first the killing of animals as nourishment for human beings (vv. 3-4), and then even the killing of human beings (in individual cases) as the penalty prescribed for murderous animals and murderous humans (vv. 5-6). In that case, however, this expansion of human "rule over creation" is expressly linked back to Gen 1:26-28: "for in his own image God made humankind" (v. 6b). Thus it here again becomes clear that the issue is the unqualified protection of life and the preservation of the earth as the house of life (v. 7).

Of course, in order that in spite of violence the earth remain the house of life willed by the creator it has need of the special protection of the living God. God promises this to the earth in the discourse in Gen 9:8-17. While Gen 9:1-7 in a certain sense governs the human contribution to the continuance of the creation, God affirms the divine contribution in Gen 9:8-17.[9]

With a solemn statement the creator God places all living things under the grace of the divine covenant:

> As for me, I am establishing my covenant with you and your descendants after you, and with every living creature that is with you . . . that never again shall all flesh be cut off by the waters of a flood, and never again shall there be a flood to destroy the earth (9:9-11).

This alliance knows no conditions, but is based solely and entirely on the God of creation who "establishes" it, that is, sets it down with unshakeable firmness. Human beings are unable to sway this covenant or to break it. They can oppose it or ignore it, but that all living things in fact live from the grace of this covenant is the one great essential statement of creation theology.

This is emphasized by the story of the image of the rainbow in the clouds:

> I have set my bow in the clouds, and it shall be a sign of the covenant between me and the earth. When I bring my clouds over the earth and the bow is seen in the clouds, I will remember my covenant . . . (9:13-15).

The father of critical Pentateuch research, Julius Wellhausen, interpreted the image of the rainbow in this way:

> The heavenly bow is originally the tool of the archer God and therefore symbol of his enmity but he lays it aside as a sign of anger put aside and of the restoration of reconciliation and graciousness. When it thundered, so that one could fear a repeated flood, then the rainbow appeared in the heavens when sun and grace again broke through.[10]

The bow laid aside signals the end of the confrontation between YHWH and creation. When YHWH would like to destroy the earth through a flood in view of the multiplying violence on the earth, the (rain-) bow shines out in the stormy sky and reminds YHWH of the covenant with creation.

In the iconography of the ancient Near East the (war) bow has a more comprehensive symbolic function.[11] It is the symbol of rule and kingship. In case of a conflict in which the creator God, in righteous anger at human evil and violence, believes it necessary to destroy the earth, the rainbow is to appear in the clouds and remind YHWH that the earth is YHWH's royal realm to which YHWH has given an unconditional "yes." To that extent this royal bow that arcs above the entire creation is *the* sign of the covenant that projects the radiant message into creation: The God of creation stands on the side of life, because God loves life.

Concerning God, it can be said that as far as God is concerned the Flood lies *behind us,* because God is the God of mercy.

The Human Being as the Image of God in the Tension Between Chaos and Cosmos

As we said in describing the compositional structure of Genesis 1–9, Noah is the pre-historical paradigm of "real" human existence. With him the primeval history makes concrete and explains the pre-history of the instruction to creation in Gen 1:28, according to which being a human being in the image of God consists in this: that people like Noah protect and promote life in the house of life. In contrast to Gen 1:1–2:3, Genesis 9 certainly insists that this life is in many ways threatened in its historical reality and must therefore be defended with disciplinary power. In Gen 9:2 our narrators express this ambivalence of life with the war metaphor that was similarly used in God's sentence of punishment in Gen 3:15. Also the deadly threat to one human being by another narratively reflected in Genesis 4 is once again affirmed as reality in Gen 9:5-6. Precisely in light of these chaotic disturbances of the cosmos and the potential for violence that breaks forth in them the world has need of the life-protecting care of the merciful God (cf. also Gen 3:21; 4:15).

The primeval history is thus aware that the life of animals and humans fails to measure up to the possibilities desired by the Creator (cf. also Genesis 3–4). When Gen 9:6 places human life *in principle* under the legal protection of God it goes beyond Genesis 1, joining the statement there about the human being as the image of God with an anthropological statement that approaches what we call human dignity and the inalienable right to life (human rights). That is the supreme meaning of the paradoxical formulation of Gen 9:6 (which seems to say the opposite), especially when it is interpreted in the horizon of the covenant that, according to Gen 9:12-17, God made *with life itself.*

Notes: Chapter 9

[1] Hans-Peter Müller, "Mythos—Kerygma—Wahrheit. Zur Hermeneutik einer biblischen Theologie," in idem, ed., *Was ist Wahrheit?* (Stuttgart: Kohlhammer, 1989) 54.

[2] Cf. on this view Erich Zenger, et al., *Einleitung in das Alte Testament* (2nd ed. Stuttgart: Kohlhammer, 1996) 74–75, 114–15.

[3] There are the following parallels or relationships between the ark and the sanctuary (cf. Exodus 26): The ark is ten times (!) as long as the wooden structure of the "habitation" in Exod 26:15-25 (300 cubits vs. 30 cubits); because the ark is to be divided into three "stories" (cf. Gen 6:16) each of which is then ten cubits high, the height of one story corresponds to the height of one of the stories of the wooden structure of the "habitation" (cf. Exod 26:15; the planks are set on end!).

[4] On the discussion about the placement of Gen 6:5-8 and Gen 8:20-22 within the history of theology (post-Priestly or end-redactional) cf. now Thomas Krüger, "Das menschliche Herz und die Weisung Gottes. Elemente einer Diskussion über Möglichkeiten und Grenzen der Tora-Rezeption im Alten Testament," in *FS-O. H. Steck*. OBO 153 (Fribourg: Universitätsverlag; Göttingen: Vandenhoeck & Ruprecht, 1997) 65–81.

[5] Othmar Keel, "Jahwe in der Rolle der Muttergottheit," *Orientierung* 53 (1989) 90.

[6] Cf. on this especially Jörg Jeremias, *Die Reue Gottes. Aspekte alttestamentlicher Gottesvorstellung*. BThSt 31 (2nd ed. Neukirchen-Vluyn: Neukirchener Verlag, 1977) 19–27, 129–32.

[7] Lothar Perlitt, "1 Mose 8:15-22," *Göttinger Predigtmeditationen* 24 (1969/70) 392; on the interpretation of the Flood narrative cf. also Erich Zenger, *Das Erste Testament. Die jüdische Bibel und die Christen* (4th ed. Düsseldorf: Patmos, 1995) 72–85.

[8] Contrary to the literary-critical limitation of Gen 9:4-6 formerly made by myself (and by many other exegetes) (cf. Erich Zenger, *Gottes Bogen in den Wolken. Untersuchungen zu Komposition und Theologie der priesterschriftlichen Urgeschichte*. SBS 112 [2nd ed. Stuttgart: Katholisches Bibelwerk, 1987] 105) Gen 9:1-7 represents an original unity; cf. this view especially in Odil Hannes Steck, "Der Mensch und die Todesstrafe. Exegetisches zur Übersetzung der Präposition Beth in Gen 9,6a," *ThZB* 53 (1997) 119–26.

[9] Formulated after O. H. Steck, "Der Mensch und die Todesstrafe," 130.

[10] Julius Wellhausen, *Prolegomena zur Geschichte Israels* (5th ed. Berlin: Druck und verlag von G. Reimer, 1899) 317 (English: *Prolegomena to the history of Israel*. Scholars Press Reprints and Translations Series [Atlanta: Scholars, 1994]).

[11] Cf. Zenger, *Gottes Bogen* 124–31; L. A. Turner, "The rainbow as the sign of covenant in Genesis IX 11-13," VT 43 (1993) 119–24.

CHAPTER 10

Israel as Revelation of the Merciful God of Creation

Even though, as we have emphasized, Gen 1:1–9:29, as primeval history of the world, is intended on the one hand to be read as a structured text with its own profile and independent message, the interpreter must on the other hand take seriously the fact that this text complex constitutes the beginning of the Pentateuch, which narrates the canonical history of Israel's beginnings. From this perspective Genesis 1–9 and Deuteronomy 34 are two primeval histories whose proper correlation is of great importance not only for understanding the Pentateuch/Torah as a whole but also for the correct understanding of the theology of creation. We have already called into question the *linear* relationship between Genesis 1–9 and Genesis 10–Deuteronomy 34. Nevertheless, these two entities need also to be understood as a connected whole.

The Connection Between the Creation of the World and the Creation of Israel in the View of the Priestly Document

While it is true that our synchronic reading perspective was previously focused on the final composition of Genesis 1–9, nevertheless a briefer diachronic look at the so-called basic Priestly document will also be helpful. For in contrast to the pre-Priestly primeval history in Gen 2:4b–8:22, which most probably originated in an independent narrative circle, the Priestly primeval history in Gen 1:1–9:29 was conceived from the very beginning as a part of the basic Priestly document. If one understands that document as a work made up of two blocks of unequal length, primeval history of the world and prehistory of Israel, the relationship of these two primeval histories can be described as follows:[1]

1. The pre-history of Israel that begins with Abraham is grounded in the primeval history of the world. The covenant with Abraham

(Genesis 17), with which the story of Israel's life begins and on which it is based, is in turn grounded in the covenant with Noah (Genesis 9), that is, in the merciful God's covenant of grace with all living things.

2. The pre-history of Israel, which extends from Abraham to Moses, differs from the primeval history of the world in that it takes place in time and space and is the historical clarification of what moved and moves the creator God to create: YHWH created the world in order that it should be a house of life for YHWH as well. What the statement "To begin with, God created heaven and earth" means in terms of the Priestly document is explained in the Shekinah theology of its Sinai narrative, where "on the seventh day" on Mount Sinai, which was thought of as the mountain of the world's creation, YHWH gives Moses the task of constructing the sanctuary in which YHWH wishes to live as the liberating God in the midst of this people. This envisages the message of creation theology: the creation of the world is realized where the world becomes the place in which the merciful God's loving care is experienced. *That* this is possible on earth (and not just in heaven) is justified and narrated in the primeval history of the world as found in the Priestly document. *How* and *why* this happens is justified and narrated in the pre-history of Israel from Abraham to Moses.

The History of the World and Israel's Pre-History

On the level of the final composition of the Pentateuch the relationship of the "primeval history of the world" and the "pre-history of Israel" can be described in still another way.

In the first place, the pre-history of Israel extending from Abraham to Moses is expressly linked with the history of the nations and of the whole world, both through Genesis 10–11 as the "stage" on which the history of Israel beginning with Abraham is played out, and also through the divine discourse of Gen 12:1-3 to Abraham ("In you all the families of the earth shall be blessed").

In the second place, Israel's history is consistently centered in the Torah. Israel's pre-history culminates in the revelation of the Torah. Inasmuch as Israel's pre-history is based on the primeval history of the world, in terms of the final composition of the Pentateuch the Torah of Israel is to be read as the revelation of the mystery of creation presented in Genesis 1–9. Creation and the Torah are interdependent and interpret each other mutually. The Torah is a key to the mystery of the creation. That is also the thesis of the texts that we want to examine more closely in what follows.

Note: Chapter 10

[1] Cf. Erich Zenger, *Einleitung in das Alte Testament* (2nd ed. Stuttgart: Kohlhammer, 1996) 98–103.

Part IV

Creation, Torah, and God's Rule
(Psalm 19)

CHAPTER 11

The Torah as the Sun of Creation

There are in Israel's Bible a variety of approaches to interpreting the Torah as a gift of God and to making it effective as a rule of life. The most significant attempt, measured in terms of its historical influence, lies in the stories of YHWH's revelation of the Torah on Sinai. In interpreting Proverbs 8 we already encountered another approach (which admittedly does not contradict that of the Sinai theology) that originated in Wisdom theology and attempts first of all to understand the Torah in terms of creation theology. According to it there is inherent in creation a God-given original order that communicates itself as the mystery of creation when one knows how to be open to it. The basic conviction of these Wisdom circles was classically formulated by Gerhard von Rad: "Creation not only has existence, but also produces truth,"[1] that is, the world announces itself as God's creation and invites to the hearing and acceptance of this creation message as instruction for life. The supporters and teachers of this theology of Wisdom saw it as

> their noblest task . . . to refer the individual to the voice that goes out through the medium of creation and to bring that individual to entrust his or her life with all its possibilities for conflict to this form of revelation. The teachers do not harbor even the smallest doubt that this self-revelation of creation can be heard. It can, as Paul also says, be "rationally understood."[2]

In addition to Proverbs 8, Job 28, and Sirach 24, Psalm 19 presents the agenda of this creation theology of Wisdom. In its final form, which may well have existed in the fourth century B.C.E., this psalm is the bold attempt to think the voice of creation and the voice of the Torah together in such a way that the voice of creation on the one hand becomes Torah and so that, on the other hand, the Torah is declared to be a concentration of the voice of creation.

The Structure of Psalm 19

Psalm 19 is a text much disputed among exegetes.[3] This is related especially to the question of whether this psalm is intended to be or can be interpreted as a unit. It is normally accepted that it contains two different psalms, the creation psalm 19A (19:2-7) and the Torah psalm 19B (19:8-15). From time to time the two parts are even interpreted as independent texts, or the question of the intent behind the combination of the two is explored. A favorite reply to this latter question is that the (newer) Torah psalm is meant to be a theological correction of the (older, pre-Yahwist) creation psalm 19A. This position is found especially among exegetes who on the basis of Reformation theology oppose and reject so-called natural theology. Essentially, what is at issue here is the reservation concerning the very relevance of creation theology that was briefly outlined at the beginning of this book.

In order to come to a well-founded decision in this controversy, we will first describe the structure of the psalm in its final form and then attempt to comprehend its world of images, for both are decisive for understanding the psalm as a whole.

1	For the choir-leader. A psalm of/for David
2a	The heavens are telling the glory of God;
2b	and the firmament proclaims his handiwork.
3a	Day to day pours forth speech,
3b	and night to night declares knowledge.
4a	There is no speech, nor are there words;
4b	their voice is not [audible];
5a	yet their voice goes out through all the earth,
5b	and their words to the end of the world.
5c	In the heavens he has set a tent for the sun,
6a	which comes out like a bridegroom from his wedding canopy,
6b	and like a strong man runs its course with joy.
7a	Its rising is from the end of the heavens,
7b	and its circuit to the end of them;
7c	and nothing is hid from its heat.

8a	The law of the LORD is perfect,
8b	reviving the soul;
8c	the decrees of the LORD are sure,
8d	making wise the simple;
9a	the precepts of the LORD are right,
9b	rejoicing the heart;

Continued from page 134

9c	the commandment of the LORD is clear,
9d	enlightening the eyes;
10a	the fear of the LORD is pure,
10b	enduring forever;
10c	the ordinances of the LORD are true
10d	and righteous altogether.
11a	More to be desired are they than gold,
11b	even much fine gold;
11c	sweeter also than honey,
11d	and drippings of the honeycomb.

12a	Moreover by them is your servant warned;
12b	in keeping them there is great reward.
13a	But who can detect their errors?
13b	Clear me from hidden faults.
14a	Keep back your servant also from the insolent;
14b	do not let them have dominion over me.
14c	Then I shall be blameless,
14d	and innocent of great transgression.
15a	Let the words of my mouth and the meditation of my heart
15b	be acceptable to you,
15c	O LORD, my rock and my redeemer.

The psalm in its present form is not to be divided into two parts, as in the traditional division between 19A (vv. 2-7) and 19B (vv. 8-15), but into three, which are meant to be read as an integrated event.[4]

1. *The first part, vv. 2-7,* is a composition of two sections that explain to what extent creation witnesses to the royal glory of the creator God. This is not, as is often said, cosmic praise that creation sings to and before the creator God. It is rather a message that is directed from heaven to earth, as the first section, vv. 2a-5b, which is skillfully framed by the double naming of heaven/firmament (v. 2) and earth/ends of the earth (v. 5), emphasizes. In a certain sense the section constructs a puzzle that is then solved in the second section, vv. 5c-7c. The message the heaven announces to the earth goes out through the sun, and by order of the creator God, as v. 5c underlines.[5]

Both sections are interwoven with one another in a variety of ways, revealing themselves as one cohesive part:

(a) The implicit subject of v. 5c is the creator God named in v. 2a; "El" is here no longer the name of the corresponding Canaanite deity, but the term for YHWH as creator God, as in (among other places) exilic/postexilic texts (for example, Isa 40:18; 43:12; 45:22).

(b) The statement of place "in the heavens" (v. 5c) where the creator God has placed the sun's tent refers back to "the heavens" in v. 2.

(c) The two sections describe the same event, though admittedly from different perspectives. Verse 2 says that the message goes out through an event in the firmament, that is, in the arch of heaven that extends above the disk of the earth. Verses 3-5 say that the proclamation consists in the continuing change from day to night; the message of the succession of days is emphasized by the prepositions. The meaning of v. 4 is unclear in the context. Either this is a non-audible message, one intended instead to be seen (v. 4 is generally translated and understood in this way: "There is no speech, nor are there words; their voice is not heard"); or, as seems more likely to me, v. 4 is a deliberate challenge to opinions like those espoused, for instance, by Qoheleth, according to which God's actions in creation are closed to human understanding in principle or in fact (see Eccl 3:11; 8:17; 11:15). In this case the text is to be translated as we did above: "There is no speech, nor are there words; their voice is not/would not be audible." Therefore, while vv. 3-4 characterize the heavenly message from a chronological perspective, v. 5ab does this in a spatial perspective: the message is universal, valid for the whole earth from end to end. This multi-perspectival description of the message event is repeated in the second section (vv. 5c-7c); this time "the sun" is deciphered as "ambassador/voice" of God in the heavens (vv. 5c-6b), whose course can be seen during the day and in the night and whose universal effective power is underlined in v. 7c.

There can be no doubt that vv. 2-7 are a cohesive unit. The sun, with its course in the heavens and the effect this produces on the earth, is a voice *sui generis* that proclaims to the earth and to all living things on it the Creator's glory and powerful creative activity.

2. *The second part, vv. 8-11,* is distinct from vv. 2-7 and forms a separate textual unit. This part no longer uses El as a name for God, but substitutes the tetragram. From a colometric perspective this part, with its short cola, has a different form from vv. 2-7. It offers a series of short hymnic nominal sentences, fashioned in a staccato style, all of which are centered on YHWH's Torah. Each nominal sentence makes a double statement: in vv. 8-9 the first colon makes a statement about the nature of the Torah while the second names the effect of the Torah on human beings. Verses 10-11 also offer statements about essential quality in the first colon, while the second colon emphasizes the effectiveness of the Torah in its chronological and spatial universality. Thus v. 10cd constitutes the climax of the sequence of six double statements about the Torah: in v.

10d a verbal sentence with a conjunction replaces the previous nominal sentences: "The ordinances of the LORD are true and righteous altogether." The concluding coda of the second part which then follows in v. 11 praises the preciousness of the Torah with two pairs of intensifying comparisons (gold/fine gold; honey/honeycomb).

3. *The third part, vv. 12-14,* distinguishes itself from the two preceding parts in that it alone is a prayer of petition framed in the I-thou style. In contrast to the two preceding sections, we now encounter a concrete social existence in the field of tension between good and evil as well as between guilt and the forgiveness of guilt by YHWH. In this part the petitioner, who twice expressly calls himself or herself the "servant" of YHWH, places herself or himself under the Torah and its blessing ("reward"), although in the consciousness of not being always and completely able to fulfill the demands of the Torah. For that very reason "the servant" asks for the grace to be able to resist the power and pressure of evil in order not to fall away from listening to the Torah and doing it. This part, which is also syntactically and poetically more complicated than the two preceding ones, is framed by the motifs of "*great* reward" (v. 12) and "*great* transgression" (v. 14).

4. *The closing formula in v. 15* takes up formulations from sacrificial theology ("be acceptable," "come before your face") and interprets the recitation of the psalm as an offering with which the praying person gives thanks for the voice of the God of creation in the heavens and in the Torah. This person experiences God in this lifegiving voice as a "rock" in the midst of chaos and as "liberator/deliverer" from the power of evil and sin.

It is true that much indicates that the third part, vv. 12-14, and the closing dedication in v. 15 were later additions to the original composition, vv. 1-10, when it achieved its present position in the book of Psalms. For our question about the creation theology developed in Psalm 19 it is admittedly much more important that Ps 19:2-11 is an original composition in which sun theology and Torah theology are combined in a significant *unified statement.* In comparison, the discussion about the origin of these two parts is of only secondary importance. In no sense is Ps 19:2-7 a "psalm of creation" that can be interpreted as such in and out of itself. If read only for itself Ps 19:2-7 would be only a fragment lacking any conclusion. Precisely this, or its theological climax, is what we find in vv. 8-11: The Torah functions as the sun of creation; through the sun and through the Torah the creator God manifests divine ordering, lifegiving, and loving care for all people on earth.

With the addition of vv. 12-15 the praying person takes his or her place expressly in the realm of life and order established by YHWH's Torah. Compositionally, with this the dynamic that begins in v. 2

reaches its goal: the voice of heaven and the voice of the Torah are heard and accepted. There are people who allow themselves to be taken into the service of the creator God, their sovereign, as emphasized by the confession, "your servant," which opens the third part (vv. 12-14). This third part also brings in a further aspect of Torah theology that becomes clear through the subtle key-word relationship between the beginning of the second part and the end of the third:

> The law of the LORD is *perfect*,
> reviving the soul; . . .
> Then I shall be *blameless* [i.e., perfect],
> and innocent of great transgression.

When "the servant" allows himself or herself to be touched by the Torah-sun and by its glowing heat (see v. 7c), when she or he is purified and renewed (see v. 8b), the perfection of the Torah, which is perfect like the round sun, is reflected in him or her. Of course vv. 12-14 add another important aspect that had become central in post-exilic piety, namely that human "perfection" comes only from the willingness to forgive of the good creator God, who is prepared to remake the damaged creation.

The Metaphorical Coherence of Psalm 19

The psalm composition in vv. 2-7, 8-11 works with the world of images of ancient Near Eastern and Egyptian cultures, evidenced also in Israel's Bible, where the sun is the real symbol of the divine gift of light, life, health, and justice. Scholarship has only recently made a thorough examination of the numerous traces of the theology of the sun that can be found in texts of the First Testament.[6] Whether the deity adored in the Jerusalem shrine in pre-Yahwist days was the sun-god Shemesh, as assumed by some researchers, can remain undecided at this point.[7] At any rate it is undeniable that especially post-exilic theology worked with the imagery of the sun in order to make statements about the active power of the creator God in creation and especially about divine creative activity exercised by means of the Torah.

A look into Israel's environment, where the sun-gods Aton (Egypt) and Shemesh (Mesopotamia) were attested in numerous texts and imaged as the givers and protecters of life, law, and righteousness, will show that the linking of sun and Torah was not something undertaken later by Israel. Especially the sun that rises in the morning and banishes the darkness is adored and pictured as judge and savior. Its midday heat, too, becomes the (mythical) real symbol of the judging and saving authority that, as divine power, rules throughout the world.[8]

Three short text examples and several pictures can verify this complex of ideas that was disseminated in the world in which Israel lived and that suggested itself to Israel as a means of expressing something about its concept of the sun-Torah that produces life and righteousness.

In a hymn for Aton from the time of Ramses it is said:

> Thou appearest beautifully on the horizon of heaven,
> Thou living Aton, the beginning of life!
> When thou art risen on the eastern horizon,
> Thou hast filled every land with thy beauty.[9]

In Akkadian prayers to the sun-god Shemesh it is said:

> You quickly throw down the wicked one,
> You choose justice and righteousness.
> The one to whom injustice was done
> who experienced violence . . .
> It is in your hand to give life, Shamesh.

And in a Hittite prayer:

> Sun-god of the heaven, my lord, shepherd of humanity,
> You come, sun-god of the heaven, out of the ocean,
> and you stride into the heavens, sun-god of the heaven,
> my lord, to the human child, to the dog, to the swine
> and to the animals of the field, O sun-god,
> you daily speak justice.

It is known that the connection of the sun-god with justice appears systematized as theology of law in the Prologue of the Codex Hammurabi, where Hammurabi presents himself as lawgiver in analogy with the sun-god:

> (. . .) At that time Anu and Enlil, in order to look after the welfare of the people, to make justice visible in the land, to destroy the wicked and the evil, not to allow the weak to be harmed by the strong, to deliver the "black heads" to the sun god and to illuminate the land, (called me), Hammurabi, pious prince and worshiper of the gods, by name.

Shemesh, who then in the Epilogue of the Codex Hammurabi is called "the sun god, the great judge of the heaven and the earth who guides living things aright," engages King Hammurabi to banish chaos and protect the cosmos through legislation. The function of the sun god who creates light = health and life, especially as the rising sun that battles evil with its heat, is also reproduced in numerous pictures.[10]

In view of this broadly verified world of ideas and images the combination of sun theology and Torah theology in Psalm 19 no longer seems unusual. On the contrary, it fits very well into the sun-imagery that is found quite frequently in Israel's Bible. Even the *beginnings* of the three stages of sun/Torah/servant of YHWH in Psalm 19 can be found, as in the Prologue of the Codex Hammurabi, where the three-part constellation Shemash/Hammurabi/law code is present. But it is precisely in the comparison with the Codex Hammurabi that the divergent conception of Psalm 19 (and of the entire biblical tradition) becomes visible. While Hammurabi is installed as lawgiver by the sun-god, in Israel it is YHWH who is the lawgiver, both in the Sinai narratives of the Pentateuch and also in Psalm 19: "the servant" in Psalm 19 is not the giver of the Torah, but its hearer and receiver. The creator God sends out an ordering and life-giving voice that can be experienced in the course of the sun and heard or read through the Torah, both of which are, strictly speaking, the two sides of one coin.

The Torah as the Light of God's Realm

The second part of Psalm 19 describes Torah, which speaks itself in creation, under many aspects. First the titular expression "Torah" is illuminated by an ensemble of other concepts: the Torah is "witness" insofar as it reflects the fundamental relationship between the creator God and God's creation. The Torah is recognized as "precept" when the authority of God that stands behind the Torah is heard. The Torah is "commandment" as the all-inclusive imperative of God. And the "decrees" are the varied instances in which the one Torah becomes concrete. The concepts are, on the one hand, ordered in "essence statements" in the first colon of each verse: perfect, sure, right, clear, pure, and true. On the other hand, in the second colon of each verse it is the Torah's way of working that is celebrated: like the sun, it renews the life force day by day; it causes eyes to see and the heart to be glad; it gives knowledge of the order and mystery of the world; it helps to integrate the individual deeds of one's life into the sound and saving order of life. The Torah is able to do all this because it opens a person, above all, to the fear of YHWH, which is "the beginning" of all life that is in accordance with creation (see Prov 1:7 and frequently in other places). Whoever surrenders to this Torah gains riches more precious than all the treasures of this world (gold and fine gold). Those who take the Torah for their own have a meal that tastes more magnificent than the best desserts of this world (honey and honeycomb were the basic elements of the most costly and luxurious desserts of the ancient Near East).

Certainly the Torah is and can do all of this because it is the self-communication of the creator God, who loves and gives life to creation. God's Torah is (like) the sun that shines day after day from heaven—like a bridegroom and like a victorious warrior.

Both metaphors stand for the creator God who is at work in the Torah. The metaphor of the bridegroom who comes festively dressed and adorned out of his tent and goes in expectant love to meet his bride is an expression for the love with which the creator God, as bringer of joy and happiness, and even life, turns toward creation. The metaphor of the "hero" emphasizes that the creator God fights the powers of chaos in order to defend life. Finally, v. 7c underscores the fundamental function of YHWH as judge. The metaphor of the noonday sun, whose glow illuminates the whole world and thus reveals everything, holds fast to the assertion that the creator God is universally competent to order all things. Those who allow themselves to be taken into the service of the Torah of this creator God (see "your servant," vv. 12a, 14a) contribute to making the world what it in fact is, the place where God reigns (see also the connections between Psalms 19 and 24). The earth becomes the realm of God's rule through the light of the Torah, and above all through human beings who allow themselves to be illuminated by this light.

Notes: Chapter 11

[1] Gerhard von Rad, *Weisheit in Israel* (Neukirchen-Vluyn: Neukirchener Verlag, 1970) 215 (English: *Wisdom in Israel.* Translated by James D. Marton [London: SCM; Nashville: Abingdon, 1972]).

[2] Ibid. 214.

[3] Cf. Frank-Lothar Hossfeld and Erich Zenger, *Die Psalmen. Psalm 1–50.* NEB (Würzburg: Echter, 1993) 128–34.

[4] In the following discussion, the verse numbering follows that given in the text, counting the header as v. 1: although the text is from the NRSV, the numbers of the verses are one higher in each case.

[5] Cf. for this understanding of vv. 2-7 especially Odil Hannes Steck, "Bermerkungen zur thematischen Einheit von Psalm 19:2-7," in idem, *Wahrnehmungen Gottes im Alten Testament. Gesammelte Studien.* ThB 70 (Munich: Kaiser, 1982) 232–39.

[6] Cf. among others Hans-Peter Stähli, *Solare Elemente im Jahweglauben des Alten Testaments.* OBO 66 (Fribourg: Universitätsverlag; Göttingen: Vandenhoeck & Ruprecht, 1985); Bernd Janowski, "YHWH und der Sonnengott. Aspekte der Solarisierung JHWHs in vorexilischer Zeit," in Joachim Melhausen, ed., *Pluralismus und Identität* (Gütersloh: Christian Kaiser/Gütersloher Verlagshaus, 1995) 214–41.

[7] Cf. Othmar Keel and Christoph Uehlinger, "Yahweh und die Sonnengotttheit von Jerusalem," in Walter Dietrich and Martin A. Klopfenstein, eds., *Ein Gott allein?: JHWH-Verehrung und biblischer Monotheismus im Kontext der israelitischen und altorientalischen Religionsgeschichte.* OBO 139 (Fribourg: Universitätsverlag; Göttingen: Vandenhoeck & Ruprecht, 1994) 269–306.

[8] Cf. Bernd Janowski, *Rettungsgewißheit und Epiphanie des Heils: das Motiv der Hilfe Gottes "am Morgen" im Alten Orient und im Alten Testament.* WMANT 59 (Neukirchen-Vluyn: Neukirchener Verlag, 1989).

[9] "The Hymn to the Aton." Translated by John A. Wilson, in James B. Pritchard, ed., *The Ancient Near East: An Anthology of Texts and Pictures* (Princeton: Princeton University Press, 1958) 227.

[10] See above, illustrations 3 and 4.

CHAPTER 12

God's Creation and the Wisdom of Jesus (Synoptic Jesus-Traditions)

The New Testament Is Not a Book of Torah Wisdom

In the New Testament one will search in vain for the Torah-Wisdom optimism expressed in Psalm 19 and other reflections about the Torah as the knowledge given by God to Israel regarding the order of creation. This has nothing to do, however, with any so-called critique of the Law. The Torah is accepted in the New Testament also as the book of the order of creation. However, in the critical view of reality that is characteristic of apocalyptic Wisdom the world is no longer regarded as the unshakeable foundation of human life guaranteed in creation. Instead, it is said of the world as it is that "heaven and earth will pass away . . ." (Mark 13:31). But this does not lead to the relativization of the Torah. "Until heaven and earth pass away, not one letter, not one stroke of a letter, will pass from the law until all is accomplished" (Matt 5:18). Whoever considers the Torah to be of little worth will also be held to be of little value in the coming world. "Whoever breaks one of the least of these commandments, and teaches others to do the same, will be called least in the kingdom of heaven" (Matt 5:19).

If there is in the New Testament no pedagogical impetus that is grounded in Torah Wisdom, that is not because of any deficient estimation of the value of the Torah. According to Paul, a Jew has in his or her hands "the embodiment of knowledge and truth." Nevertheless, such a one cannot "boast of [his or her] relation to God" and cannot therefore pretend to be "a guide to the blind, a light to those who are in darkness, a corrector of the foolish, a teacher of children" (Rom 2:17-20). This is not because of the Torah, but is due to the constitutional incapacity of the human being to give expression to the wisdom of the Torah by a life in accordance with creation.[1] For as a deed of the human being, doing the Torah is always an expression of subjection to the law of sin and death. Precisely as a creature, in his or her frailty as "flesh" the human being is exposed to the chaotic powers of sin and of death. For this reason one does not do what he or she knows and desires in agreement with the wisdom of the Torah (see Rom 7:14-19). No pedagogical *elan* can help us in this situation, as Paul shows by reference to himself and his biography (see Gal 1:13-14; Phil 3:3-9). It may be that by virtue of his radical rejection of his earlier option[2] for Torah wisdom Paul takes an extreme position. Nonetheless his skepticism about the possibility of a life in accordance with creation and Torah is grounded in a basic conviction found in the apocalyptic tradition and in other New Testament conceptions.

It is obvious that the conditions under which the Jewish population of Palestine existed in New Testament times did not correspond to the Torah. The land that God had given to the people in order that they live there in accordance with the life-promoting will of God was ruled by the Romans and by a traditionless Herodian tetrach. The land belonged in large measure to foreigners, so that the instructions of the Torah concerning property rights were obsolete. Uncertainty predominated on all sides concerning the tithes and other things that affect the purity of the land. There was collaboration and accommodation with illegal circumstances everywhere. The list of offenses against the order consistent with the Torah could be continued. Life in accordance with the Torah under such conditions in Palestine—the diaspora had long ago accommodated itself to alien-determined realities—could be led at best in social niches and under less rigorous standards. In this respect it was the Pharisees who had developed their concept most convincingly with the synagogue as a house of instruction at the center and the house of the Pharisaic family as solid basis of cooperative self-sufficiency in all things having to do with economics and cultic purity. Life in accordance with the Torah in these niches, however, represented a rule of God over creation that is hidden rather than manifest. The task was to bear the yoke of heaven, now hidden, but to be manifest in the future.[3]

In New Testament texts one does not find this model of cooperation in the coming of God's rule that is grounded in a life consistent with the Torah.[4] God and the human world are here considered so estranged from one another that the way to a lived reality in accordance with the creation, on the contrary, is hoped for as the coming of God for the deliverance and liberation of creation. The New Testament documents in the most varied ways that the foundation of this hope for the first Christians was Jesus of Nazareth.

The Creative Power of God and the Charisma of Jesus (Exorcism and Therapy)

In the gospel it is above all Jesus' healings that are understood as manifestations of God's present action in creation. The basic assumption underlying this is the understanding of sickness and healing in the First Testament and early Judaism.[5] As living creatures, human beings participate continually in a relationship to God, who breathed the breath of life into them and takes it from them again in death. God is the creative and sustaining power for the totality of human life. "In his hand is the life of every living thing and the breath of every human being" (Job 12:10). This relationship can be disturbed at any time during the whole length of human life by anything that separates the human being from the life of God, inevitably also by impurity and sin. Sickness is considered a symptom of this. It causes sick people to come close to Sheol, the place where human beings are utterly separated from God. Sickness, like healing, is considered to be an act of God. It is God who kills and makes alive, who tears apart and binds together, strikes with illness and heals (see Deut 32:39-40; 1 Sam 2:6; 2 Kings 5:7; Hos 6:1; Job 5:18-19). "I am the LORD who heals you" (Exod 15:26).

In the perspective of apocalyptic literature this understanding of illness and healing had changed in that affliction with illness was not attributed to God but to powers hostile to God, the demons or contrary chaotic powers personified as sin and death that threaten created life. The ability to heal from illness is accordingly considered a gift of superhuman power. The corresponding knowledge led Flavius Josephus, in his detailed description of the praxis of the Jewish exorcist Eleazar, to refer to the legendary wisdom of Solomon (*Ant.* 8.42-46; see Wis 7:20). Also according to Josephus the Essenes in particular made use of healing roots and stones and for this had recourse to "the work of ancient writers" (*Bell.* 2.136). This is consistent with the explanation the Book of Jubilees offers for the origin of medical knowledge (*Jub.* 10:10-14). According to that book medical knowledge goes back to the secret instruction Noah received from angels and left to later generations in a book. The art of healing is thus based on secret knowledge from the time of the Flood and possesses a heavenly quality. According to 1 Enoch 7:1; 8:3, however, such knowledge is to be traced to the fallen angels.[6] According to 2 Enoch 7:1 they transmitted demonic wisdom, especially the acquaintance with magical charms, incantations, and root-cutting, to the women with whom they had intercourse. In this version too this kind of knowledge is primeval knowledge about creation, but of demonic origin.

Against this background it is understandable how the suspicion arose that the exorcisms attributed to Jesus in the synoptic tradition were to be attributed to demonic powers.[7] This confirms first of all that in the Jesus tradition illness is considered a symptom of the rule of demonic power in the human world, while healing is a sign of their apocalyptic and definitive disempowerment. For the healings of sick people by Jesus of Nazareth stand expressly in the interpretive context of his message of the inbreaking of the reign of God and thereby achieve their unambiguous expressive force.[8] If illness is a symptom in which the contemporary rule of forces inimical to God manifests itself over the human being, the healings become in this context a signal in which God's eschatological turning to God's people announces the establishment of divine rule. Jesus' healings reveal God's interference in the previous violent control of the human world by forces inimical to God. Accordingly, in the synoptic tradition the healing of people who are ill is portrayed in two differing literary genres: either as exorcism[9] or as therapy.[10] The exorcism genre places the healing of human beings under the aspect of depriving the demons of their power through the word of the charismatic (Mark 1:21; 5:8; 9:25; Acts 16:18); the therapy genre locates it under the aspect of the healing touch of the person by the power of God (see Mark 1:31, 41; 5:25-28, 41; 7:33; 8:23 and many other places). Thus the miracles of healing not only show that Jesus is equipped with the divine power of healing, but that the claim associated with it in Jesus' message says that in the healings of Jesus the very acts of God for the deliverance of creation from the power of chaos have begun. "But if it is by the finger of God that I cast out the demons, then the kingdom of God has come to you" (Luke 11:20). In consequence of their apocalyptic interpretation the healings are therefore the good beginning of the fulfillment of the creation in the reign of God.

"The Earth Brings Forth Fruit by Itself": Creation and God's Rule in the Parables of Jesus

In the Jesus tradition in the gospels the saving deeds of God in the activity of Jesus are reflected, in terms of creation theology, in Wisdom forms. This is true, for example, of the three parables brought together in Mark 4. All three use the illustration of sowing seed to make the same basic statement, namely that with the deeds of Jesus the good beginning has been made; its inexorable end will be revealed to be the reign of God. Everyday experiences[11] are thus reflected in such a way that in the parable they open our eyes to the reality of creation.[12] If the beginning has been made, the decisive work is already done. By itself the earth produces fruit—the human being does not know how—until the harvest has come (see Mark 4:26, 29). The parable refers to normal sowing and growing in a manner reminiscent of the promise made in connection with the sabbatical year (Lev 25:20-22), that God will see to it that during the time when the earth lies fallow the food necessary for the life of the people will be brought forth without the participation of human beings themselves (see Lev 25:6). But the point of the parable about the growing of the seed without human participation is not the special experience of the sabbatical year, which recalls God's sovereignty as the ruler of the land during the idleness of the fields (see Lev 25:4a). Rather, it has to do precisely with the rules governing the normal economic year, for the parable allows the land worked by human hands to become the showplace for the activity of God in the creation, at the same time manifest and secret. The parable makes this experience transparent for God's activity for the deliverance of creation that becomes manifest in the deeds of Jesus. Much the same is the case in the parable of the mustard seed. The mustard seed has no specific symbolic meaning that could be posited by the parable. An ordinary mustard seed that is the smallest at its planting and yet, when it has been sown, becomes bigger than all the plants and puts forth branches like a tree (see Mark 4:30-32), becomes in the parable the image of the reign of God that offers its protection to living things. As soon as it is sown, the beginning of the great thing is already present. Similarly the parable of sowing on many kinds of ground (Mark 4:3-8) emphasizes the contrast between the inconspicuous beginning and the ending, the whole purpose of the sower's work. Here, however, a new aspect comes into play. The series of seeming failures that the parable lists in order to portray the process of sowing as something unsure and risky—the seeds on the path, where the plow was not used, are eaten by the birds; the stones in the rocky ground prevent much of the seed from growing; with the beginning of the early rains the thorny weeds in the field sprout just as fast as the seed, so that in such places the wheat does not grow tall—this series of everyday failures is presented so dramatically in the parable that the question arises as to whether what the farmer does is not absurd. The answer is given with the fourth and last stage of this parable of contrast: the farmer harvests his crop. It is not the farmer, therefore, for whom at the beginning everything seems to go wrong, who is the fool when he relies on the fertility of the earth, but it is whoever thinks the farmer is a fool. With the experience of the inbreaking of the reign of God the criteria for what is considered wise and foolish are changed.

Learning from the Lilies and the Ravens: Didactic Wisdom Discourse in Luke 12

A large part of the synoptic Jesus tradition deals with this question. What is wisdom, what is foolishness in the crisis of radical change[13] that accompanies the establishment of the rule of God, when God turns to the poor and the rich have as much difficulty in entering the reign of God as a camel has in passing through the eye of a needle? What is then considered foolish is, for example, that a farmer brings in a ripe harvest and believes he can guarantee himself a happy life by replacing his old barns with larger new ones, thus optimizing the means of his previous existence (see Luke 12:16-21). Here the principle that God's rule will again turn the original creation into the foundation for the life of created things is practically caricatured. The proper action is not to enlarge the old barns but to act in the certainty that the previous ground of human existence no longer functions. Wise are they who, knowing of the impossibility of their present position, nevertheless act decisively in that position, doing whatever they can to make themselves ready for a new existence. The example for such unconventional wisdom is to be found in the parable tradition of the manager of an agricultural business who when his dishonesty is revealed is forced to muster all his cleverness in order to save his neck from the noose by means of one great final fraud (see Luke 16:1-8). But they are also wise who find the measure of the Creator's care for creation in the lilies and the ravens, creatures who do not attend at all to their own life support.

This reading stands within the context of a Wisdom discourse on the theme of concern for life that was already present in the Sayings Source, Q (see Matt 6:25-33 par. Luke 12:22-31) in the context of encouragement to fearless confession of Jesus. Luke expands this concept into a great teaching discourse of Jesus about folly and wisdom in view of the coming reign of God (12:1–13:9). The discourse has the following structure:

Part 1 Concerning unavoidable conflicts (directed to the disciples)

12:1-3	Warning against hypocrisy
4-7	Admonition to fearlessness
8-12	Confession and denial before the court

Part 2 Concerning foolish attitudes (directed to the crowd)

13-14	Chreiae about inheritance disputes and their settlement
15-21	Parable about the rich fool

Part 3 Concerning wise attitudes (directed to the disciples)
22-34 Concerning vain worry and the search for true treasure
35-48 Concerning necessary vigilance (with intervening question in v. 41) and the new social responsibility
49-53 The coming of Jesus as a crisis of the "household" order

Part 4 Concerning the attitude to the present crisis (directed to the crowd)
54-59 The final deadline for reconciliation
13:1-5 The lesson from the most recent catastrophes
6-9 Final parable about the unfruitful fig tree

The section concerning vain worry about life opens the central passage of the instruction of the disciples about wisdom, a text in which the concept of an apocalyptic-Wisdom orientation to life is readily evident:

22 He said to his disciples,
"Therefore I tell you,
do not worry about your life, what you will eat,
or about your body, what you will wear.
23 For life is more than food, and the body more than clothing.
24 Consider the ravens: they neither sow nor reap,
they have neither storehouse nor barn,
and yet God feeds them.
Of how much more value are you than the birds!
25 And can any of you by worrying
add a single hour to your span of life?
26 If then you are not able to do so small a thing as that,
why do you worry about the rest?
27 Consider the lilies, how they grow:
they neither toil nor spin;
yet I tell you,
even Solomon in all his glory was not clothed like one of these.
28 But if God so clothes the grass of the field,
which is alive today and tomorrow is thrown into the oven,
how much more will he clothe you—
you of little faith!
29 And do not keep striving for what you are to eat
and what you are to drink, and do not keep worrying.
30 For it is the nations of the world that strive after all these things,
and your Father knows that you need them.
31 Instead, strive for his kingdom,

and these things will be given to you as well.
32 Do not be afraid, little flock,
for it is your Father's good pleasure to give you the kingdom.
33 Sell your possessions, and give alms.
Make purses for yourselves that do not wear out,
an unfailing treasure in heaven,
where no thief comes near and no moth destroys.
34 For where your treasure is, there your heart will be also."

The structure of the text becomes visible in its segmentation. Two examples from Nature are presented as argument in such a way that their fundamental importance emerges. The opening prohibition, "Do not worry about your life," is formulated in such basic form that the sentences that follow can be read as elementary reflections about wisdom. The point is not merely to encourage those addressed in view of a particular dangerous situation, but more generally and fundamentally about the worry that human existence as a whole demands.

That people must secure their lives through energetic work is one of the traditional themes of Wisdom pedagogy.

> A child who gathers in summer is prudent,
> but a child who sleeps in harvest brings shame (Prov 10:5).

Insights of this kind are found by the Wisdom traditions also in examples from Nature, evidently with the intention of confirming the cultural models in force.

> Go to the ant, you lazybones;
> consider its ways, and be wise.
> Without having any chief
> or officer or ruler,
> it prepares its food in summer,
> and gathers its sustenance in harvest.
> How long will you lie there, O lazybones?
> When will you rise from sleep? . . .
> . . . poverty will come upon you like a robber,
> and want, like an armed warrior (Prov 6:6-11).

The opposite lesson is taught by the natural examples of the ravens and the lilies. The opening sentence with which the section begins already shows that the philosophy presented here contradicts the traditional insights of Wisdom. Here it is basically denied that the human being can somehow ensure his or her existence through precaution. This was already shown with the example of the foolish rich farmer in the previous context (Luke 12:16-20).[14] Now this maxim is developed positively for Jesus' disciples of those days. From the example of the ravens and the lilies they are to learn that the kinds of work that were generally considered to be necessary for life in agrarian culture for men (sowing and reaping) and women (housework in general and spinning in particular) cannot ensure life at all, for only God's care for God's creatures is able to do this. What applies to the ravens and the short-lived[15] beautiful flowers is even more valid for a pupil of Jesus (the *Qal wa-ḥomer* ending argues from the smaller to the greater). Is idleness then recommended as the consequence of the wisdom that corresponds to trust in God's care for creation?

That this is an open provocation of sound human Wisdom understanding becomes even clearer through the two rhetorical questions inserted between the two examples from the natural world. Rhetorical questions are formulated with the presumption that they will answer themselves. Accordingly, the first states as incontrovertible that no human being can prolong his or her life even slightly. With scarcely-concealed irony the second follows with the conclusion that when a person is unable to do even the least thing—the prolonging of life—then he or she no longer needs to concern himself or herself with the rest, either. The rejection of human worry in v. 23, the first argument in the initial sentence of the discourse, was not formulated so provocatively. Life and the body appear as the greater goods in comparison with food and clothing. Concern about the lesser things is here at first seemingly only subordinated to concern for the greater things. But in vv. 25-26 other criteria are applied. The "least" that it denies that human beings are able to do is to lengthen *life.* The irony is obvious. Should one who knows this not rather die of hunger at the outset? How cynical (Cynic) is this teaching?[16]

The assertion in the first rhetorical question (v. 25) cannot be rejected out of hand. It is the key point of the entire argumentation with the ravens and lilies as examples of wise behavior in the eschatological crisis. Contemporary Stoic philosophy could also have agreed with this thesis. Among the "things that are not within our power," Epictetus, in the first chapter of his "Little Handbook of Morality,"[17] reckons "our bodies, our property, our reputation, our position in society." But because human beings do not decide freely about these things, being dependent on alien influences, they should not make their happiness depend on them, but recognize them as alien. "Think about it, therefore: If you hold that which depends on Nature to be free and that which is alien to be your own, your plans will be thwarted and you will lament, lose your composure, and be at odds with God and the world. But if you consider your property only what[18] really belongs to you, but what is alien to be alien as it actually is, then no one will ever compel you, no one frustrate you, and you will not chide anyone or blame anyone, and never do anything against your will; you will have no enemies and no one will hurt you, because you cannot suffer any loss." For the wise person will not consider something that happens without his or her free choice as something that concerns him or her.

If Epictetus had been able to review the apocalyptic Wisdom reflections in Luke 12:22-34 he might have agreed with the examples from Nature, but only if the discourse had continued according to his inclinations. That one should not "worry"[19] about "things that are not within our powers" is ultimately grounded for Epictetus in the idea that the gods "exist and rule the universe well and justly."[20] Therefore one can be ready to obey them and to accept everything that happens. This can be done freely and spontaneously when one has from the gods the just-named "correct ideas." "For then you will never criticize the gods and accuse them of not caring about you" (*Enchirideion* 31). But it is precisely in this sense that the discourse in Luke 12:29-31 does *not* continue. The world as it exists is not there interpreted as being guided by a good divine rule that leaves nothing to be desired. Rather the royal rule of God is here just breaking in. As such it is what a disciple of Jesus is to "seek," and precisely in place of the other things that are additionally given in the royal reign of God. For the disciple who finds God's reign, God is then also the Father who knows of people's needs, an idea that Epictetus certainly does not allow. Wishing and longing, on the other hand, according to Luke 12:29-31, are not necessarily the expression of insufficient instruction, and especially not then when the longing is directed to what is "not in our power" but in God's unique decree, God's righteous royal rule over creation, for whose *coming* Jesus' disciples pray in the Lord's Prayer. With the coming of God's rule will be fulfilled even those desires whose fulfillment it would now be foolish to seek, according to the Jesus tradition.

The Mercy of God as the Measure of Righteous Action

At the end of this section of the discourse (vv. 32-33) the evangelist Luke[21] introduces his practical ideas about the theme of worry. He explains to his readers how the treasure of the knowledge of God's royal reign, by which they distinguish themselves as a cognitive minority ("little flock") from the "peoples of the world" (v. 30), is to present itself through its social engagement as something that will change the world. This opens up a further aspect of the theology of creation in the synoptic Jesus tradition.

The trust in God's care for creation through the establishing of divine rule in the world of human beings, which is awaited in the near future and newly experienced in its breaking into the present, provides the certainty and confident assurance one needs in order to personally cooperate in the fulfilling of God's righteousness by means of a behavior toward one's fellow human beings that corresponds to God's activity.

The ideal of conduct that mirrors God's actions, of becoming similar to God (ὁμοίωσις θεῷ, *imitatio Dei*),[22] can produce widely-varying orientations depending on how God's relationship to the world is conceived. In the Holiness Code the entire congregation of Israel is obligated to God's holiness:

> You shall be holy, for I the LORD your God am holy (Lev 19:2).

This sentence opens a sense unit (19:1-37) that is considered in the rabbinic exegetical tradition to be a compendium of the entire Torah. The life of the people guided by the Torah is the path of *imitatio Dei.* Distance from the polytheistic cults is only one aspect of this among others (see Lev 19:4).

In Plato's dialogue *Theaetetus* becoming like God is an "escape route" by which one can escape from evil. Thus distance from the world becomes the essential characteristic of the *imitatio Dei.*

> But it is not possible, Theodorus, that evil should be destroyed—for there must always be something opposed to the good; nor is it possible that it should have its seat in heaven. But it must inevitably haunt human life, and prowl about this earth. That is why a man should make all haste to escape from earth to heaven; and escape (φυγή) means becoming as like to God as possible (ὁμοίωσις θεῷ κατὰ τὸ δυνατόν); and a man becomes like God when he becomes just and pure (δίκαιον καὶ ὅσιον), with understanding (*Theaetetus* 176a,b; cf. *Laws* IV 716a-d).[23]

There is a similar expression of the concept of imitation of God in the preamble of the *Community Rule* of the Qumran Essenes. Here, too, the basic idea is one of separation. However, a flight from the mutually contending principles is inconceivable.

> . . . [book of the Rul]e of the Community: in order to *(2)* seek God [with all (one's) heart and with all (one's) soul; in order] to do what is good and just in his presence, as *(3)* commanded by means of the hand of Moses, and his servants the Prophets; in order to love everything *(4)* which he selects and to hate everything that he rejects; in order to keep oneself at a distance from all evil, *(5)* and to become attached to all good works; to bring about truth, justice and uprightness *(6)* on earth . . . in order to love all the sons of the light, each one *(10)* according to his lot in God's plan, and to detest all the sons of darkness, each one in accordance with his blame *(11)* in God's vindication.

The members of the Essene community commit themselves according to this program to an either-or by which they seek to be in accord with God's partiality in regard to light and darkness, truth and falsehood, holiness and sin. Concretely this is the program for a communal life according to priestly ideals but distinct from the real Temple and its order of worship.

Sirach 4:10 gives a very different prescription for how a "son of the Most High" is to behave according to the example of God and how God will deal accordingly with him:

> Be a father to the orphans
> and be like a husband to their mother;
> you will then be like a son of the Most High,
> and he will love you more than does your mother.

Here God becomes the example for compassionate attentiveness to those who are socially weak. The father's mercy toward his children is the attitude of the Creator toward creatures.[24] To those who act according to the measure of divine kindness God gives special care. Philo of Alexandria (ca. 15 B.C.E. to 50 C.E.) says the following on the subject:

> This premise of mine is confirmed by the law, where it says that they who do "what is pleasing" to nature and what is "good" are sons of God. For it says, "Ye are sons to your Lord God," [Deut 14:1] clearly meaning that He will think fit to protect and provide for you as would a father. And how much this watchful care will exceed that of men is measured, believe me, by the surpassing excellence of Him who bestows it.[25]

It is clear from these different presentations that as regards the ideal of basing one's behavior on the standard of divine action the crucial question is what is meant by divine action. Shortly before the Jewish War the anti-Roman resistance group of Zealots had identified itself with the "zeal" with which their model, Aaron's grandson Phinehas, proceeded violently against a couple living in an illicit union (see Num 25:6-13). Numbers 25:11 evaluates this as imitation of God's zeal. In the Mishna treatise *Sota* (*b. Sota* 14a), on the other hand, in connection with the topic of suspicion of adultery, the question of the imitation of God's zeal is stated with much greater caution.

> Is it then possible for a human being to follow the Shekina?[26] It says, after all: For YHWH your God is a consuming fire (Mark 4:24). Rather (it is meant) that one should follow God's manner of working *(middot).* As he clothes the naked (Adam and Eve, Gen 3:21), you also ought to clothe the naked. As he visits the sick (the sick Abraham, Gen 18:1), so you, too, should visit the sick. As he comforts the bereaved (Isaac after Abraham's death, Gen 25:11), you, too, ought to comfort the bereaved. As he buries the dead (burial of Moses, Deut 34:6), so you, too, ought to bury the dead.[27]

In the New Testament God's judgment on the world is expected in the near future. But how will God encounter the sinful world when the last things come, and what human conduct corresponds to God's activity in the eschatological situation of crisis? Will it be zeal or mercy? When the ideal of the *imitatio Dei* is related to the idea of judgment, as is unavoidable in the New Testament texts, it must appear in what is specific in the experience of God that is expressed in the Jesus-tradition of the synoptic gospels. The most prominent statements about this are to be found in the Lord's Prayer and in the Sermon on the Plain or the Sermon on the Mount.

The Lord's Prayer has been transmitted in two Greek versions of differing length (Matt 6:7-15 and Luke 11:1-4). A synoptic comparison allows us to reconstruct the source of both in the Sayings Source, Q. The following translation corresponds to the recovered text.

1 Father,
2 hallowed be your name;
3 your kingdom come;
4 give us today the bread we need
5 and forgive us our debts,
6 as we, too, have forgiven our debtors;
7 and do not lead us into temptation.

According to the synoptic tradition Jesus gave his disciples this short prayer as an expression of the new relationship to God he had opened for them. The relationship is that of a familial immediacy expressed in the address as Father. The petitions that follow do not, however, understand this relationship as a self-evident condition, but as a dynamic process in which God's relationship to God's sons and daughters and their relationship to God as their Father is realized. God's realm, God's coming kingdom, and the situation of the one who prays are not yet congruent. The hallowing of God's name is not realized until the arrival of God's rule among human beings, and the expression of these petitions makes it present. The sphere of the one who prays is open to God's rule. It is expressed as the sphere defined by privation and guilt (lines 4 and 6), but now through God's just mercy it becomes a place where the care and forgiveness of the Creator are experienced. This gives the norm according to which God's sons and daughters are to conduct themselves in the eschatological crisis. The only indicative sentence of the prayer (line 6) gives expression to this. It implies that the persons who pray are themselves already acting and have acted according to the measure of the mercy for which they themselves pray ("as we, too, have forgiven" is in the perfect tense). There is no calculation involved, but rather the new experience that God's mercy liberates the human being for mercy. No one can forgive guilt but God alone. That forgiveness is now pronounced also by the disciples of Jesus permits them to have a share in the mercy by which

God, at the judgment, will reveal to the world of human beings the faithfulness of its divine Creator.

The new idea of *imitatio Dei* contained in the Lord's Prayer becomes a key concept in the Lukan Sermon on the Plain (Luke 6:20-50).[28] This can be seen in the composition of the discourse.

6:20-26. Exposition: Invitation to Wisdom: Beatitudes and Woes	
Part 1	Part 2
vv. 27-35: Acting according to the golden rule	vv. 36-45: Acting according to God's example
The norm: love of enemies (27-28)	The norm: mercy (36)
Concretization: giving and receiving (29-30)	Concretization: forgiving and receiving forgiveness (37-38)
Final statement: the golden rule (31)	Final statement: logion about the measure with which one measures (38d)
Argumentation: negative: distancing from the principles according to which sinners act (32-34); positive: love of enemies as *imitatio Dei* (35)	Argumentation: negative: self-critique as precondition of fraternity/sorority (39-42); positive: action as the criterion for good and evil (43-45)
6:46-49. Conclusion: Parable of Building the House	

The *imitatio Dei* motif is found at the center of the discourse. It closes Part 1 and opens Part 2. At the end of Part 1, which deals with love of enemies as the form of love necessary in the eschatological crisis, this is brought into relationship with the "kindness" with which God encounters "the ungrateful and the wicked." Those who follow this norm in their actions are and become "children of the Most High."

The parallel passage in Matthew's Sermon on the Mount (Matt 5:44-45) shows the creation-theological background of these ideas more clearly than does the Lukan Sermon on the Plain.

> But I say to you,
> Love your enemies
> and pray for those who persecute you,
> so that you may be children of your Father in heaven;
> for he makes his sun rise on the evil and on the good,
> and sends rain on the righteous and on the unrighteous.

The special significance of this statement consists in the justification of love of enemies[29] as acting according to the same norm by which God acts in the eschatological crisis. God encounters human beings precisely in this last, definitive turning to them with the merciful fidelity of the Creator to creation. Imitation of God in the eschatological crisis, therefore, does *not* consist in Jesus' disciples assuming the role of those appointed to carry out God's judgments on other human beings, not even within the congregation (see Part 2 of the Sermon on the Plain). The imitation of God's mercy is the norm of living together with others, with "your" enemies. Thus Jesus' wisdom makes a disciple of Jesus an ethically sovereign actor, one in charge of the situation so far as his or her own action is concerned, precisely in the confrontation with the unjust reality in which he or she had at first seemed to be only the victim of enmity, violence, rapacity, and disrespect, utterly inferior and at the mercy of injustice (see Luke 6:29-30 par. Matt 5:39b, 40, 42).

The wisdom of Jesus introduces a way of acting creatively according to the golden rule and the measure of divine mercy, even now within unjust reality, as if the reign of God were already the basis for the interactions of all people with one another. That one already dares to behave in this way has to do not only with the expectation that God will soon put things in order, but above all with the fact that through Jesus his disciples have themselves experienced God's merciful turning to the chaotic world of human beings.

The Other Fence of the Torah: The Sermon on the Mount as Interpretation of the Torah

In the Sermon on the Mount the commandment of love of enemies is expressed in the form of an antithesis (Matt 5:43-48):

43 "You have heard that it was said,
'You shall love your neighbor and hate your enemy.' [Lev 19:18]
44 But I say to you,
Love your enemies
and pray for those who persecute you,
45a so that you may be children of your Father in heaven.

In the antithesis form the norm formulated by Jesus confronts another rival understanding, and in fact in the sense of correcting it.[30]

What is corrected in this case is not the statement cited from Lev 19:18: "you shall love your neighbor," but rather an interpretation of this statement that does not allow the commandment of love to prevail in its original and complete sense, but limits it in the sense of "you shall hate your enemy."[31] The antithesis of this thesis formulates and stresses the original and full demand of Lev 19:18, and specifically, as shown above, in a creation-theological context. The instruction to love the enemy, founded in the theology of creation, therefore, restores the original demand of the Torah[32] in opposition to a truncated understanding of loving the neighbor. This yields a connection between creation-theological argumentation and Torah interpretation such as that characteristic of the *Torah-Wisdom* concept. The antitheses of the Sermon on the Mount are, therefore, as becomes clear at this point, to be understood as Wisdom-Torah interpretation. Matthew makes a fence for the Torah out of the *apocalyptic Wisdom* Jesus tradition.

"Making a fence for the Torah" is one of the three principles of Pharisaic and rabbinic Torah-Wisdom that, according to *Pirqe ʾAbot* 1.1, is said to have been formulated after the exile by "the men of the great synagogue." The metaphor "a fence for the Torah" describes the entire tradition developed by Pharisaic-rabbinic Torah scholarship in order to discover and transmit the creative wisdom of God contained in the Torah (see *Pirqe ʾAbot* 3.13a).

In Matthew's gospel, too, it is taken for granted that the Torah-Wisdom interpretation of the Law is the honorable task of the scribes and Pharisees that establishes their authority:

> "The scribes and the Pharisees sit on Moses' seat; therefore, do whatever they teach you, and follow it . . ." (Matt 23:2, 3a).

The scribes and Pharisees are thereby not only respected as authorities as far as the teaching of the Torah is concerned; it is also assumed that the hearers of Jesus' message in the Sermon on the Mount and in the discourse in Matthew 23 are also hearers of the scribes and Pharisees. This explains Matthew's antithetical form. Situations are presented to readers of the gospel in which Jesus and the scribes and Pharisees compete as authorities for the best interpretation of the Torah. The Matthaen Jesus obviously represents the correct interpretation, which leads his disciples to that righteousness that far exceeds that of the scribes and Pharisees and that alone makes it possible (cf. Matt 5:20) to attain the royal reign of the heavens, while the competing authority is severely criticized in the "woes" in Matthew 23, especially because they close the royal reign of the heavens to human beings (see 23:13). Jesus' competitors are making the wrong use of the key they hold in their hands.

The superiority of Torah interpretation in the context ("fence") of Jesus' wisdom in contrast to the Sadducean and Pharisaic interpretations is revealed in the last antithesis of the Sermon on the Mount; as was clear above, here the Torah (in this case Lev 19:18) is interpreted in its full meaning, namely in accord with creation. In the declaration of principles that precedes the antithesis both aspects are formulated in their claim to universality.

5:17 "Do not think
that I have come to abolish the law or the prophets;
I have come not to abolish
but to fulfill.
5:18 For truly I tell you,
until heaven and earth pass away,
not one letter, not one stroke of a letter,
will pass from the law until all is accomplished."

The New Testament is not a book of Torah-Wisdom. Matthew is the borderline case that confirms this thesis. In this conception the relationship of creation, Torah, and divine rule is established through the apocalyptic Wisdom-theological interpretation of the Torah. It is this interpretation of the Torah through the Wisdom of Jesus that, according to Matthew, is proclaimed as Torah for Israel and the nations (see Matt 28:19-20) to the end of the world.[33]

Notes: Chapter 12

[1] More details on this below in ch. 13.

[2] In Phil 3:3-9 Paul distances himself from his past as a Pharisee (v. 5); accordingly, the "Judaism" from which he disassociates himself in Gal 1:13 is not to be identified with the Judaism to which Christianity would be an alternative.

[3] A detailed description of the socio-economic situation in Palestine and the Jewish people's religious-cultural strategies for coping are furnished by Ekkehard W. Stegemann and Wolfgang Stegemann, *Urchristliche Sozialgeschichte. Die Anfänge im Judentum und die Christusgemeinde in der mediterranen Welt* (Stuttgart: Kohlhammer, 1995) 97ff.

[4] On the absence of the rabbinic terminology of taking upon oneself the yoke of heavenly rule cf. Helmut Merklein, *Die Gottesherrschaft als Handlungsprinzip: Untersuchungen zur Ethik Jesu.* FzB 34 (Würzburg: Echter, 1978) 117.

[5] On the understanding of sickness and healing in the First Testament cf. Klaus Seybold, *Das Gebet des Kranken im Alten Testament. Untersuchungen zur Bestimmung und Zuordnung der Krankheits- und Heilungspsalmen.* BWANT 99 (Stuttgart: Kohlhammer, 1973); Claus Westermann, "Heilung und Heil in der Gemeinde aus der Sicht des Alten Testaments," in idem, *Erträge der Forschung am Alten Testament. Gesammelte Studien III,* ed. Rainer Albertz. ThB 73 (Munich: Kaiser, 1984) 166–77; Hans Walter Wolff, *Anthropologie des Alten Testaments* (Munich: Kaiser, 1973) 211–20 (English: *Anthropology of the Old Testament.* Translated by Margaret Kohl [Philadelphia: Fortress, 1974]); Klaus Seybold and Ulrich B. Müller, *Krankheit und Heilung.* BiKon 1008 (Stuttgart, Cologne, and Mainz: Kohlhammer, 1978 (English: *Sickness and Healing.* Translated by Douglas W. Stott [Nashville: Abingdon, 1981]); Norbert Lohfink, "'Ich bin Yahweh, dein Arzt' (Exod 15:26). Gott, Gesellschaft und menschliche Gesundheit in der Theologie einer nachexilischen Pentateucherzählung (Exod 15:25b-26)," in idem, et al., *"Ich will euer Gott werden" Beispiele biblischen Redens von Gott.* SBS 100 (Stuttgart: Katholisches Bibelwerk, 1981) 11–73 (English: "'I am Yahweh, your Physician' [Exodus 15:26]. God, Society and

Human Health in a Postexilic Revision of the Pentateuch [Exod. 15:2b, 26]," in idem, *Theology of the Pentateuch. Themes of the Priestly Narrative and Deuteronomy.* Translated by Linda M. Maloney [Minneapolis: Fortress, 1994] 35–95).

[6] In 1 Enoch 8:1-3 the types of demonic knowledge are listed; in the first group are the ability to manufacture weapons, jewelry, and cosmetics; in the second group are the art of conjuring and of root-cutting, releasing from curses, as well as various mantic arts.

[7] Cf. Mark 3:22 parr.; Matt 9:34; 12:24. The controversy is thus not about the fact of the miraculous healings, but about their nature.

[8] Cf. Rainer Kampling, "Jesus von Nazaret: Lehrer und Exorzist," *BZ* 30 (1986) 232–48. For further understanding of exorcisms and healings in contemporary charismatic Judaism cf. Geza Vermes, *Jesus the Jew: A Historian's Reading of the Gospels* (London: Collins, 1973).

[9] Mark 1:23-28; 5:1-20; 7:24-30; 9:14-29; Matt 9:32-34; Acts 16:16-18; 19:13-17.

[10] Mark 1:29-31, 40-45; 2:1-12; 5:21-24, 25-34, 35-43; 7:31-37; 8:22-26; 10:46-52; Matt 8:5-13; 9:27-31; Luke 7:11-17; 17:11-19; John 5:2-9; 11:1-44; Acts 3:1-10; 9:32-35, 36-43; 14:8-10; 20:7-12; 28:7-10.

[11] This is emphasized by Dan Otto Via, *The Parables: Their Literary and Existential Dimension* (Philadelphia: Fortress, 1967) 98. See also H. J. Meurer, *Die Gleichnisse Jesu als Metaphern. Paul Ricoeurs Hermeneutik der Gleichniserzählung im Horizont des Symbol "Gottesherrschaft/Reich Gottes."* BBB 111 (Bodenheim: Philo, 1997) 64.

[12] It is true of the parables in general that as "extended metaphors" they radiate simultaneously both an alienating and an innovative power that permits one to see reality in a new way. Cf. Meurer, *Gleichnisse* 308–14. It becomes especially clear in the examples discussed above that in light of the parables the world of daily experience itself reveals the primeval reality of creation.

[13] That Jesus was a teacher of Wisdom is to a great extent accepted. Controversial is how the Jesus-Wisdom-traditions are related to the programmatic theme of the proclamation of the rule of God, that is, whether original sayings of Jesus of the Wisdom type are related to apocalyptic Wisdom. Max Küchler, *Frühjüdische Weisheitstradition. Zum Fortgang weisheitlichen Denkens im Bereich des frühjüdischen Jahweglaubens.* OBO 2 (Fribourg: Universitätsverlag; Göttingen: Vandenhoeck & Ruprecht, 1979), who for the first time really grasped the significance of apocalyptic Wisdom as an early Jewish phenomenon, suggests in a "look to the future" (572–92) an apocalyptic Wisdom interpretation of Jesus' Wisdom logia. Hermann von Lips, *Weisheitliche Traditionen im Neuen Testament.* WMANT 64 (Neukirchen-Vluyn: Neukirchener Verlag, 1990) does not follow this approach, either for the interpretation of the Jesus tradition or for any other New Testament material, but continues to posit a "side-by-side juxtaposition of Wisdom and prophetically-marked texts" in the Jesus tradition in the synoptics (241). He establishes their relationship in terms of creation theology (247–54): "It is the creator God who desires to establish full dominion in the world. Hence the activity of the Creator represents the positive point of contact for eschatological preaching and its roots in experience. . . . Thus a Wisdom view can serve as a pointer to eschatological action in light of the present experience of creative activity" (25–26). Because the basic problem of determining the relationship of Wisdom and apocalyptic cannot be discussed here, especially not in relation to the historical Jesus, the following remarks refer to sections of the gospels of Luke and Matthew that present the Jesus-Wisdom-tradition in its whole breadth and variety, each within its own theological program.

[14] The farmer is a fool because he thinks there is a cause-and-effect relationship between taking precautions and a guaranteed enjoyment of life. The secondary v. 21, however, retracts the radicality of this idea when it adopts an ethical stance and accuses the foolish farmer of greed.

[15] What thrives "today" will be burned "tomorrow" (v. 28). Here apocalyptic crisis thinking is clarified with an example from nature.

[16] On the question energetically discussed in the United States of whether Jesus was a Jewish Cynic, cf. Hans Dieter Betz, "Jesus and the Cynics: Survey of Analysis of a Hypothesis," *Journal of Religion* 74 (1994) 453–75.

[17] For a recent critical edition see Gerard Boter, *The Encheiridion of Epictetus and Its Three Christian Adaptations, Transmission and Critical Editions* (Leiden and Boston: Brill, 1999).

[18] With this metaphor Epictetus refers to the "things that lie in our power," namely "our understanding, our initiative to act, our desire and avoidance," in short, everything "that goes out from us." The list makes clear that Epictetus' concept of freedom is to a considerable extent concerned with human ability to control the perception of things, i.e., to what extent one wishes to permit material reality to affect oneself.

[19] The expression Luke chooses here takes up a familiar Hellenistic usage.

[20] Naturally Luke thinks differently about this. In the temptation narrative the Devil, contemplating all the empires of the world, their power and glory, says ". . . it has been given over to me, and I give it to anyone I please" (Luke 4:6).

[21] Especially the contrast between the "nations of the world" (v. 30) and the "little flock," as well as giving alms out of a fortune that has been sold (v. 33) go back to him.

[22] Cf. Gerhard Schneider, "Imitatio Dei as Motiv der 'Ethik Jesu,'" in Helmut Merklein, ed., *Neues Testament und Ethik: für Rudolf Schnackenburg* (Freiburg: Herder, 1989) 71–83.

[23] Plato, *Theaetetus*, ed. and intro. Bernard Williams. Translated by M. J. Levett. Revised by Myles Burnyeat (Indianapolis and Cambridge: Hackett, 1992) 46.

[24] Cf. Prov 14:31; 17:5.

[25] Philo, *The Special Laws* 1.318. Translation in *Philo* with an English translation by F. H. Colson. LCL (Cambridge, Mass.: Harvard University Press; London: William Heinemann, 1937).

[26] With the word *shekinah* (literally "habitation") the rabbis designate the manner in which God is present in the people of Israel and their institutions. Cf. Clemens Thoma, *Das Messiasprojekt. Theologie jüdisch-christlicher Begegnung* (Augsburg: Pattloch, 1994) 82–84.

[27] Text with explanatory glosses according to Hans Joachim Schöps, "Von der Imitatio Dei zur Nachfolge Christi," in idem, *Aus frühchristlicher Zeit. Religionsgeschichtliche Untersuchungen* (Tübingen: Mohr, 1950) 286–301, at 290 n. 1.

[28] For an interpretation in this context cf. Karl Löning, *Das Geschichtswerk des Lukas. I: Israels Hoffnung und Gottes Geheimnisse* (Stuttgart: Kohlhammer, 1997) 204–13.

[29] Cf. Peter Dschnulnigg, "Schöpfung im Licht des Neuen Testaments. Neutestamentliche Schöpfungsaussagen und ihre Funktion (Mt, Apg, Kol, Offb)," *Freiburger Zeitschrift für Philosophie und Theologie* 40 (1993) 125–45, at 126–27. Loving one's enemies also belongs to the Wisdom tradition (cf., for example, Prov 25:21-22; *TJos* 18:2; *TBenj* 4:3) and can be traced back to the second half of the second millennium before Christ. Cf. Dieter Zeller, *Die weisheitlichen Mahnsprüche bei den Synoptikern*. FZB 17 (Würzburg: Echter, 1977) 57–58, 104–106.

[30] The form of the polemic antithesis is not usual in Judaism either. Cf. Heinz-Wolfgang Kuhn, "Das Liebesgebot Jesu als Tora und als Evangelium. Zur Feindesliebe und zur christlichen und jüdischen Auslegung der Bergpredigt," in Hubert Frankemölle and Karl Kertelge, eds., *Vom Urchristentum zu Jesus: für Joachim Gnilka* (Freiburg: Herder, 1989) 194–230, at 213–17; Lawrence H. Schiffman, "The New Halakhic Letter (4QMMT) and the Origins of the Dead Sea Sect," *Biblical Archeologist* 53 (1990) 64–73 introduces a polemic letter text that discusses contrary Torah interpretations in antithetical form ("you . . . but we . . .").

[31] This merely formulates a popular conception. It is not included either in Lev 19:18 or in the program of any of the religious parties of early Judaism.

[32] According to a stubborn Christian bias, the opposite is true. On this see Hubert Frankemölle, "Die sogenannte Antithesen des Matthäus (Mt 5:21ff). Hebt Matthäus für Christen das sogenannte 'Alte' Testament auf? Von der Macht der Vorurteile," in idem, ed., *Die Bibel. Das bekannte Buch, das fremde Buch* (Paderborn: Schöningh, 1994) 61–92

[33] Cf. Hubert Frankemölle, "Die Tora Gottes für Israel, die Jünger Jesu und die Völker nach dem Matthäusevengelium," in Erich Zenger, ed., *Die Tora als Kanon für Juden und Christen* (Freiburg: Herder, 1996) 379–419, at 395–401.

CHAPTER 13

The Patience of Creation: On the Relationship Between Creation, Torah, and Eschatological Revelation of the Righteousness of God (Paul's Letter to the Romans)

The relationship between Torah, creation, and the reign of God constructed by Matthew's gospel through its interpretation of the Torah in the context of the wisdom of Jesus is also of fundamental significance for the train of thought in Paul's letter to the Romans and the creation-theological statements in Rom 8:18-23. The structural affinity of these two great theological conceptions is no accident; it makes visible the elementary foundational relationships that are characteristic of New Testament theologies.

The Apocalyptic-Wisdom Structure of New Testament Soteriologies

In the Gospel of Mark the creation-theological motifs are set within a soteriological context.[1] The main theme is the establishment—through Jesus, the crucified Son of God—of God's rule in opposition to the seemingly still unbroken violence of the power of death in the darkness of the world that is distant from God. The theology of creation is implicit in this principal theme, and this is true of Mark's gospel as a whole. This is apparent from the fact that the role of Jesus in the exposition of the book is that of the guarantor of peace in the entire creation. Accordingly, soteriology and the theology of creation stand in an indissoluble relationship that is, however, so constituted that the theology of creation, as an implication of soteriology, generally moves into the background.

In the hierarchy of theological themes in New Testament texts, however, soteriology, for its part, occupies "only" second place. The discourse about God's redemptive activity in the world is fundamentally a reaching out beyond the world as it is, a discourse about what no eye has seen and no ear has heard. One can only speak about God's saving activity at the end of the age when there is knowledge about the end and God's ultimate plans that is superior to all knowledge that can be gained as wisdom drawn from experience of the present world. Therefore the apocalyptic-Wisdom structure of a theology concedes the first place to the theme of knowledge and the justification of knowledge before all matters of content. A classic example of this is the theological conception of the Fourth Gospel, whose exposition of the mission of Jesus as the revealer of God's glory is derived from the figure of the λογος, the personified word of creation.[2]

The transformation of soteriological statements at the level of knowledge is the distinctive mark of apocalyptic-Wisdom conceptions, and is generally characteristic of all New Testament soteriologies. Statements about God's turning to creation always appear in New Testament texts in revelation-theological transformations as statements about God's revelation or about the gift of saving knowledge through Jesus. The story told in Mark's gospel about the struggle of the Son of God to establish the reign of God is at the same time the story of the secret epiphanies of God, and simultaneously a history that was planned from eternity in God's eternal dialogue with divine Wisdom, presented in Scripture as the *mysterion* of divine power. What was "hidden from eternity" is "now revealed," as this is didactively formulated in the New Testament scheme of revelation (see Col 1:26-27; Eph 3:8-12; Rom 16:25-26; 2 Tim 1:9-10; Titus 1:2-3; see 1 Pet 1:20), where theologies of creation and revelation stand in close relationship to one another. The section that follows also has to do with this concept of an apocalyptic-Wisdom soteriology and its creation-theological implications.

The Place and Value of the Creation Theme in Romans

The creation-theological statements in Rom 8:18-23, which clearly illustrate the connection between creation-theological and revelation-theological aspects of Pauline soteriology, are not in isolation within the letter to the Romans.[3] The letter's train of thought is established from the outset in such a way that the statements about the liberation of creation turn out to be the point of the entire argumentation. Therefore we must begin with the introductory chapters.

The *proemium* of Romans (1:8-17) with its statement of the proof to be proposed (*propositio*, vv. 16-17) leads directly into the first principal section:

16 For I am not ashamed of the gospel;
it is the power of God for salvation to everyone who has faith, to the Jew first and also to the Greek.
17 For in it the righteousness of God is revealed
through faith for faith;

as it is written,
"The one who is righteous will live by faith" [Hab 2:4].

From the start, therefore, the conversation on the level of knowledge is about the saving "power" of God. "God's power" is the predicate noun in a statement about "the gospel." "Everyone who has faith" experiences deliverance.

This initial thesis is expanded in the first main part of the letter (1:18–3:31) on the level of knowledge and in accordance with the *propositio*. The overarching theme of this main part is the situation of eschatological crisis, which is analyzed along two lines. The first (Rom 1:18–2:16) deals with the situation of the human being under the *revelation of the wrath* of God.[4] The second (2:17–3:31) raises the question of the meaning of Torah-Wisdom in the eschatological process of the *revelation of the righteousness* of God. The first section contains the creation-theological statements that are of special interest here.

18 For the wrath of God is revealed from heaven against all ungodliness and wickedness of those who by their wickedness suppress the truth.
19 For what can be known about God is plain to them,
because God has shown it to them.
20 Ever since the creation of the world his eternal power and divine nature, invisible though they are, have been understood and seen through the things he has made. So they are without excuse;
21 for though they knew God, they did not honor him as God or give thanks to him,
but they became futile in their thinking,
and their senseless minds were darkened.
22 Claiming to be wise, they became fools;
23 and they exchanged the glory of the immortal God for images resembling a mortal human being or birds or four-footed animals or reptiles.
24 Therefore God gave them up in the lusts of their hearts to impurity, to the degrading of their bodies among themselves,
25 because they exchanged the truth about God for a lie and worshiped and served the creature rather than the Creator,
who is blessed forever! Amen.

The structure of the thought process that begins with this section of the text can be sketched briefly. The initial thesis (v. 18) is argumentatively developed in two sense units according to its two principal aspects (God's wrath and the unrighteousness of human beings). The first (1:19-25) describes the permanent fall into sin, the second its effects (1:26-32). This corresponds to the Wisdom scheme of action and result. It is the basis not only of vv. 22-25 but determines the relationship of the first series of arguments (1:19-25) to the second (1:26-32), since the phenomena of degradation described in 1:26-32 are understood as God's punishments, and thus as expressions of divine wrath. The second series of arguments, therefore, develops the first aspect of the initial thesis (revelation of the wrath of God), while the first series of arguments—the text given above—develops the second aspect (the unrighteousness of human beings).

The first series of arguments contrasts two proposed sets of facts, each of which is argumentatively supported: the possibility of knowing God (1:19-20) and human refusal of that knowledge (1:21). The latter is concretized by means of the scheme of action (1:22-23) and result (1:24-25).

The situation of humanity before God is presented in poster-fashion in this text as an apocalyptic crisis of the end time. However, God's wrath, which is directed against humankind, does not express itself as a flood or a fiery judgment, but in a manner befitting the unrighteousness spoken about here. The human unrighteousness against which God's wrath is "revealed"—the first word of this major section!—consists in this, that it "suppresses the truth," that it represses the knowledge of the power of God that is revealed in creation. God's action consists accordingly in delivering over the people who have scorned to recognize God (οὐκ ἐδοκίμασαν) to their futile thinking (εἰς ἀδόκομον νοῦν, v. 28), causing them to behave contrary to creation. It is the leading principle of Stoic anthropology that it is mind (νους) that refuses to recognize the revelation of God's power in the creation (cf. νοούμενα, v. 20) and is thereby itself perverted, with corresponding expression in the wrong actions of all human beings. Therefore it is impossible for any human being to escape God's judgment (cf. 2:1-16).

It would be a mistake to separate this part of the letter to the Romans as an independent tractate on the natural knowledge of God *(theologia naturalis)* from the subsequent context.[5] The weight of the creation-theological statements in this connection is not evident outside the total context of chs. 1–3. The refusal of the knowledge about God that is accessible to all human beings when they recognize the world as God's creation leads, in the following section of the letter (2:17–3:31), to the question of the significance of Jewish knowledge in the context of the event of the apocalyptic revelation of God's righteousness. Circumcision and Law are named as the essential achievements of Jewish religious culture. In this context statements about the Law and the knowledge it contains have the predominant place. In the Torah the Jewish religion possesses the formulated knowledge and truth (μόρφωσιν τῆς γνώσεως καὶ τῆς ἀληθείας) about God that would make a Jew educated in the Torah an ideal teacher of all other people. In Paul's judgment, however, this does not apply in the way that Torah-Wisdom thinks (see 2:17-20 vs. 2:21-24). What really constitutes the advantage of the Torah and the knowledge it contains, according to Paul,[6] is discussed in a three-stage argument (3:1-31). The thesis (3:1-8) states: The Jews have a significant advantage "in every respect" inasmuch as in the Torah, God's "oracles" are entrusted to Israel (v. 2). This is valid also from the perspective of apocalyptic deficit analysis. As God's word the Torah is not robbed of its truth just because the people to whom it is entrusted are "liars" (v. 4). The antithesis (vv. 9-18) counters: "we [Jews]" (said under the fictitious assumption that a diatribe-discussion is taking place here with Jewish addressees)[7] "are no better off at all," because "all, both Jews and Greeks, are under the power of sin." This is verified through quotations from the Scriptures (vv. 10-18). The synthesis (vv. 19-26)[8] leads to the decisive statement ("Now we know that . . ."): the knowledge that those to whom the Torah speaks really have is "the knowledge of sin" (see vv. 19-20). This knowledge is the background against which the revelation of God's righteousness *happens,* without the Torah having *thereby* played any role (χωρὶς νόμου). But this revelatory event is "attested" by "the law and the prophets," the revelatory knowledge of Scripture. God's eschatological revelation reveals no other truth than that attested in Scripture, even when the revelation of God's righteousness is something that Torah-knowledge was not able to bring about (see Rom 8:3).

In summary, the theological structure of the triad creation/Torah/end-time revelation (of the righteousness of God) in the letter to the Romans can be thus characterized: creation, Torah, and end time revelation are seen as the substantive gifts of knowledge in which God is self-revealed to humans. It is characteristic of the apocalyptic starting point that these are not understood as the unshakeable eternal decrees of God, as in the creation theology of the Priestly document. Rather they are presented in the context of an end-time drama in the course of which the thing that was not realized as the original plan is once again in play. According to Rom 1:19-32 this is the perfection of creation in the human knowledge of God spoken of in Rom 1:19-20. The soteriology developed in the letter to the Romans is a confrontation with the permanent fall into sin, the refusal of this knowledge on the part of human beings described in Rom 1:21-32.

The Revelation of the Glory of the Children of God as the Liberation of Creation (Romans 8:8-27)

The fundamental-theological connection between the knowledge of creation, the knowledge of the Torah, and the eschatological revelation of God's righteousness established in the opening section of the letter to the Romans is made more explicit in the second section of the letter (Romans 5–8, followed by the excursus on Israel in chs. 9–11), after the digression regarding Abraham in ch. 4, but this time from the perspective of the *new* knowledge, justification by faith. The creation-theological aspect that is of interest here is repeatedly and explicitly expressed, first in the Adam-Christ typology (5:12-21): the peace with God newly grounded in justification by faith abolishes the rule of death over creation "from Adam to Moses" (5:14). The thought process in Romans 7–8 is especially instructive. After liberation from the rule of death and the power of sin, liberation from the old rule of compulsive observance of the Torah is here thematized along with its effect on humankind and creation. The compulsion does not proceed from the Torah but from the powers of sin and death, which so dominate human action that it cannot bring to expression what the Torah contains. In the seventh chapter the despair this provokes comes to the fore. The Torah, which as revelation of the will of God is "holy and just and good" (7:12), cannot prevent the power of sin from causing the very "law of God," which the reflecting I certainly follows with its mind (νους), to become the "law of sin" by means of the created nature ("the flesh") of the human being (see 7:25b). To this the eighth chapter contrasts gratitude for rescue from this alienation of the human being from self and from God. Now the connection between creatureliness, Torah-observance, and divine righteousness, whose problematic nature is so thoroughly explored in Romans 7, can be positively developed: liberation from "the law of sin and of death" occurred, according to 8:2-4, so that the goal the Torah could not reach because of the creaturely weakness of the human being could nevertheless be attained by the judgment of sin that was accomplished in the death of the Son, "so that the just requirement of the law might be fulfilled in us, who walk not according to the flesh but according to the Spirit" (v. 4). The life that is guided by the Spirit is ultimately the life that perfectly corresponds to the Torah. Out of this comes the hope of perfection that still stands in tension with the present suffering of believers (v. 17). But the perfection of the believers will at the same time be the liberation of creation from the slavery of temporality (vv. 18-23). Here the fundamental connection between created reality and human knowledge introduced in Rom 1:18-32 is applied in a positive sense.

18 I consider that the sufferings of this present time
are not worth comparing with the glory about to be revealed to us.

19 For the creation waits with eager longing for the revealing of the children of God;

20 for the creation was subjected to futility, not of its own will but by the will of the one who subjected it, in hope
21 that the creation itself will be set free from its bondage to decay and will obtain the freedom of the glory of the children of God.

22 We know
that the whole creation has been groaning in labor pains until now;
23 and not only the creation,
but we ourselves, who have the first fruits of the Spirit,
groan inwardly while we wait for adoption, the redemption of our bodies.
24 For in hope we were saved.
Now hope that is seen is not hope.
For who hopes for what is seen?
25 But if we hope for what we do not see, we wait for it with patience.

26 Likewise the Spirit helps us in our weakness;
for we do not know how to pray as we ought,
but that very Spirit intercedes with sighs too deep for words.
27 And God, who searches the heart, knows what is the mind of the Spirit,
because the Spirit intercedes for the saints according to the will of God.

The initial thesis (v. 18) of this section[9] contrasts the hoped-for definitive deliverance of believers with their continuing painful present situation. In the suffering that marks the existence of believers during the still continuing time of this passing age the coming glory is concealed. Accordingly, fulfillment is seen in the fact that the status as sons and daughters already received (see 8:14-16) will become apparent in believers. Then Paul will be proved right in his thesis that the crushing load of suffering is not to be compared with the freedom of the children of God that has already been given and will become visible in the age to come. Out of this comparative evaluation of the situation of believers in the contemporary eschatological crisis situation come the statements about the fulfillment of creation.[10] The motif of suffering is thereby the point of connection. The suffering of the believers who have already been freed for status as sons and daughters makes them exponents of the suffering creation and thereby bearers of the hope of its fulfillment (cf. the key-word link "in hope" between v. 20 and v. 24).

The argumentative development of the initial thesis proceeds in three steps on whose relationship to one another everything depends. The first (8:19-21) is related to creation and its interconnection with human destiny. Creation is personified and decked out with anthropomorphic features, the capacity for suffering and hope, both of which come together in the motif of yearning. Creation has a destiny that it shares with human beings.[11] It is subjected to the "futility" (8:20) that corresponds to the erroneous thinking of human beings by which they suppress the truth they should have recognized in the works of creation (see 1:18-20). Between the permanent human fall into sin and the subjection of creation to "futility,"[12] there is the same relationship as between the revelation of the status of believers as sons and daughters of God and creation's fulfillment. For this reason the creation longs for the perfection of the human being.

In the second step (8:22-25) the knowledgeable we-group (v. 22) achieves solidarity with creation, which in its groaning and its sighing links itself to humanity. It is now the knowledgeable we-group, as whose representative the author speaks, that articulates its own longing expectation of the ransom of the body from enslavement to the power of death. This it shares with the patiently waiting creation.[13]

In the third step (8:26) it is finally said *who* gives expression to this harmony between the human being and the creation in their hope for fulfillment. The Spirit, the principle of creation and of its deliverance out of the nullity and ruin of death, takes upon itself the creaturely "weakness" of the knowledgeable "we-group," their still-persisting affiliation with the world as the sphere of the power of sin and death. The activity of the Spirit for the conclusive fulfillment of creation has thereby shifted entirely into the interior of the believers. The Spirit, in its unutterable speech, articulates the requests that bring the hope of the suffering creature before God in a way that really corresponds to God's creative will. This has nothing to do with a world-averse internalization. The idea that God begins the work of the fulfillment of creation by placing the divine Spirit within human beings means that believers are guided in their thinking, speech, and actions entirely and before every personal human stirring by the Spirit. The Spirit of God begins to re-create creation by taking up an abode in believers (see 8:9), thus finally making creation the place of God's revelation and of the human being's acknowledgment and response, as it should have been from the beginning.

Notes: Chapter 13

[1] Cf. Part I, ch. 4, "Motifs of Creation Theology Within the Framing Conception of the Gospel of Mark."

[2] Cf. Part II, ch. 6, "The *Logos* as the Revelation of God's Creative Glory (Gospel of John)."

[3] Cf. Nikolaus Walter, "Gottes Zorn und das 'Harren der Kreatur.' Zur Korrespondenz zwischen Röm 1,18-32 und 8,19-22," in Karl Kertelge, Traugott Holtz, and Claus-

Peter März, eds., *Christus bezeugen: Festschrift für Wolfgang Trilling zum 65. Geburtstag*. Erfurter theologische Studien 59 (Leipzig : St. Benno-Verlag, 1989) 218–26, especially 224–25.

[4] Cf. Günther Bornkamm, "Die Offenbarung des Zornes Gottes (Röm. 1–3)," in idem, *Studien zum Neuen Testament* (Munich: Kaiser, 1985) 136–60.

[5] Cf. Karl Kertelge, "'Natürliche Theologie' und Rechtfertigung aus dem Glauben," in Walter Baier, et al., eds., *Weisheit Gottes, Weisheit der Welt: Festschrift für Joseph Kardinal Ratzinger zum 60. Geburtstag* (St. Ottilien: EOS, 1987) 1:83–95; reprinted in Karl Kertelge, *Grundthemen paulinischer Theologie* (Freiburg: Herder, 1991) 148–60.

[6] Cf. Peter von der Osten-Sacken, *Die Heiligkeit der Tora. Studien zum Gesetz bei Paulus* (Munich: Kaiser, 1989).

[7] That those addressed are not thought to be Jews, but Gentile Christians, is apparent from the particular form of address used in Rom 11:13a.

[8] Romans 3:19-25 is *one* sense unit. Verse 21 ("But now . . . the righteousness of God has been disclosed") is not the beginning of a new section, but is a further thought within the same argument. This is not narrative, but argumentation. For this reason "now" is not an episodic marker, but introduces the second thought within the scheme "once—but now" (cf. Rom 6:22: 7:6, 17). The following should serve to clarify the arrangement within the text of Rom 3:19-24:

19 Now we know that
whatever the law says, it speaks to those who are under the law, so that every mouth may be silenced, and the whole world may be held accountable to God.
20 For "no human being will be justified in his sight" by deeds prescribed by the law.
For through the law comes the knowledge of sin.
21 But now, apart from the law, the righteousness of God has been disclosed, and is attested by the law and the prophets,
22 the righteousness of God through
faith in Jesus Christ for all who believe.
For there is no distinction,
23 since all have sinned and fall short of the glory of God;
24 they are now justified by his grace as a gift, through the redemption that is in Christ Jesus.

[9] Cf. the analysis of Jacques Schlosser, "L'ésperance de la création (Rom 8:18-22)," in Raymond Kuntzmann, ed., *Ce Dieu que vient. Études sur l'Ancien et le Nouveau Testament offertes au Professor Bernard Renaud à l'occasion de son soixante-cinquième anniversaire.* LD 159 (Paris: Cerf, 1995) 325–43.

[10] Cf. Anton Vögtle, *Das Neue Testament und die Zukunft des Kosmos* (Düsseldorf: Patmos, 1970); Walter Bindemann, *Die Hoffnung der Schöpfung, Römer 8:18-27 und die Frage einer Theologie der Befreiung von Mensch und Natur.* NStB 14 (Neukirchen-Vluyn: Neukirchener Verlag, 1983); Erich Gräßer, "Das Seufzen der Kreatur (Römer 8:19-22). Auf der Suche nach einer bbiblischen Tierschutzethik,'" *JBTh* 5 (1990) 93–117; Hans-Jürgen Findeis, "Von der Knechtschaft der Vergänglichkeit zur Freiheit der Herrlichkeit. Zur Hoffnungsperspektive der Schöpfung nach Röm. 8:19-23," in Thomas Söding, ed., *Der lebendige Gott: Studien zur Theologie des Neuen Testaments; Festschrift für Wilhelm Thüsing zum 75. Geburtstag.* NTA n.s. 31 (Münster: Aschendorff, 1996) 196–225; Hans Weder, "Geistreiches Seufzen. Zum Verhältnis von Mensch und Schöpfung in Röm. 8," in idem, *Einblicke ins Evangelium. Exegetische Beiträge zur neutestamentlichen Hermeneutik. Ges. Aufsätze aus den Jahren 1980–1991* (Göttingen: Vandenhoeck & Ruprecht, 1992) 247–62.

[11] "Depicted as a living being, Nature reaches out to the first human being, from whom she can never be separated, nor it from her." Joachim Gnilka, *Paulus von Tarsus. Apostel und Zeuge.* HThKNT, Suppl. Vol. 6 (Freiburg: Herder, 1996) 200.

[12] Ματαιότης is a Wisdom concept that really refers to mistaken thinking, also in Rom 1:21, for example. It formulates on the level of knowledge what on the object level in Rom 8:21 is called "transitoriness."

[13] Cf. Hans Weder, "Geistreiches Seufzen."

CHAPTER 14

The Activity of the Spirit of God *(rūaḥ)* for the Fulfillment of Creation (Isaiah 11:1-10)

Isaiah 11:1-10 is considered one of the "great" texts of the First Testament. On the one hand it is read together with Isa 7:10-17 and 9:1-6 as messianic or christological. For this reason the text has its "seat" in the seasons of Advent and Christmas in the Christian liturgy. On the other hand, the text has been newly discovered as a "creation text" in ecological discussions. It does in fact seem, more than any other biblical text, to give a programmatic summary of the themes mentioned in the "conciliar process of responsibility for justice, peace, and the protection of creation."

A Creation-Theological Utopia

Within the exegetical landscape Isaiah 11 tends rather to create difficulties. More than a few exegetes doubt that 11:1-5 and 11:6-8 ever constituted an original unity, and even if 11:6-8, 9 was later added by a redactor as commentary and continuation of 11:1-5, it is said that here two themes are brought together that *really* do not belong together.[1] Against the opinion that 11:1-5 and 11:6-8 constituted an original conceptual unity these scholars cite not only tradition-historical considerations but also the content of the text itself: "It would have been appropriate to the *ductus* of 11:1-5 if the wild animals had been wiped out along with the violent people in 11:4, as in Lev 26:6; Ezek 34:25-28."[2]

Another point of controversy is the precise limitation of the text to be interpreted. Because 11:1 begins adversatively ("But . . ." in the original) it is usually assumed that the textual unit begins at 10:33, for 10:33-34 contains the image of the violent cutting down of trees, which could well be followed by 11:1 with its image of the regrowth of a young shoot out of the tree stump. At the level of the final composition 11:10 is assumed to be the end of the textual unit. Even if 11:10 is to be understood in a diachronic sense as reductional continuation, with this verse the section arrives at the statement that is decisive for the overall interpretation and is indispensable for our creation-theological reading of the text.

10:33	Look, the Sovereign, the LORD of hosts, will lop the boughs with terrifying power; the tallest trees will be cut down, and the lofty will be brought low.
10:34	He will hack down the thickets of the forest with an ax, and Lebanon with its majestic trees will fall.

11:1	[But] a shoot shall come out from the stump of Jesse, and a branch shall grow out of his roots.
11:2	The spirit of the LORD shall rest on him, the spirit of wisdom and understanding, the spirit of counsel and might, the spirit of knowledge and the fear of the LORD.
11:3	His delight shall be in the fear of the LORD. He shall not judge by what his eyes see, or decide by what his ears hear;
11:4	but with righteousness he shall judge the poor, and decide with equity for the meek of the earth; he shall strike the earth with the rod of his mouth, and with the breath of his lips he shall kill the wicked.
11:5	Righteousness shall be the belt around his waist, and faithfulness the belt around his loins.

11:6	The wolf shall live [as a guest] with the lamb, the leopard shall lie down [peacefully] with the kid, the calf and the lion and the fatling together, and a little child shall lead them [as their shepherd].
11:7	The cow and the bear shall graze, their young shall lie down together; and the lion shall eat straw like the ox.
11:8	The nursing child shall play over the hole of the asp, and the weaned child shall put its hand on the adder's den.

11:9	They will not hurt or destroy on all my holy mountain; for the earth will be full of the knowledge of the LORD as the waters cover the sea.

11:10	On that day the root of Jesse shall stand as a signal to the peoples; the nations shall inquire of him, and his dwelling shall be glorious.

The text combines images from royal theology and creation theology into a thrilling utopia.

The young shoot that surprisingly grows out of the hewn down trunk of the Davidic dynasty (Jesse is the father of David; see 1 Sam 16:1) and becomes a thriving fruit tree is a metaphor for the royal figure whose activity to restore the troubled order of life and salvation is then described in various ways. He carries out justice and righteousness in his entire land, and with the power of his word he eliminates the wicked and wickedness—for no one does anything evil or corrupting any more.

This royal shoot brings creation to its fulfillment, as Isa 11:6-9 emphasizes with its subtle allusive references to the biblical primeval history:

1. Isaiah 11:9 alludes to the flood story. What is named in Gen 6:5 and Gen 6:11-12 as precipitating the flood will be brought to an end by the royal shoot, first on YHWH's holy mountain (Zion) and then in the whole land of Israel. Because in the future announced here there will be no more evil and corrupt deeds, the judgment of the creator God on creation no longer needs to be, as in Gen 6:12, "And God saw that the earth was corrupt; for all flesh [that is, both human *and* animal life] had corrupted its ways upon the earth." Instead it can be said, in accordance with the idea of creation developed in Genesis 1 (see above): "And God saw everything that he had made, and indeed, it was very good" (Gen 1:31).

2. While in Gen 6:13 the creator God says, "I have determined to make an end of all flesh, for the earth is filled with violence because of them," it is now said in Isa 11:9 that "the earth will be full of the knowledge of the LORD."

3. Because through the work of the royal shoot the corruption of human being and animal comes to an end, so now also the war between human being and animal (as well as between animal and animal) conceded by the creator God because of their tendency to violence comes to an end as described in the peaceful images from Isa 11:6-8. These images of peace, as we know, often allude to the primeval history: That infants and weaned children play peacefully with dangerous snakes is the counter-image to the primeval-historical disruption that in Gen 3:15 is characterized as "eternal" enmity between

serpent and human being. That the lion eats grass and straw like the ox signals through a paradigm the realization of the vision of cosmic peace (see above) projected in Gen 1:29-30. And when predatory animals and domestic animals, strong and weak, live peacefully side by side and dwell with one another the condition has been attained that Gen 1:28 envisioned with its instruction regarding creation: "Have dominion over the animals . . . ." The note in Isa 11:6d, "a little child shall lead them" (as shepherd), often neglected in the interpretation of the chapter though it stands at the center of the composition 11:6-7, can on the one hand be connected with the "task of shepherding" in Gen 1:28; on the other hand we cannot rule out the possibility that it is meant as an allusion to the royal youth in Isa 7:14-15 and 9:51.

In view of these relationships between Isaiah 11 and the primeval history in Genesis 1–9 there should be no doubt that Isaiah 11 is meant to be read as a creation-theological utopia—as a word of promise that is at the same time meant to empower for life in accordance with creation. With the figure of the shoot from the stump of Jesse, which we now want to examine more closely, Isaiah 11 projects how life in harmony with creation ought to look.

Revitalization of the Beginning

The figure depicted in Isaiah 11, the one who grows out of the stump of Jesse, is certainly to be seen within the horizon of the Davidic tradition. His coming is a revitalization of the source from which David came. The image of the little shoot that grows up unexpectedly into a fruit-bearing tree is to be seen as a contrast to Isa 10:38-39. The collapse of the terrifying world empire in whose epochal collapse the Jerusalem kingdom also disappeared does not mean, as far as YHWH is concerned, the end of the relationship between YHWH and the people of Israel or between YHWH and creation. It is that very epochal collapse that reveals how inexhaustible is YHWH's creative vigor: YHWH is both willing *and* able to revitalize the *beginning as a new beginning* so that as a goal it becomes reality.

For this reason YHWH will again send out the divine "spirit," that is, the creative breath of divine life by means of which YHWH can fill everything with new life (see Gen 1:2-3; Ezek 37:1-11; Ps 104:30).[3] With this spirit YHWH will continually bless the sprout from the root of Jesse. Differently than with Saul, from whom the Spirit of God departed (see 1 Sam 16:14), and differently than with the Davidic line of the pre-exilic dynasty, which with the destruction of Jerusalem was itself swept into the catastrophic abyss, the creative power will this time abide—and in six- or sevenfold abundance, as developed in 11:2-3. What is important here is that "wisdom" and "understanding" are named as God-given charisms, that is, the capacity to recognize the order of life and righteousness that is inherent in the world and to act in accordance with it. The second pair of charisms, "the spirit of counsel and might," is to be understood in the same sense as the capacity to fight against all wicked people and every evil that threatens the order of creation. This is the spirit that enables one to do justice. As a fundamental condition of these two pairs of charisms our text then names in the third place the gift of the spirit of knowledge and the fear of YHWH. All this is to be found integrally in the Wisdom tradition, according to which the fear of YHWH is the basic principle ("the beginning") of wisdom (see Prov 1:7; 9:10 and numerous other places), and that means, in the horizon of the book of Isaiah, the cancellation of that troubled relation to YHWH in which the non-recognition of YHWH had made Jerusalem and Mount Zion places of injustice and depravity (see Isa 1:3; 6:9).

In the power of this "new" creative Spirit, the original order of all-encompassing life and salvation that dwells in creation will come to prevail in Jerusalem and on Mount Zion. A royal tree of life will grow on YHWH's mountain; its fruits will be justice and righteousness for all, especially for the humble and the poor. There will be a royal authority through whose application both evil and wicked people will disappear from the land.

That the end of violence, oppression, and enmity is now occurring in a new, creative manner is the message of the world of images in Isa 11:6-8. That this passage does *not*, as one would expect, see the end of enmity as coming by the annihilation of predatory animals and mortally-dangerous snakes, but by their transformation into peaceful companions in the pasture and playmates is the special point of the creation-theological utopia of Isa 11:1-10.

Jürgen Ebach has summarized the point of the bringing together of the two image constellations of the rule of peace in 11:1-5 and the peace between animals in 11:6-8 in the following manner:

> With v. 6 the view passes from the figure of the ruler to the effects of his rule in the realm of nature. The description of the "peace among the animals" represents both a transcendence of the political dimension and an extension of the political level. The passage about the peace among the animals begins with a sentence that doubly emphasizes the reversal of existing norms: *"The wolf shall live [as a guest] with the lamb. . . ."* This describes the peaceful life together of former deadly enemies. The utopia points . . . to the conquest not of the enemy, but of the state of enmity. And the image contains still more: we should note the role of each animal in the situation in which enmity has been overcome. "To be a guest" (the Hebrew word *gūr* can mean "to dwell as a foreigner, as a person to be protected") applies not to the weak animal dwelling with

> the strong, but just the *opposite:* the wolf will live with the lamb, the leopard with the kid . . . . The idea of the secure protection the weak receive from the strong would affirm and idealize the prevailing power relationships (for which reason it is an enduring *topos* in royal ideology); but the constellation in Isa 11:6 constitutes an overturning of prevailing norms. The image thus reveals itself as the extension of the previous expectation of the peaceful ruler, in which everything depends on the raising up of the weak and their receiving their rights, that is, that they do not remain dependent on kind treatment from the powerful.[4]

That all living things attain the *right to life* that was given to them along with their life, in accord with the original order that has dwelt in the world since its "beginning," is the "messianic" charism that YHWH will pour out from YHWH's holy mountain in order, beginning from that point, to bring fulfillment to creation.

But who is the recipient of this creation-perfecting charism? On the level of the text in 11:1-9 one can see a renewed kingdom that fulfills its royal commission to mediate comprehensive *shalom.* That the activity of the king as the agent of the creator God brings *shalom* even to the fertility of the animals and the fields is a widely-attested concept in the ancient Near East. In particular, the beginning of the reign of a new king was considered a renewal of creation. The "messianic" Psalm 72 is a beautiful biblical example of this.[5] The motif of a royal figure subduing predators for the benefit of creation is also frequently attested, as can be seen from the three following illustrations.[6] Figure 8, a Persian seal (from the fifth century B.C.E.), shows in an artful composition the powerful royal figure of a (divine) hero who rules over and controls the animal world. That this "king of the animals" is

Figure 8

flanked on the seal by luxuriant trees of life opens up the deeper meaning of the motif: "the king of the animals" brings order to the world and promotes healthy life.

Figure 9

Figure 9, a middle-Assyrian seal (14th/13th c. B.C.E.) shows the "lord of the animals" in the midst of the animals in a "paradisiacal" landscape.

Figure 10, a Syrian seal (ca. 800 B.C.E.) shows at the left a hero with six locks of hair (cf. the biblical Samson), with a deer held fast in each

Figure 10

arm and with each hand holding a gazelle by its hind feet. Alongside this figure is a constellation of other figures with the motif of the "intact world." This includes in the first place the highly stylized tree of life at the earth's center, representing the earth and its sound order. Then, suspended above the tree of life/the earth, we see the heavens, supported by two sky-bearers; on it can be seen the heads of the three gods of Ur (the lord of heaven accompanied by the gods of sun and moon). The scene is flanked by two adorers. If one takes the two scenes on the seal together the composition can only mean that the hero who "pastures" the wild animals carries out his assignment *in such a way* that the earth as a whole becomes a sound and blessed place.

We have already encountered this motif of "rule of the animals" for the good of the world above in the interpretation of Gen 1:26-30 and Gen 9:1-7.[7] It also stands in the background of Gen 2:15-20. To this thought world also belongs the idea, developed especially in Assyrian, Persian, and Hellenistic royal ideology, of royal paradise-parks as "miniatures" of a creation ordered and made peaceful by the king.[8] Within this perspective Isa 11:1-9 therefore hopes that YHWH will give YHWH's people a new kingdom endowed with the authority to establish the sacred order of creation in YHWH's realm and on YHWH's holy mountain.

On the level of the final text, of course, Isa 11:1-9, as we said before, does not reach its real climax and focal point until 11:10. Here the royal figure is transformed into a metaphor for the royal/messianic people living on Zion and in Israel that will become the mediator of creation for the peoples and the nations.[9] In this perspective the utopia of Isa 11:1-10 corresponds with the utopia of Isa 2:1-5, to which it is linked through the relationship of key words *and* through the common idea of peace through transformation (swords into plowshares, lances into vintners' knives, changing the weapons of death into instruments of life).

The Renewal of Creation Begins with the New Creation of the People of God

In contrast to the interpretations that see in Isa 11:1-4 the utopia of the *universal* fulfillment of creation, we must emphasize with Odil Hannes Steck[10] that here (as in Isa 2:1-5) the discussion is "only" about Zion and its surrounding land. *Here* YHWH will begin, through the outpouring of the divine creative Spirit, to carry through the divine ordering of justice and peace as the perfected form of God's creation.

This utopia is described in Isa 32:15-20 with images related to those in Isaiah 11:

32:15	until a spirit from on high is poured out on us, and the wilderness becomes a fruitful field, and the fruitful field is deemed a forest.
32:16	Then justice will dwell in the wilderness, and righteousness abide in the fruitful field.
32:17	The effect of righteousness will be peace, and the result of righteousness, quietness and trust forever.
32:18	My people will abide in a peaceful habitation, in secure dwellings, and in quiet resting places. . . .
32:20	Happy will you be who sow beside every stream, who let the ox and the donkey range freely.

The outpouring of the Spirit leads here to paradisiacal fertility and to a peace that includes the animals. (The domestic and useful animals can be allowed to walk around without fear that they will be attacked by predators or eaten.) Wherever and whenever this happens it astonishes the peoples, and they move to this wonderful place in order to learn peace there (see Isa 2:1-5), to experience the goal of creation—and to allow themselves to be transformed by the "glory" of the creator God that appears there (cf. Isa 11:10).

Notes: Chapter 14

[1] Cf. Hans-Jürgen Hermisson, "Zukunftserwartung und Gegenwartskritik in der Verkündigung Jesajas," *EvTh* 33 (1973) 54–77.

[2] Cf. Odil Hannes Steck, "'. . . ein kleiner Knabe kann sie hüten.' Beobachtungen zum Tierfrieden in Jesaja 11:6 und 65:25," in Jutta Hausmann and Hans-Jürgen Zobel, eds., *Alttestamentlicher Glaube und Biblische Theologie: Festschrift für Horst Dietrich Preuss zum 65. Geburtstag* (Stuttgart: Kohlhammer, 1992) 107.

[3] Cf. above, pp. 18–19 and pp. 42–43, but also Part IV, ch. 15 below.

[4] Jürgen Ebach, *Ursprung und Ziel. Erinnerte Zukunft und erhoffte Vergangenheit* (Neukirchen-Vluyn: Neukirchener Verlag, 1986) 78–79.

[5] Cf. also Erich Zenger, "'So betete David für seinen Sohn Salomo und für den König Messias.' Überlegungen zur holistischen und kanonischen Lektüre des 72. Psalms," *JBTh* 8 (1993) 57–72; Bernd Janowski, *Stellvertretung. Alttestamentliche Studien zu einem theologischen Grundbegriff.* SBS 165 (Stuttgart: Katholisches Bibelwerk, 1997) 41–66.

[6] Illustrations from Othmar Keel, *Jahwes Entgegnung an Ijob.* FRLANT 121 (Göttingen: Vandenhoeck & Ruprecht, 1978): Plates 8 and 9, p. 121; Plate 10, p. 89.

[7] Cf. above pp. 111–13 and pp. 124–25.

[8] Cf. Christoph Uehlinger, "Vom *dominium terrae* zu einem Ethos der Selbstbeschränkung. Alttestamentliche Einsprüche gegen einen tyrannischen Umgang mit der Schöpfung," *BiLi* 64 (1991) 59–74.

[9] On this level of reading the Immanuel in Isa 7:14-16 and the child of the king in Isa 9:1-6 are also figures of the royal people of God.

[10] Odil Hannes Steck, ". . . ein kleiner Knabe" 109–113.

CHAPTER 15

Renewal of the Creation and the Reestablishment of Israel (Acts of the Apostles)

The Acts of the Apostles, the second book of the Lukan historical work, begins with a great vision of the fulfillment of creation. Although there is no reference made here to Isaiah 11 by the very nature of things there are connections between the two texts. The Lukan portrayal of the Pentecost event also combines creation-theological motifs with the concept of the reestablishment of Israel within the horizon of the Davidic tradition. Here, too, the renewal of creation is linked to the assumption of rule by the eschatological David, and the power of the creative Spirit of God is understood as the gift that makes the mass of pious Jews from the entire world now assembled in Jerusalem to be witnesses to God's action for all nations. The renewal of creation in the Spirit begins, according to the thesis of Acts, as the renewal of the historical role of Judaism as the people of God who are a sign for the nations.

The historical process portrayed by the Acts of the Apostles proceeded, of course, differently than was foreseen in the promising beginning. It is true that the post-Easter rule of the exalted Messiah will reach the ends of the earth in the message of Jesus' witnesses. But this story is at the same time that of the division between Jews and Christians brought about through the conflicts precipitated by the word of Jesus' witnesses in Jerusalem and in the Jewish Diaspora. Is it Luke's opinion, then, that the dream of the restoration of creation through the reestablishment of Israel was a failure? If that were the case, what would be the point of the great vision of the fulfillment of creation at the beginning of the book? Is the second volume of Luke's historical work the balance sheet of the failure of this hope? Or is for Luke the ideal beginning the commencement of an unstoppable and certain good ending that has not yet happened? Or was Luke interested only in giving the Christian church a theologically legitimizing foundational myth?

The Reestablishment of the Kingdom in Israel

The first theme of the Acts of the Apostles is the expectation of the reestablishment of the kingdom for Israel. It is formulated as a question of the apostles (Acts 1:6) in the context of a forty-day period of instruction by the resurrected Jesus "about the kingdom of God" (1:3). The question of whether God's rule will bring back the kingdom for Israel at "this time" (v. 6) is partially rejected in Jesus' reply ("It is not for you to know the times or periods that the Father has set by his own authority") but also partially confirmed ("but you will receive power when the Holy Spirit has come upon you") (vv. 7-8). The answer leaves a lot open. The rejection of the question about the date of the reestablishment of the kingdom for Israel can also be understood as the confirmation that this is anchored in God's plan of salvation and can therefore be expected with certainty.[1] Also unanswered is what the "power of the Spirit," with which the apostles will be equipped, has to do with the reestablishment of royal rule for Israel. The immediate context deals with the empowerment of the apostles as witnesses of the resurrection; their report, going out from Jerusalem, is to be proclaimed throughout the world. But in Jesus' farewell discourses before his death he "confers" on these same disciples the "kingdom" that the Father had conferred on him, and promises them in addition to participation in the messianic meal that they will judge the twelve tribes of the people of God (Luke 22:29-30). This function is probably not the same as that assigned to them in Acts 1:8. It is nevertheless clear that the question of the reestablishment of royal rule for Israel is not foolish. Instead it contains the real explosive material of the exposition in the book of Acts, the energy that produces tension to the very end of the book.

In the sense of the expectations laid down in the exposition of Acts the first episode describes a process that symbolically anticipates the complete restoration of the twelve tribes of Israel: the reestablishment of the group of Israel's designated judges, the circle of the Twelve, through the addition of Matthias (1:15-26). The replacement of Judas by another witness to Jesus (see vv. 21-22) is justified with a quotation from Ps 109:8 ("Let another take his position of overseer"). In Luke's scriptural hermeneutics[2] this means that the restoration of the group of the Twelve is part of God's eternal plan for the deliverance of God's people. The realization of the reestablishment of Israel predetermined in God's plan of salvation begins with the Pentecost event.

The Ideal Role of Judaism

The Acts of the Apostles depicts the pouring out of God's Spirit over all flesh (see Acts 2:17 = Joel 3:1) as the gathering of a cosmogonic storm from heaven that is at the same time an event of communication and speech.[3] The roar of the storm fills the house in which all are sitting together (v. 2). Tongues of fire appear and divide, placing themselves on every individual in the house (v. 3). They are filled with the Spirit and begin to speak. The Pentecost event is accordingly and above all the event of the liberation of the speech of Jesus' witnesses. By means of their speech the renewal of the creation through God's Spirit is proclaimed.[4]

To the Pentecost event also belongs the understanding of this speech. This, too, is portrayed as a miracle of the renewal of the human world. The scene in the house opens with the language miracle of the comprehension of Spirit-induced speech (2:5-11). A great multitude hears and understands the words spoken by the Galilean witnesses of the Spirit, each in his or her own tongue, "in our own languages" (v. 11). The miracle of God's message for the renewal of creation continues on the level of the ability to receive communication.

The list of nations (2:9-11) that describes the origins of the polyglot hearers of the Pentecost event and Peter's Pentecost discourse is interpreted in a particular way by the narrator through the introduction to the scene in v. 5. These, accordingly, are "devout" Jews from the Diaspora who are living in Jerusalem.[5] They do not represent the nations whose languages they speak; on the contrary: with their non-Jewish mother tongues they are the born mediators of the revelation of God's Spirit to all peoples under heaven. As witnesses of God they can proclaim the work of the renewal of creation, transmitting God's message to all people to the ends of the earth.[6]

Peter's discourse brings the decision as to whether this ideal role will really be assumed. This speech is intended not only to be understood word for word, but to have its content accepted. It develops the great utopia of an Israel inspired by the Spirit of God. On the other hand, it formulates the conditions for the acceptance of this role.

The ideal image of the people entirely filled with this Spirit corresponds to the idea that is first projected in Num 11:29 by an angry Moses: "Would that all the LORD's people were prophets." The introduction to Peter's speech (2:14b-21) interprets the Pentecost event in its twofold nature as miracle of speech and of understanding as a realization of this ideal. The speaker thereby appeals to Joel 3:1-5a (LXX; Hebrew 2:28-32), an unambiguously eschatological text that announces the great day of the Lord. Two aspects are evident in the extensive quotation (Acts 2:17-19). On the one hand the Pentecost event is understood with Joel 3:1-2 [2:28-29] as the eschatological filling of the entire people of God with the spirit of prophecy. On the other hand the eschatological day of the Lord is understood with Joel 3:3-5 [2:30-

32] as a shaking of the cosmos, a cosmic catastrophe out of which everyone who calls on the name of Lord will be saved. Accordingly, Peter's address interprets the situation that came about with the Pentecost event as a situation of crisis in which Israel's ideal prophetic role is at stake.

Peter's speech addresses this question. The final sentence formulates the condition that from the Lukan perspective must be fulfilled: "Therefore let the entire house of Israel know with certainty that God has made him both Lord and Messiah, this Jesus whom you crucified" (Acts 2:36). The ideal role of God's witness among the nations is to be assumed by Judaism in that it recognizes in the Pentecost event the beginning of the reestablished Davidic royal rule. It is the knowledge of this new beginning that sets in motion the process of renewal of creation, precisely the knowledge proclaimed to the people for the first time in Peter's speech.

Jewish Christianity as a Sign for the Nations

Acts describes Peter's Pentecost speech as a great success. The number of those baptized is counted in the thousands (2:41) and at the end of Acts in the tens of thousands (21:20). But the numbers given by Luke do not symbolize the full number of the twelve tribes of Israel. The vision of the day of Pentecost is not realized, at least not in the events reported in Acts. Luke makes the Temple aristocracy responsible for this. According to his description they prevented the Temple from placing itself at the service of the world's renewal (see Acts 3–4). The rule of divine Wisdom over creation, renewed through the Jesus exalted as Lord and Messiah, will indeed reach the nations, but not by way of the Temple. Nevertheless the great vision of Acts 2 is not thereby abandoned. The relevance of the meaning of this concept does not become clear until one realizes that Luke's historical work already looked back on the Jewish War and the destruction of the Temple after the interval of about half a generation. The vision of the restoration of creation and Israel's role as witness in that process is also a confrontation with the fact of the catastrophe of the Temple and of the city of Jerusalem. Luke places the question about Israel's role in the eschatological process of the renewal of creation against this background. How does Israel's history attain the good end envisioned for it?

Acts offers its readers one answer to this open question in the description of the Apostolic Council (Acts 15), specifically in the discourse of James, which establishes the connections between the new experience of God's saving acts toward the Gentiles and the canonical knowledge of the Jewish religion.[7] Amos 9:11-12 is cited, a text that in the book of Amos follows the threat of the destruction of the Temple (at Bethel). The prediction of the destruction of the Temple is juxtaposed to the promise of rebuilding.

> "After this I will return,
> and I will rebuild the dwelling of David, which has fallen;
> from its ruins I will rebuild it, and I will set it up" (Acts 15:16).

What is announced as a promise in the book of Amos is not a vision in the context of the discourse of James, but a realized fact. The holy place that has risen out of the rubble is the Jewish-Christian community in Jerusalem. It is here understood as the place where divine Wisdom has again become accessible for the nations:

> ". . . so that all other peoples may seek the Lord—
> even all the Gentiles over whom my name has been called"
> (Acts 15:17 = Amos 9:12 LXX).

Luke's historical work is written for a Gentile-Christian readership and furnishes an answer to their question about their Christian identity. The heart of this answer is formulated here, with a sober look at the fractures and catastrophes that have previously hindered the realization of the great vision of the renewal of creation in the Spirit and the ideal role of Israel. The answer is given out of the canonical knowledge of Jewish religion. It shows the Gentile-Christian readership that they have found a relationship to God only because God had allowed Godself to be found by them in the midst of God's people.[8]

Notes: Chapter 15

[1] This is indicated by the context of Acts 3:21. The "apokatastasis" (cf. Acts 1:6 ἀποκαθιστάνεις) as the key concept of the exilic/postexilic hope for a"reestablishment" out of destruction of the Davidic realm in the end time has, beyond its political connotation, the comprehensive meaning of the inclusive and saving inclination of God in the new age, the definitive restoration of creation. That this—especially against the apocalyptic-Wisdom background—will be realized *with certainty* is attested by the immediately following reference to God's commitment to the word that was given "through his holy prophets"; cf. also Franz Mussner, "Die Idee der Apokatastasis," in idem, *Praesentia salutis: Gesammelte Studien zu Fragen und Themen des Neuen Testaments* (Düsseldorf: Patmos, 1967) 223–34; originally published in Heinrich Gross and Franz Mussner, eds., *Lex tua veritas; Festschrift für Hubert Junker zur Vollendung des siebzigsten Lebensjahres am 8. August 1961, dargeboten von Kollegen, Freunden und Schülern* (Trier: Paulinus, 1961) 283–306.

[2] Cf. also Karl Löning, *Das Geschichtswerk des Lukas. I: Israels Hoffnung und Gottes Geheimnisse* (Stuttgart: Kohlhammer, 1997) 26–47.

[3] The Lukan description of the Pentecost event coincides in its central motifs with the description of the Sinai theophany (Exod 19:16-25) and especially with the revision

in Philo, *Decalogue* 11: "Then from the midst of the fire that streamed from heaven there sounded forth to their utter amazement a voice, for the flame became articulate speech in the language familiar to the audience, and so clearly and distinctly were the words formed by it that they seemed to see rather than hear them. . . ." The voice of God is here classified with the visible phenomena. In Luke it is the contrary. The tongues of fire do "appear," but for the balance of the action it is not the visible that is important, but rather that it has to do with "tongues" that make one capable of charismatic discourse. Cf. the relationship of the key-words in v. 3a and v. 4b. Even though Luke's description of the Pentecost event could have alluded to a Sinai tradition, his conception of the eschatological revelatory event is nevertheless not primarily that of a theophany.

[4] Cf. on this as a whole the contribution of Ulrich Busse, "Aspekte biblischen Geistverständnisses," *BN* 66 (1993) 40–57.

[5] Their piety and their dwelling in Jerusalem are indications of their messianic hope. This and the speaking in foreign tongues are treated positively, without any connotations of exclusivity. The natives of Jerusalem are included in the addressees of Peter's discourse (cf. vv. 22-23).

[6] Cf. Karl Löning, "Das Verhältnis zum Judentum als Identitätsproblem der Kirche nach der Apostelgeschichte," in Ludwig Hagemann and Ernst Pulsfort, eds., *"Ihr alle aber seid Brüder": Festschrift für A. Th. Khoury zum 60. Geburtstag.* Würzburger Forschungen zur Missions- und Religionswissenschaft. Religionswissenschaftliche Studien 14 (Würzburg: Echter; Altenberge: Oros, 1990) 304–19, at 308.

[7] The point of departure for the debate described in Acts 15:5-21 is the question about the legitimacy of the Law-free mission to the Gentiles that became acute following the baptism of Cornelius. Its solution in the "provision of James" governed the "communion of two expressions of the *vita christiana* in differing cultural traditions" and freed it from any possible soteriological or ecclesiological relevance. Cf. Karl Löning, "Das Evangelium und die Kulturen. Heilsgeschichtliche und kulturelle Aspekte kirchlicher Realität in der Apostelgeschichte," *ANRW* II.25.3 (1985) 2604–46, at 2627.

[8] That the inclusion of the Gentiles in God's *basileia* is not developed programmatically until the second half of the Acts of the Apostles and that Luke at no point abandons the salvation-historical primacy of Israel was noted for the first time by Gerhard Lohfink, *Die Sammlung Israels. Eine Untersuchung zur lukanischen Ekklesiologie.* StANT 39 (Munich: Kösel, 1975).

PROSPECT

Impetuses for a Biblically-Inspired Culture of Creation

In our overview of the multiform worldviews of the two-and-yet-one Christian Bible we have seen throughout that biblical theologies of creation by no means express the uncritical naïveté or childish optimism of ancient peoples that we, on the threshold of the third millennium, can no longer accept in light of the catastrophes we have already suffered and those we still fear. It is historically correct—so we maintain in concluding—that the biblical theology of creation attained its maturity and solidity precisely in light of catastrophes suffered. The great creation-theological designs were first formulated in the crisis of the Babylonian exile in the sixth century B.C.E. After this the social upheavals of the fifth and fourth centuries B.C.E. led in the book of Job, but also in numerous psalms, to a creation-theological confrontation with individual sickness, privation, and suffering. Finally the social and religious disruptions that appeared after the second century B.C.E. precipitated an apocalyptic intensification of the creation-theological traditions in whose horizon the New Testament texts should also be read. God and the human world are now experienced as so estranged from each other that the way to a creation-worthy life is hoped for only as the coming of God for the deliverance and liberation of creation from the power of evil. It is the hope that the origin that the creator God desired "to begin with" will finally come to its goal, not in the process of a linear evolution but through the creative personal intervention of God. The New Testament documents show in the most varied ways that the *ground* of this hope in primitive Christianity is Jesus of Nazareth.

What is common to the biblical voices we have heard is that in spite of all painful, chaotic experiences they manage to say their fundamental "yes" to the world and to life in the world. In the midst of privation and anxiety, doubt and desperation, the people of the Bible seek to recognize, share in forming, and celebrate the earth as the location of the saving rule of God and as a the realm wherein life is given to them, as cosmos within the chaos. Thus the biblical creation theologies are, on the one hand, expressions of a realistic-critical view of the world and of human beings *and,* on the other hand, the expression of a determined trust in the sovereignty of God as the creator and perfecter of the world. The biblical theologies of creation are therefore a passionate "yes" to life—in view of and despite death in all its forms.

In the context of the *entire* Bible the theology of creation and soteriology are therefore inextricably linked. Precisely in the New Testament texts we have repeatedly seen that in sending Jesus God intends the renewal and perfection of the *world as creation.* According to the witness of the whole Bible, the establishment of God's rule in Israel and in the Church is to be understood and accepted as God's life-creating action against the seemingly still-unbroken power of death, so that even now life can be lived out of the power of the inbreaking reign of God—in imitation of the merciful God of creation.

In view of the continually intensifying ecological crisis a new paradigm for dealing with creation is demanded by the biblical theologies of creation. The paradigm of the last centuries was the principle of "progress" that has brought global changes to our world, whereby "progress" was massively defined and justified by anthropocentric standards. There is no doubt that nature and many dimensions of human life have thereby been damaged. That the biblically-inspired communities of Judaism and Christianity have applied too little of their own particular traditions to exposing and combating the destructive consequences of this model of progress is also beyond discussion. The time has come, therefore, for us again to rediscover "life," the paradigm that dominates the Bible, as the interdependent context of everything and make this paradigm the basic starting point of our culture. That is meant neither as a nostalgic conjuring of nature romanticism nor as a belligerent appeal of "Back to Nature." Rather it means an option that seeks to recognize the world as a living organism and in its multiplicity of life-forms the secret of the saving divine rule itself. Creation *is* the place where the healing and saving God wishes to be revealed and encountered. The earth *is* the space in which God's royal rule desires to communicate itself as "life in abundance." And human beings are to be collaborators in this event.

When, in the Easter night, the liturgy chooses the story of creation in Genesis 1 as its first reading, it emphasizes that the earth is the place where God's saving activity is experienced. This is not to be understood as a naïve linear-historical reading of salvation; instead, it here becomes clear that in the resurrection of Jesus the *origin* of the world narrated in Genesis 1 as its "beginning" is finally revealed as the *meaning and goal* of creation. Christian liturgy is therefore shaped to the core by creation theology. Though we need no special "creation feast" in the liturgical calendar, we should certainly cause the creation dimension of our great festivals of Christmas, Easter, and Pentecost, as well as our celebration of the Eucharist (bread and wine as gifts of life) to emerge more clearly and shine more intensely. Creation and salvation are not two disparate dimensions of God's activity, but "are blended together . . . in our central festivals. None of them can any longer be celebrated without the other."[1]

The message of the biblical theology of creation, that God *never* gives up on creation because God loves it, desires to inspire and alter the way we deal with creation.

> Those who say, "I love God,"
> and hate their sister the Earth
> are liars;
> for those who do not love their sister whom they have seen,
> cannot love God whom they have not seen. . . .
> those who love God
> must love their sister, the Earth, also (cf. 1 John 4:20-21).

Note: Prospect

[1] Norbert Lohfink, "Altes Testament und Liturgie. Unsere Schwierigkeiten und unsere Chancen," *Liturgisches Jahrbuch* 47 (1997) 12.

Index of Scriptural References

Subject and Name Index